Retirement Planning E:

2025

Plan more, save more, earn more, live better and achieve a better retirement.

Fully updated for the UK 2025/26 budget and covering your planning for a glidepath (not cliff-edge) retirement. Retirement Planning Expert 2025 covers, in depth, your leisure time, well-being, flexible working options, cutting costs and debt in readiness for retirement, UK tax planning in the light of the budget announced in October 2024, pensions and property. This could be your re-set moment in 2025 and you might even retire 5 years earlier. The 5th edition of this bestselling UK retirement planning book will help you achieve a better retirement.

by

Allan Esler Smith, Fellow of the Institute of Chartered Accountants ("FCA")

Publisher's note, disclaimer and terms of use agreement

Every possible effort has been made to ensure that the information contained in this book is accurate at the time of going to press (January 2025), and the publisher and author cannot accept responsibility for any errors or omissions, however caused. No responsibility for loss or damage occasioned to any person acting, or refraining from action, as a result of the material in this publication can be accepted by the publisher or the author. The publisher and author make no representations or warranties with respect to the accuracy, applicability, fitness, or completeness of the contents of this book. Importantly, this book is only a guide and it is neither legal nor financial advice; it is no substitute for taking professional advice from a financial adviser or other professional adviser. Any potential UK tax advantages may be subject to change and the 2025/26 budget announced in October 2024 remains subject to approval. Much will depend upon your individual circumstances and, again, individual professional advice should be obtained that is appropriate to your individual circumstances.

The publisher and the author do not warrant the performance, effectiveness or applicability of any websites or other resources listed in this book. Fifth edition published in Great Britain and Northern Ireland in 2025 by Quartertoten Productions Limited.

Apart from any fair dealing for the purposes of research or private study, or criticism or review, as permitted under the Copyright, Designs and Patents Act 1988, this publication may only be reproduced, stored or transmitted, in any form or by any means, with the prior permission in writing of the publishers, or in the case of reprographic reproduction in accordance with the terms and licenses issued by the Copyright Licensing Agency. This publication may only be used on a training course with the prior written permission in writing of the publishers.

CONTENTS

ESSENTIAL STEP 3: EARN MORE

ESSENTIAL STEP 4: LIVE BETTER

ACKNOWLEDGEMENTS

I am indebted to my father, Stanley Smith, a retired senior civil servant and my wife Karen, whose assistance and guidance were invaluable. Frances Kaye introduced me to writing books on this subject and provided me with the greatest of help and support over many years and I remain very grateful. I also value incisive professional input and in this regard Martin Gorvett, a Chartered Financial Planner of Lavender Financial Planners Ltd, cuts an effective knife through the complexities and language of investments and pensions. And on legal matters, wills and powers of attorney I thank Tom Bottomley of Ewart Price Solicitors of Hertfordshire as legal issues are so vitally important to smoothing the path of an estate.

Allan Esler Smith FCA

Introduction and top ten opportunities in 2025/26

2025/26 could be your re-set moment and armed with this book it may be time to start putting yourself first. You might even retire five years earlier. Fifty years ago retirement books were a scarcity as everything was relatively simple with a fixed income being received over a shorter period of time. To-day we have increased life expectancy, more complex pension arrangements and more flexible access to pensions. On the plus side we also have more opportunities around flexible working to help provide some additional income into the retirement years (you can retire more than once!). On the negative side in the UK we have a state pension age that keeps getting raised. Eroding public services around 'care and welfare' adds a worry. Have we lost touch with the whole purpose of our later years being the most enjoyable? Is it time to put yourself first, 're-set' to save more, earn more and embrace new lifestyle opportunities? If yes- this is the book for you and with better knowledge you will harness the opportunities that are out there in the UK and achieve a better 'glidepath' rather than 'cliff-edge' retirement.

Retirement Planning Expert 2025 is updated for the UK 2025/26 tax year (subject to approval of the October 2024 budget) and will help you achieve a better retirement. It's all about spotting those opportunities (and there are hundreds) to improve your finances <u>and</u> lifestyle in retirement. There is plenty of focus in this book on just living better as **a good retirement does not have to mean rich but it can mean 'content'.**

Opportunity is what it is all about after we have been battered in the UK for the last five years by Covid-19, a tidal wave of inflation (albeit now reducing), a cost-of-living crisis, eroding public services and stealth taxes (the freezing of key tax thresholds resulting in a higher proportion of your income going on tax). I wanted to make this a book **packed with straightforward, hard-hitting, practical advice and easy to understand information** on the opportunities that could help you in 2025/26.

If you are reading this in your 30s or 40s you are in a great place as you have plenty of time to pull the different levers explained in this book and can make a dramatic difference to achieving a better retirement. **It's never too early to start that plan!** For others in their 50s and early 60s you may just need help with a **'re-set'** moment. You've realised retirement is approaching but you don't want a cliff-edge retirement and, instead, want to glide into the retirement years and through it. This book will offer you so much. I retain an absolute focus on helping <u>you</u> to **achieve a better retirement by following my four essential steps**. You will understand where you are now, where you want to get to and how <u>you</u> **can achieve a better retirement by making better choices based on better knowledge**. My first and possibly most important **"top tip"** is to trigger that 're-set' moment and give yourself time to think.

Top tip
We are often so busy with life that we don't stop and think about what we really want ahead in life. A re-set and then a glidepath retirement can be achieved so give yourself time to think and plan.

The longer you have until retirement, the more you can do to improve your prospects, as so much flows from increasing your knowledge around pensions, investments and how they interlink with tax. This throws up an immediate challenge as the **UK has one of the most complex tax regimes in the world** and we cope with the impact of 'stealth taxes'. These are changes which avoid the headline income tax rates and, instead, result in you paying more tax- the key stealth tax is the freezing of income tax bands so that as you **'earn more'** you may enter a higher tax band (as the band has not moved in line with earnings or inflation) and you pay more in tax. Other tax pain has been caused by the slashing of capital gains tax reliefs and tax-free dividend amounts in recent years. The freezing of tax allowances and tax thresholds until 2028 will be a slow, tough squeeze. Add in the biggest tax raising budget since 1993 as announced in October 2024 and the challenge gets tougher. Capital Gains Tax increases and the slashing of business asset disposal relief will result in retirement plans being changed. The wealthy are hit hard in the October 2024 budget with changes announced around pensions and other reliefs which is intended to increase Inheritance Tax.

   In addition to taxation we have **relatively high mortgage rates** and **cost of living problems** for many. On the flip side there are hundreds of opportunities outlined in my book to improve your retirement by planning your way through a complex tax regime, saving more and earning that little bit better. I do also have to say right at the start that all the clever financial stuff ignores the more important goal of creating the life you seek from a **great home**, focusing on your **health** and **personal relationships** and enjoying great **experiences, hobbies**, **new interests** and maybe **volunteering** (and giving something back to society).

   A quick word on how you might make best use of my book and get the best out of **the four essential steps**. As you will see, perhaps I should call it a workbook or manual for your retirement plan. Most of the chapters are relatively self-contained. It is not like reading a novel with a beginning, a middle and an end which you read in sequence. You can pick your way through the chapters depending on what is of most interest and relevance to you and then work out your plan and take some incisive actions based on my **top tips** (which you can't miss in the **TOP TIP boxes**).

   Having said all that, you probably should read through the **opening two chapters** first. **Chapter 1** deals with the key issues of basic **financial planning and establishing your net wealth and a budget** and asking **'Could you retire five years earlier?'**. **Chapter 2** deals with the central part of most people's lives – **their home**- and also the 'magic wand' of retirement planning if you own the property and are prepared to consider a change. The chapter on **well-being and personal relationships (Chapter 10)** could also be important as an early read as health and relationships may need adjustment as you glide towards retirement. I should explain up-front my favourite word in the whole book and which governs my approach- **'glidepath'**- it underpins everything. I have presented seminars for nearly two decades where I got the sense that many people were approaching a **'cliff-edge'** retirement. Suddenly they were on a course and maybe retirement came 6 months later - that's a cliff-edge! Others on my courses in their 40's and 50's realised they could plan a **glidepath** and that there was so much more they could do to plan and achieve a better retirement. They realised that you can 'retire' (or '**re-set**') more than once on a journey that commences from around 55-58. They also realised that it was time to put themselves first. Also looking at the work I do with my personal tax clients over the two decades I underline the concept of a **glidepath** into retirement as it gives a better chance to create the lifestyle you want and a better retirement. Just a thought to take away right at the start of this book! Let me outline my **four essential steps.**

THE 'PLAN MORE' ESSENTIAL STEP. I start by explaining the basics. There are **three phases of retirement** that you will travel through: the *'active retirement years'*, then *'the passive retirement years'* and finally *'retirement with care'*. The three phases could easily cover a thirty-year period if you '**re-set**' and 'retire' from 55-58 and your income, expenditure, opportunities and risk will change radically as you move through each phase. Few people really grasp the three phases and what this means for their finances and what they can do about it. Next, I peel back the sometimes-complex world of doing the retirement sums (establishing your net wealth and a budget) and show you how to do it. You then have the basis of a financial plan that is developed by the next three essential steps of retirement planning.

THE 'SAVE MORE' ESSENTIAL STEP. Having defined your net wealth and a basic financial plan the focus shifts onto demystifying 'financial speak' and assessing the opportunities for you to **'save more'** by starting with one of your biggest assets - **Your Property and Home (Chapter 2).** The next big potential savings in most retirement plans will come from **Pensions (Chapter 3), Savings & Investments (Chapter 4) and Tax (Chapter 5)**. I try to cut through the waffle and get you focused on where you can really save money with loads of precise **'top tips' in a book that is updated for the 2024/25 budget announced in October 2024**. I should also warn you that I expect more predators stalking your wealth, so I provide some points to help avoid their pension traps and the risk to your wealth around this. The UK has a magnificent financial services safety net that could just help you in recessionary times. Straying outside the regime and its protections could cost some readers a fortune if a financial institution goes bust or you encounter a rogue adviser. By the way, my tips come from experience as I worked in Insolvency and Corporate Recovery during the 1989 to 1993 recession and then as the Manager of the Investigations and Recoveries Unit at the UK's Investors Compensation Scheme (predecessor of the Financial Services Compensation Scheme). My other very relevant experience comes from over two decades advising, as a Fellow of the Institute of Chartered Accountants, clients on their businesses and tax. I have presented at Retirement Planning Courses since 2018 and have written Retirement Planning books since 2012. This has given me a useful perspective!

I didn't want to go over the top on cutting costs as we all need to try and live a bit better but I do recognise that your plan could be improved with improving how you handle and slash down ugly debt **(Chapter 6, Clear debt)** and better knowledge on **Cutting costs, Raising complaints** and fending off **Scammers (Chapter 7).** The extent to which you find the **'save more'** chapters on this book useful will depend on your personal circumstances. If you are newly retired with a good final salary scheme you may skim over the pensions chapter as you have a fixed and strong pension base. On the other hand, if you are in your 40's and are a higher rate taxpayer in a defined contributions pension scheme the pensions chapter may save you thousands of pounds (as I see many times every year in my day-to-day work).

THE 'EARN MORE' ESSENTIAL STEP. The third essential step is considering how you can **'earn more'**. This is the other side of the economic equation on balancing the retirement plan. It may involve **Starting Your Own Business (Chapter 8)** or maybe the solution **to start putting yourself first and re-model your existing job through flexible working or find a *'better'* job (Chapter 9**) as you glide towards retirement**?**

THE 'LIVE BETTER' ESSENTIAL STEP. The fourth essential step is perhaps the most important section of all. It's about living better as we glide into and through retirement. It's about retuning your **Well-being, Personal Relationships and Health (Chapter 10)** and perhaps the best of the lot, **Experiences, Leisure and Holidays (Chapter 11)**. Life, however, comes with some inevitable bumps and bruises and challenging or sad times. Taking care of our young people or elderly relatives can also present financial and emotional challenges. For many readers these may happen at the same time and hence the tips for the **'Sandwich Generation' (Chapter 12)**. This chapter also covers wills, power of attorney and executors to help you start these difficult conversations. I close the **'live better'** step with three final pages that are all about **Your Plan (Chapter 13)**. It is where <u>you</u> make notes to plan <u>your</u> actions and follow up research to help achieve a better retirement. I have also left some extra space in the margins of each page throughout the book (a bit like a workbook) for you to make any extra notes.

I can also **guarantee** that **I have never and will never take a commission or other**

inducement to tip something. The hundreds of highlighted tips are simply because I think they are worth looking into. To get you started I've set out my top 10 tips for 2025/26.

MY TOP TEN TIPS FOR 2024/25 AND INTO 2025/26

1. **Put yourself first** and **'re-set'** your thinking towards a **glidepath** and not a cliff-edge retirement. Start your plan, put those key numbers into it and then create a glidepath and not a cliff-edge retirement. Could you start your retirement 5 years earlier than you planned? **(Chapter 1)**

2. Give yourself good quality **time to think** what you (and any partner) really want in life. It is choice and not chance that usually shapes a better retirement. **Good choices** flow from better information so start increasing the quality information on retirement and start to make a plan **(Chapter 1).**

3. Trade some of your wealth for experiences as "you'll be more disappointed by the things you don't do than the ones you did do" (Mark Twain). A good retirement doesn't have to mean 'rich' but it can mean 'content' and there is a wealth of free experiences to tick off. Make a list of the experiences that you really want to happen or achieve over your retirement glidepath and put them in your plan. **(Chapter 11).**

4. Property prices have grown by more than average earnings and RPI since October 2001. Well done if you have reaped the benefit as a homeowner. They now appear to be stabilising, but I have no crystal ball on the next move. I think, however, the really key question during **'re-set'** thinking around a glidepath retirement is about **rightsizing or relocating** to free up a 'fun pot' and get the right home closer to the location/services/lifestyle you will need in the future **(Chapter 2).** Property can be the magic wand of retirement planning.

5. Get a **health MOT** with your GP or privately. Find opportunities that address any identified health risks and those common older age risks around isolation, lack of activity and poor diet. Make commitments to any necessary lifestyle changes and obsess about each change until it becomes a new habit **(Chapters 10).**

6. Whilst still in work make sure you are getting all the **'free money' your employer is providing** via pension and share saving plans within HMRC limits **(Chapters 3 and 4).**

7. **Tax. Use your UK tax-free limits and thresholds.** Know your tax bands and rethink who holds the investments/ savings (between a husband and wife or civil partners). Use Individual Savings Accounts ('ISAs') to ensure the interest and dividend earned are exempt from tax in both 2024/25 and 2025/26. Re-focus on how to fund pensions to 'play' the tax bands and reduce your tax as there are some very generous pension related tax breaks that may not survive future budgets if the UK economy does not grow as hoped. Capital Gains Tax has been slashed in recent years. The October 2024 budget announced significant taxes to be raised from pensions, farms and business disposal through inheritance tax. This could see the biggest gifting away of wealth at an earlier stage by the wealthy. So, the unexpected beneficiaries of the October 2024 budget could by the children of the wealthy who may receive the money at the time when it is needed more. Planning with a specialist Independent Financial Adviser is probably underway already albeit the budget changes remain to be completed as I write (December 2024). **(Chapters 3 and 5).**

8. The ongoing cost of living issues may hurt your finances. Make sure you stay within the **UK financial services safety net** and that means only dealing with advisers registered with the Financial Conduct Authority. Re-carve your savings and investments so you stay within the Financial Services Compensation Scheme limits. Protect yourself with the 'Section 75 magic wand' on credit card purchases **(Chapter 7).** Cut costs **(Chapter 7)** and slash ugly debt **(Chapter 6)** and reconsider how you can '**earn more**' (or better) via **Chapters 8 and 9** via paid work and starting a business.

9. **Make a will** and take out powers of attorney **(Chapter 12).**

10. Public services, the care system and health service seem to be crumbling causing issues for our younger and older relatives. You may be caught in the middle **(the 'sandwich' generation)** but there are things you can do to help both generations and yourself **(Chapter 12).**

Give yourself time to think and start your plan and actions as early as possible so that you do not have a cliff-edge retirement. Start putting yourself first, have that **'re-set'** and aim for a glidepath into the life you want to create. Maybe even start the retirement journey 5 years early? Life has changed for all of us over the last few years and, overall, my **four essential steps** of **plan more, save more, earn more** and **live better** will help you **'re-set'** and achieve a better retirement as we progress through some challenging times ahead in the remainder of 2024/25 and as you then move through 2025/26 **- guaranteed!**

Allan Esler Smith FCA
December 2024

Chapter One

Could you retire five years earlier? Plan more!

"Excellence is never an accident. It is always the result of high intention, sincere effort, and intelligent execution; it represents the wise choice of many alternatives - choice, not chance, determines your destiny."

ARISTOTLE

Folk that know me wouldn't say that I go around quoting philosophers, but in a break with tradition and immediately above I've started with a powerful quote. In simple terms Aristotle is saying you should think straight and start making better choices based on better knowledge rather than crossing your fingers and leaving things to chance. If you do that things should be better. In other words, live life by design and not by default. This book will help you in that **'re-set'** moment and once you realise that retirement can be more about a glidepath rather than a cliff-edge you will start to see the opportunities. It's quite simple and boils down to my four essential steps where you **plan more, save more, earn more, live better** and, ultimately, achieve a better retirement. The earlier you start the better. Could this be the year where you gather in more knowledge, put yourself and your family first and make better choices that pave the way to a brighter retirement. **I want to cut through the waffle and give you unbiased, straightforward, hard-hitting, practical advice in easy-to-understand information.**

Choice
not chance
determines
your destiny

I'm starting with information to help you understand how much income you are likely to need in retirement. Firstly, with some averages and then we are going to work this through, so you get something more tailored to your circumstances. Armed with these numbers you'll pretty much know if your finances are sufficient to get you through retirement and, if not, then what you can do about it. The finance numbers can look daunting, but they are easy once you know how. It just needs a clear head, some straight thinking, and the ability to add up.

Let's start with some high-level numbers and take it from there. I like to use the Pensions and Lifetime Savings Association's *'Retirement Living Standards update'* (the most recent one at the time of writing this 2025 edition of my book in December 2024 was dated February 2024) to provide a starting point for thinking about the amount you may be spending in retirement. The 'standards' set the cost of three retirement lifestyles: Minimum, Moderate and Comfortable. Each lifestyle has an approximate annual cost determined by a basket of goods made up of household bills, food and drink, transport, holidays and leisure, clothing and personal care and helping others. The categories, amounts and what life could look like are below and you can dig into more detail at retirementlivingstandards.org.uk and use this as a good starting point for your own plan.

	2024 'cost' per annum of the living standard *	What life could look like
Minimum Single Couple	 £14,400 £22,400	Around £50 a week on groceries, £25 a month eating out and £15 a fortnight on takeaways. A week's holiday in the UK. Basic TV and broadband and 1 streaming service. About £630 for clothing and no car. £20 for each birthday and Xmas present. £50 a year charity donation.
Moderate Single Couple	 £31,000 £43,100	Around £55 a week on groceries, £30 a week eating out and £10 a week on takeaways. Around £100 a month taking others out to eat. A fortnight's 3* all inclusive holiday in the Med and a long weekend break in the UK. Basic TV and broadband and 2 streaming

		services. Up to £1,500 for clothing. 3 year old car replaced every 7 years. £30 for each birthday and Xmas present. £200 a year charity donation and £1,000 to support family members e.g. paying for grandchildren activities.
Comfortable Single Couple	£43,100 £59,000	Around £70 a week on groceries, £40 a week eating out and £20 a week on takeaways. Around £100 a month taking others out to eat. A fortnight's 4* holiday in the Med with spending money and 3 long weekend breaks in the UK. Extensive bundled TV and broadband subscription. Up to £1,500 for clothing. 3 year old car replaced every 5 years. £50 for each birthday and Xmas present. £300 a year charity donation and £1,000 family support.

*IMPORTANT: the figures shown are the amounts of annual expenditure required to achieve the living standard (they are not gross income figures before tax).

Now for the tough bit. It's the vitally important difference between what is achievable versus desirable. You may aspire to a comfortable retirement now that you can see what it translates to in financial numbers but are those numbers achievable based on your net wealth and future income prospects? If you are about to start retirement, do you already have the net wealth and funds in pensions and savings to meet or exceed the living standard that you aspire to using the above as a rough starting point and refining it to better suit your circumstances? **Importantly** it's the money you need to spend <u>after</u> tax as the numbers are the amount you actually spend. This is often misunderstood so I'm underlining the point twice. Advancing things a little further: are you also happy that your net worth and income during retirement will fund that sort of annual expenditure for all the retirement years ahead (subject to both funds and spending moving in line with inflation)? Then for the even tougher bit – and we might as well get into the big issues straight away - the great unknown of the length of time ahead of us. It's the subject that actuaries could write a whole book on but for now let's keep it simple and just give you a starting point. The UK government's Office of National Statistics ("ONS") have a 'life expectancy calculator' on their website which estimates that a male aged 66 in December 2024 has a life expectancy of 85, a 25% chance of reaching 92 and a 3.1% chance of reaching 100. A female of the same age has a life expectancy of 87, a 25% chance of reaching 94 and a 5.5% chance of reaching 100.

If the starting point of the review yields a resounding yes to your income and net worth in retirement being more than sufficient to fund the likely expenditure of the lifestyle you aspire over your likely retirement years then you are basically there- well done! You can focus more on the lifestyle and 'living better' sections of this book.

For others there will now be some thinking, planning and looking at the living standard that is actually achievable and/or what levers can be pulled to rebalance your retirement plan and budgets. Some of the levers I'll outline might radically reshape your plans and you might even be able to start your glidepath into retirement 5 years earlier. Making this happen and determining your destiny (as the Aristotle says in the quotation I use to introduce this chapter) will come from you improving your knowledge and then making better **choices and not by leaving it all to chance**. This all starts with improving your planning, the first of the four essential steps, and this book will look in detail at all the levers you can pull to make a difference by planning more, earning more, saving more and living better (the four essential steps of the Retirement Planning Expert 2025 book). Bringing this all together will help you achieve a better retirement as you learn about and act on these levers (opportunities and/or avoiding the risks). This is even more important in the UK in 2025/26 as retirees are facing some of the toughest financial challenges for a generation, including over the last 5 years:

- Dealing with the Covid-19 pandemic from Spring 2020 onwards- both from the health care and wellbeing perspective.
- Then dealing with the cost-of-living crisis started by the surge in fuel prices in 2022 and then the inflation tidal wave in 2023 (albeit now starting to reduce).
- If you still have a mortgage on a property, 2023 saw mortgages rise to levels not seen since the last financial crisis in 2008. Mortgages continue to be relatively high when looking back over the last decade. The drag effect will squeeze the spending power of those who renewed their mortgages in 2024 and this may continue to sting in 2025.
- Stealth taxes will also squeeze out more of your disposable income with the freezing of key tax allowances and tax thresholds until 2028 (unless changed beforehand by a new budget).
- The pensions landscape is tougher than it was for the previous generation.

Gold plated final salary pensions have reduced and the state pension age keeps increasing.
- Personal pressures arise from deteriorating public services around care for the elderly which increases the pressure points on you- the next generation- to fill the gap. At the other end of the spectrum our adult children are returning to the nest and often remaining until their 30s as property prices and rents prove a barrier to moving on.
- Economic growth in the UK may be the magic wand to improving public services. But if growth falters or the 'black hole' in the UK government funds deepens we may find that taxes may increase or that tax reliefs are tuned down.

Against this the retirement landscape is also improving and providing opportunities that may allow your retirement glidepath to be more rewarding, including:
- Pensions freedom and the ability to access some pensions at an earlier age.
- Flexible working arrangements that may allow you to start your retirement glidepath earlier (maybe even 5 years earlier).
- Improving your planning for your retirement glidepath with this book.

To help with your '**re-set**' and plans to navigate through the complexities of a modern retirement more is explained in this book with **'TOP TIPS'** highlighted in boxes to give you the knowledge in an unbiased way that is straightforward, hard-hitting, and easy to understand. You are now ready to start making some better choices.

This chapter at a glance

- *Understand the three phases of retirement (active, passive and with care) and, ultimately, the life you wish to lead in <u>each</u> of these retirement phases.*
- *Use a simple approach to doing the sums and start to refine your own retirement plan.* The word 'budget' or 'plan' can send some folk running to the hills. But let's face facts from the start of this book. The life you wish to lead in each phase of retirement will come at a cost. What you may desire in retirement may be completely different from what you can actually achieve. The simple fact is that getting to the reality of your retirement net wealth, income and expenditure can be difficult but you'll get there with a bit of time and effort with this book. This chapter therefore sets out an approach to help put you in a better position and provides signposts to further help.

Pre-retirement planning- it's never too soon to start

It's never too soon to start your pre-retirement planning and, indeed, you may have embraced financial life planning long ago. Martin Gorvett, Chartered Financial Planner, of Lavender Financial Planners Ltd, helps you get to grips with the simple reality of this. Financial worries do not necessarily derive from lack of money, but more often from lack of planning. "If you want to make the most of your money, putting it to good use by investing in your future self, then a plan is needed. This needn't be set in stone, in fact it's important to allow your plan to be adaptable, because life is certainly not a straight line drawn on a piece of paper with various events along the way. Your plan needs to be broad and address all the key moments that you target in life (buying your first house, funding children in education and then on to the housing market, establishing your own business, eventual retirement etc). It should also consider those moments that bring financial worry (sickness, unemployment, early death etc). This isn't something you can ask AI to do for you – your circumstance and attitudes are unique to you – but it's something that above all can bring a sense of financial well-being for the journey ahead".

Ideally you are reading this in your 30s or 40s as the earlier you start the more time you have to build plans and adapt them. In your 50's and 60's there are still lots of things you can do to achieve a better retirement so read on. As mentioned at the start of this chapter, what life do you want to create as you move into retirement – how does it look in terms of location, lifestyle, holidays and use of time? Everyone will be different, and each lifestyle will have a different standard of living. As you get older the money you will need to achieve it will change as, indeed, will your activity levels. This is the starting point of your retirement plan. Martin Gorvett, Chartered Financial Planner summarises the challenge. "The earlier you can start planning the more choices you will have. If you want to retire at 60, there is no point in starting to plan at 59….! Beginning your planning early makes things like budgeting habitual, allowing more flexibility for any bumps in the road. It can also generate surpluses that can be spent on achieving your financial goals earlier than expected – with time being the most valuable commodity, this will feel like a huge win".

The three phases of retirement after your 're-set' moment

Here is the vital bit. Your finances and lifestyle will change significantly as you advance through, say, a thirty-year retirement glidepath. Your finances, activity levels, opportunities and risks change as you progress through 'retirement' and each of the three distinct phases of that retirement journey. You will achieve a better outcome with a plan to help leverage the opportunities and manage the risks during each phase.

The first phase is ACTIVE retirement (also known as "having a whale of a time")

This is so important. Once you understand this point about the first of the three phases of retirement you're on your way. Your active retirement years start when you leave or adjust your regular full-time work. This might be in your mid to late 50s. The ten to twenty years after this are your 'active retirement years'. I say adjust as you may choose to 'just' downsize the regular job to a less stressful position with perhaps less hours so that you maintain a very active life and enjoy a decent income to supplement your pension and savings. You may still be working but, importantly, you have '**re-set**' your life and your retirement glidepath has started. This '**re-set**' and putting yourself first is becoming increasingly available from more progressive employers who understand the benefits of retaining and rewarding experience. This approach is needed in a relatively full employment economy where employers really do need you more than you might realise. Positive and progressive employers leverage employment positive policies such as flexible working (part-time working, compressed hours); buying extra holiday; working school-time only; allowing unpaid leave or career breaks (for that holiday of a lifetime travelling while you still have loads of energy and an income afterwards) or allow late starts or early finishes. Not all of these will be available at every workplace but if some are then they give you an opportunity for more time off (time to put yourself first) to start building your glidepath into retirement (more at **Chapter 8, Career Transition: Paid Work and Volunteering**).

In the 'active years' you are still 'buzzing' (or having a 'whale of a time' as I like to say in the courses I run) and enjoying a great social life with more holidays, more hobbies and you may even relocate within the UK or abroad as part of unlocking a 'fun pot' from your property (more at **Chapter 2, Your Home and Property**). It will still be an expensive time and you may also eat into those savings you had built up so that you can enjoy these years to the full. It should be an expensive, but rewarding, period of your retirement and is probably the best of the three phases of retirement. Remember the important word in that last sentence 'expensive' and that will need to factor in your plans.

The second phase is PASSIVE retirement

Your passive retirement years are generally in your seventies and eighties. Work income may have largely dried up and you are now mostly reliant on pension income and any savings that are left after you were having a whale of a time during the active retirement phase. Finances will be tighter (although spending will be lower) and you will also probably have to accept there will inevitably be changes in what you can and cannot do as medical issues arise. Associated with this will be questions about your property location and proximity to social and medical facilities (it's that **Chapter 2**, Property again but don't worry that comes next and is only a few pages ahead). Overall, you will be reassessing if your home remains cost efficient to your lifestyle, manageable and in the right location. The passive phase is nearly always the least expensive of the three retirement phases.

The third phase is retirement WITH CARE

Medical and other care needs may dictate what you do and where you live. Your savings will probably be gone (gifted away?) and your income may rely solely on state and occupational pensions. Your day-to-day spending will be lower or will need to be cut to meet your income. Your home may need to be used to underwrite care at home costs or some form of residential care. The average cost of residential care in the UK is £60,320 per annum (£1,160 per week) while average fees at a nursing home are £73,320 per annum and vary depending on geographical location and the quality of the service provided- more at Chapter 12, Sandwich Generation and 'planning for care home fees'. At this stage all your possessions may be reduced to a bedroom or bedroom and attached living room. Your space may be bigger and the costs may be less if care is arranged in a home environment. Handle these figures with care as there can be huge variations depending on location, lifestyle choices and amenities provided. The addition of the cost of care/ a care home can make this stage the most expensive phase of retirement. In very broad terms if you have 'capital' (savings, investments and assets) of more than £23,250 (again, more in Chapter 12) you are expected to pay the fees for your care. The cost may come initially from any savings that are left and then from eroding the equity in any house you may own each year. This may conflict with your ultimate inheritance and gifting plans and so you may now see how the whole 'picture' comes together in your plan as you progress through this workbook (and read Chapter 2, Your Home and Property, Chapter 5, Tax and Chapter 12 Sandwich generation).

Top tip

Grasp and understand the three phases of retirement and how your lifestyle, income, savings and expenditure patterns will change over the three phases. 'Do the sums' and then increase your knowledge around retirement planning and the related opportunities and risks so that you can make better choices and achieve a better retirement.

Know your net wealth and how it changes

Net wealth takes me back to my earliest days in finance. It is a simple but important concept if you strip it back to the basics. On the one hand it is everything you own (assets) and on the other it is everything you owe (liabilities). The assets less liabilities calculation varies over your lifetime and probably peaks in your late 50s for homeowners. You may have up-sized over several house moves, paid off the mortgage, have investments and savings, pension funds and other assets. If you are lucky there may be little or no debt (maybe a small bank loan and a bit on a credit card). You should know your net wealth and when it peaks and how that overall wealth could be applied as part of your retirement plans, any gifting and any inheritance.

Know your £ numbers - money in/money out

Once you retire there will inevitably be changes in your financial affairs over the three distinct retirement phases. Your lifestyle and income will change but as mentioned earlier so, too, will your pattern of expenditure. Many people worry about this, but the good news is that provided you are prepared to do a little planning, things will work out better. The earlier you do this the better as you will have more time to plan your **'re-set'** and future lifestyle. You will be able to achieve a better retirement through quality information and then better choices. You will plan more, save more, earn more and live better.

This is where we try to refine and improve the approximate figures generated by the Pensions and Lifetime Savings Association's *'Retirement Living Standards update'* that I set out at the start of this chapter. It's a two step process. Firstly, establish a reality check on your likely income over your retirement glidepath. Secondly, assess how much you currently spend a year and how that might need to change (this brings me back to the point I made earlier about what is achievable versus what is desirable). You might want a drive a top of the range convertible sports car, have a holiday home in Spain, go on three cruises a year, dine out twice a week and gift £50,000 to each child or grandchild- it may all be desirable but it may not be achievable – it might just be pie in the sky. Once you get a grasp on what is more likely and achievable you can then start to plan to adjust things and make it that bit better- and sometimes radically better. And remember it's not just about achieving a better financial plan it's just as much about achieving a better lifestyle (and much more on the lifestyle aspects in the second half of the book). The steps in this book will take a bit of time and effort but it will give you peace of mind and will help you identify improvements to your plan that you can implement straight-away or in the future for a better retirement. It's all about spending time putting together an annual budget and assessing your predicted pension income at the start of your expected glidepath into retirement; also, your expected savings at that point (potentially for the 'big one-offs that I'll flag up in a moment) and other assets in your net wealth that could be leveraged in your plan. If you are someone who has always had a personal budget then things should be pretty straightforward and you simply need to take a hard look at your expected income and expenditure pattern once you retire and over the three phases of retirement. Things will change on retirement and very few forty and fifty year olds grasp the reality of their pension and savings plans and what that will mean in reality for their retirement years. Before you know it you are at a cliff-edge retirement and maybe attending a retirement planning course 6 months before you retire and wishing you had planned a glidepath retirement a decade earlier.

For three decades I've watched retirees stumble into a cliff edge retirement and I've also watched accountants and financial advisers claiming this sort of planning and budgeting as their own territory. It's actually fairly easy and you should be able to do it with a bit of time and effort and this book will get you off to a good start. It becomes much easier once you have the basic figures in place for the first time and you can then build it and refine it from there.

Step 1. Work out your likely income

Let's start with your income calculations, which should be relatively straightforward. You start by inserting on the template at the end of this chapter your current income - nothing could be easier.

Then set out your estimated retirement income based on the year you will start your retirement glidepath. This needs some more work to get an estimate of any pension entitlements. However, what should be a simple task can be complex and sometimes it seems like wading through treacle due to the jargon and sometimes slow and convoluted communications with pension providers but I have set out more help and 'jargon-busters' in Chapter 3, Pensions. Those pension entitlements will come from your state pension and any previous employment or private pension provision you might have made. Such pensions are, however, taxable so don't fall into the trap of pension income might equal retirement spending power. In your calculations you would need to make an allowance for any tax due on them, less tax allowances such as the tax free 'Personal Allowance' (much more in Chapter 5, Tax). State Pensions are not taxable at source. However, the tax authorities will usually adjust your Personal Allowance to take account of what you receive in State Pension and use that to set an appropriate tax code for your employment or private pensions which usually means those pensions are paid net of basic rate tax (and currently there is no national insurance on pension income). I know, I know... it's starting to get complex but hang in as this bit was never going to be easy and as I said a moment ago this needs a bit of work and effort but that's probably the most difficult bit sorted.

An additional point about a State Pension is that many people '**re-set**' and retire before pensionable age. In those circumstances they may have to use any savings and investments to balance the books until such time as they become eligible for their State Pension. One positive thing about this is that when the State Pension does eventually arrive they may feel better off.

You then need to estimate any income you expect from investments or savings– again taking account of any tax that may be due, albeit there are beneficial tax breaks that allow you £1,000 of interest tax free if you are a basic rate taxpayer and £500 for higher rate taxpayers (£0 for additional rate taxpayers).

Finally, you may have prospects of some further paid work (employed or from your own new small business) after you start your retirement. Or perhaps you may plan to serve as a non-executive director on some advisory body or quango or just take a little job doing something you've always fancied. Any income from such sources should be included in your plan – again allowing for Income Tax and National Insurance (the latter continues on earned income until you reach state retirement age).

As you work through the chapters that follow your knowledge will improve on the above and, as a result your plan will improve and you will be able to start making better choices rather leaving it to chance.

Step 2. Work out your likely expenditure

You start by inserting on the template at the end of this chapter your **current** expenditure based on the categories below. Don't guess or estimate. Determine the numbers now based on you bank accounts and credit cards over a year. Extracting data via a csv file into excel is relatively easy from most accounts. Otherwise, it's more time needed to manually review and extract the data from your bank statements and credit cards. In reality, and in my experience, most people significantly underestimate their expenditure. Don't fall into this trap and do the work to get the correct starting point.

This is another complex bit but bear with me... ignore inflation and in accounting terms base it on the present days value and I'll explain why later in this chapter. Then set out your best estimate of what the expenditure may look like in the future during your active retirement years based on the life standard and cost that is achievable. Estimating expenditure in the future, while perhaps slightly more complex and less precise than income, is also relatively straightforward providing you have a decent starting point based on current expenditure and the following notes provide some more guidance.

Food and drink

What is purchased and what it costs can vary greatly from family to family. Your eating and drinking habits may increase in the active retirement years, reducing in the passive years and then again reducing further in the retirement with care years. Remember to include eating out and take aways and those coffees and a cake that don't seem expensive but can add up quickly. If you have not done this before the total may surprise you but don't be put off.

Household and property

The obvious items are utilities, rent, council tax/rates, water rates and insurance. If you own a property factor in any outstanding mortgage although many plan to end mortgage payments well before or around the time they are due to retire so that should represent a major saving in retirement. It is always the major repair and maintenance household costs that tend to trip up any budget from updating bathrooms and kitchens to needing roof repairs. Ideally these one-off major spends will come out of an existing savings pot (see the section 'savings and the big one-offs' below) rather than your annual income. If not, you may need to start setting something aside each month before starting your retirement glidepath to create a 'reserve'/ savings pot. Or is it time to right-size the property (as big and old properties cost more to maintain) or relocate to a cheaper region? Both tactics can release significant funds to create a better retirement. A property can be the biggest component in your overall net wealth and it can be leveraged to reduce costs, increase disposable income and help create the living standard you aspire to. More in Your **Home and Property, Chapter 2**.

Travel

Cars are expensive and if you have two cars it's time to ask if you really need 2 cars especially if you right-size and relocate your property (more in Your Home and Property, Chapter 2). If you were provided with a company car while working this could mean quite significant additional expenditure starting at the purchase price and adding road tax, insurance, servicing, replacement parts, MOT and any subscriptions to motoring organisations. Cars don't keep going forever, so you may need to think about a replacement every 5 years. The good news is that many new cars come with exceptionally good three-, five- or even seven-year warranty provision so do shop around and look for value here – even if you do have to give up that cherished 'brand' that you have always bought. If you prefer a monthly budget a 'Personal Contract Purchase' ("PCP") loan or Contract hire may work better over 24, 36 or 48 months. You can pay a one-off fee (called the final balloon payment) to take ownership of the car at the end of the contract or hand it back and your obligations end. There are too many pros and cons on PCPs and Contract hire to go into here but you can start to explore the option on moneysaving expert (search for 'personal contract purchase'.)

Leisure and donations

The whole idea of a '**re-set**' and glidepath retirement is that you should have more time to enjoy yourself. While some of the most enjoyable things in life are free others do require some expenditure. Club fees and any other social clubs you are involved with or join to broaden your horizons will come with some cost but this is possibly what you have been waiting for so pay and enjoy. Much more is set out in **Chapter 12, Experiences, Leisure and Holidays**. But probably the main item of expenditure could be holidays and weekend breaks. If there is a big holiday of a lifetime that you have promised yourself maybe this comes out of your 'savings and big one-offs' as per the section below. You will almost certainly have more time for these, and this cost may rise significantly in the active retirement years. This is a difficult area to estimate but you should not ignore it and should make your best guess as this may underpin another quality side of your better retirement. If you are overly ambitious you can cut back, and conversely if you are overly careful you may find you can afford to do more than you anticipated. Don't forget holiday insurance and the fact that premiums tend to increase as you get older and as your medical history and disclosures increase. You will need to set aside something to cover sundry expenditure. These may be relatively small amounts that, taken individually, you may scarcely notice but which can mount up. For example, if you buy a newspaper every day of the week this could well amount to something in the region of £500 over the whole year. There is also the occasional gift or not so occasional if it involves grandchildren and, indeed, presents and gifts are another big component of this category - underestimate this at your peril. Donations may also increase as you use this time of your life to reflect on organisations that do good work and you feel that it is time to give something back to help them on their way. The list could go on and on. You need to look at the lifestyle standard you aspire to and that is achievable and determine the cost and that you can afford it. This could be one area where there is an element of trial and error and it may just take a little time to work out but once it is in your plan you can refine things over time and with better knowledge and experience.

Savings and the big one-offs

I've already mentioned how the big one-offs tend to wreck even the best retirement planning. In the last few pages I have mentioned: significant property costs (new roof, kitchen, bathroom); replacing the car every 5 years or so and a holiday of a lifetime. There may also be health related costs or property adaptions. The life stages of your family members also need some thought. The millennials and Generation Z (more at **Chapter 12, Sandwich Generation**) have never had it so tough (student debt, unaffordable houses, inflation not matched by wage increases and higher taxes through the stealth tax of freezing tax bands). Do you wish to help children or grandchildren with wedding costs? The average cost of a wedding is £20,700. University costs (fees, accommodation, and maintenance costs) run, potentially, to £50,000 over 3 years. Maybe there is also a house deposit (£20,000)? This can be where the importance of savings and investments comes into focus. When planning your retirement glidepath you will need to assess the potential for 'big one-offs' and how you pay for them. If this has not been done there are still opportunities to do this from, perhaps savings and investments, any pension tax free lump sum, building up a pot from some part-time working (remember you can retire more than once) or tax planning or maybe even right-sizing/relocating your property. There are levers that can make a big difference and this book will help you with more information and tips as you work through it.

At the same time older generations may look at gifting away inheritances at a much earlier stage than may have happened in previous generations with improved knowledge and planning around inheritance tax and the seven year rule (more at **Chapter 5, Tax**). Maybe that's another route to cover those big-one offs that involve helping children or grandchildren or good causes i.e. gifting away at an earlier stage when they may actually need it more? At this point you may be feeling that the challenge of preparing your retirement plan is getting a little daunting. But as you work through the chapters that follow your knowledge will improve and, as a result, you should be able to make better choices and achieve a better retirement.

Balancing your books

If at the first count income balances with expenditure and your savings and investments look like you can cover any big one-off payments then you are either very lucky or you are a financial genius. If income and savings exceed expenditure you have no problems and, after checking that there are no errors in your figures, you can go and book an extra holiday! The likelihood is, however, that you will find that expenditure exceeds income and savings.

In these circumstances you might find you still have time to save more by perhaps increasing your pension income in the future. One way is by deferring income now that you pay a higher rate tax upon to a later point in time when you may be paying a lower rate of tax (more at **Chapter 3, Pensions**). Or maybe you go and earn more. All will become clear as you work through the next two essential steps on retirement planning about 'save more' and 'earn more' so that you can then go on to enjoy the best step of all 'living better'. Again, the earlier you start these actions the better.

How to go about it

The table at the end of this chapter gives a proven outline of how you might do this. Just look at the general headings and ignore the detail of splitting it into months at this stage. The headings are not set in stone as people have differing patterns of income and expenditure and you need to tailor it to your own personal needs and circumstances.

While you may be able to get by with a yearly budget, it is probably worthwhile to take just a little more time and set everything out on a monthly basis. This also has the advantage that you can see if things are not quite working out as you go along, rather than being surprised at the end of the year. All of this is easier to deal with if you can adjust things on a monthly basis to compensate for what will probably be inevitable changes.

Finally, estimate how your savings and investments become diluted (if expenditure exceeds income) and what happens as you progress through the active years and into passive years (perhaps less expenditure) to then the retirement with care years (when your home may be used to finance care home fees).

I'd suggest putting it all on a spreadsheet. If you have been used to dealing with spreadsheets in your working life this will not be difficult. The sort of very simple spreadsheet suggested at the end of this chapter is easy to set up in an hour. It would certainly be worthwhile as it enables you to update things quickly and roll forward year on year.

A final word on doing the sums

Don't be put off by all of this – you do not need to follow the suggestions slavishly. The intention has been to start you thinking about the way your financial affairs might change when you retire and then pass through the three phases of retirement. Those more used to financial modelling will spot that I have not mentioned the effects of inflation and how this can erode your finances (and budget). They are probably right but for now I just want to get you thinking more clearly about the numbers around known income and expenditure. I've assumed that inflation will affect both income and expenditure in broadly the same way in the longer term albeit I appreciate there was quite a gap in 2023 with inflation soaring to 10% but now moderating and equalising.

Everyone has different circumstances and will have different retirement lifestyle ambitions, so you just need to pause and think about your own situation. If you follow the suggestions in this chapter, adjusted as necessary to your own personal needs, then you should have a better understanding of your future finances as you glide through retirement and can also start to identify opportunities to adjust the numbers. But don't forget that personal budgeting is not a precise science; you have to be flexible and prepared to make adjustments as you go along. If things just seem too complex then the answer is very simple and you just need to engage the services of a good financial adviser or accountant who will be used to shaping these sorts of projections and can also adapt quite easily for 'what if' scenarios. The earlier in life you do this sort of exercise the better chance you have of achieving the retirement you seek.

Top tip

The key to improving your retirement plan lies in the four sections of this book: plan more, save more, earn more and live better and you will ultimately achieve a better retirement. If you turn now to the final pages at Chapter 13 you will see possibly the most important pages of all for you. It's a space for you to start setting down your own actions and choices and remember the quote at the start of this chapter which is repeated below. Is it time to make your first entry and start to prepare your financial plan based on this chapter? It's your choice.

"Choice not chance determines your destiny."

ARISTOTLE

Useful reading

For further help and information the following should prove useful:

www.moneyhelper.org.uk
www.retirementlivingstandards.org.uk

RETIREMENT PLANNING EXPERT 2025 BUDGET AND PLANNER

BUDGET AND PLANNER	Current annual income and expenditure	Annual income and expenditure from starting retirement	Annual income and expenditure from state pension age
INCOME			
Paid work (after tax)			
State Pension (less any tax due)			
Pension 1 (after tax)			
Pension 2 (after tax)			
Dividends from investments (after tax)			
Interest on savings (after tax)			
Any other income			
Total income (A)			
EXPENDITURE			
Food and drink			
Groceries			
Drink			
Meals out and takeaways			
Total food and drink			
Household and personal			
Mortgage or rent			
Council tax/ rates			
Water rates			
Insurance			
Electricity, gas and oil			
Clothing			
Telephone, mobile and broadband			
TV packages			
Routine decorating, repairs and maintenance			
Garden upkeep and maintenance			
Hair, nails, beauty and health			
Cash spending			
Other/ contingency			
Total household and personal			
Transport and car			
Petrol/fuel			

Tax			
Insurance and breakdown cover			
Service, parts and repairs			
Any other regular transport costs (train, taxi etc.)			
Total transport and car			
Leisure and donations			
Fitness and gym			
Clubs and hobbies			
Theatre, cinema and cultural			
Annual holidays and weekend breaks			
Pets- food, vets, insurance, boarding			
Sundries, gifts and presents			
Donations			
Total leisure and donations			
Total expenditure (B)			
Surplus/deficit (i.e.total income – total expenditure)			
NET WEALTH			
Property (asset value less mortgage)			
Investments			
Savings			
Other assets (including car value)			
Loans or other liabilities including overdraft, credit cards, car leasing costs, store cards etc			
Future big one-off costs Major house improvements New cars Holiday of a lifetime Gifting on major life events (education, weddings, house deposits etc)			

Attach notes and calculations. Aim to set up the above template as an excel spreadsheet.

Reminder: Take any action points or follow up points to Chapter 13, Your Plan For A Better Retirement.

Chapter Two
Your home and property

"Home is the place that goes where you go, yet it welcomes you upon your return. Like a dog overjoyed at the door. We've missed you is what you hear, no matter how long you have been gone."

MICHAEL J ROSEN

If you own a house one of the biggest opportunities on saving more <u>and</u> achieving a better retirement can flow from property and right-sizing or relocating for a tax-free windfall. It gets even better as the property change can (if you get it right) radically reduce your ongoing energy, repair, maintenance and other property costs going forward. The right location may also help you transform the lifestyle you are seeking to achieve in a positive way. Property can be the magic wand of retirement planning and it will always be an early 'save more' chapter in my books. It deserves this place due to the transformative impact it can have on your retirement planning.

Property can be the magic wand of retirement planning

One of the biggest opportunities on **saving more** and achieving a better retirement can flow from property. It can be the magic wand of retirement planning and propel your plans and may even help you start your retirement glidepath 5 years earlier if you get your planning right. Re-tuning your property can provide you with a tax-free windfall and can also let you address personal and social issues that have been burning away in the background. This is especially the case if your children have flown the nest and you are now an empty nester. Remember the essential four steps as you work through this book; plan more, save more, earn more, live better and achieve a better retirement.

Your home is likely to be a significant part of your wealth if you own it (or costs if you rent) and is usually at the centre of your social and family life. The 'reset' and glidepath into retirement offers a perfect opportunity to reappraise your home, your values and priorities around 'the home'. This re-set has been brought more into focus by experiences or thoughts during the Covid-19 pandemic and then the inflation tidal wave that hit us in 2022 and 2023 and an economy that now appears to be struggling.

This chapter at a glance

As a quick guide, this chapter covers in detail the main aspects of home and property that you should consider:

- *Future proofing the place you call home is important.* This means taking an in-depth look at where you currently live and deciding if it will work for you in your retirement - it is called 'right-sizing' and/or 'relocating your home.
- *Rightsizing your property costs.* The pros and cons of property costs and how to reduce these.
- *Moving abroad or taking a second home abroad* can look brilliant through rose-tinted glasses. Find out more and some options in this chapter.
- *Using your home to earn money.*

The home is a central part of lives for both economic and sentimental reasons. The sentimental reasons are emphasised by some old familiar sayings *'Home is where the heart is'*, and *'There's no place like home'* and by Michael J Rosen as quoted at the head of this chapter - I love that quote! Home is our space, our comfort, our shelter, our retreat and a place to welcome family and friends. That is not likely to alter once you retire and it is likely to remain at the centre of your social and domestic life. Let's start with the four basics:

Property prices have risen and risen over the last four decades with the exception of a few bumps along the way (the recession in the early 1990's and the 2008 banking crisis). Property may represent your biggest investment and the biggest part of your overall net wealth which you may now be able to leverage to good effect.

Home owners may hope to have cleared their **mortgage** as part of their plan towards their glidepath retirement- this can be a transformative moment on finances.

Economic factors flow from the **size and age of the property** – big and old properties cost more (energy, repairs and maintenance) and can become unsuitable as you age.

Property prices vary massively across the UK. The Office of National Statistics House Price Index summary available at gov.uk could prompt a rethink on the **location** of your future home as part of a plan towards a better retirement.

Country and government office region	Annual change	Average price October 2024
UK	3.4%	£292,000
England	3.0%	£308,781
Northern Ireland (Qtr 3)	6.2%	£190,553
Scotland	5.5%	£197,451
Wales	4.0%	£222,316
East Midlands	3.9%	£250,605
East of England	2.7%	£344,434
London	0.2%	£519,579
North East	4.7%	£167,132
North West	4.4%	£225,360
South East	1.7%	£381,566
South West	2.7%	£324,709
West Midlands Region	3.7%	£256,384
Yorkshire and The Humber	4.6%	£217,146

Source: Office of National Statistics: UK House Price Index summary, October 2024. Note the Northern Ireland House Price Index is quarterly, not monthly. Contains HM Land Registry data

Crown copyright and database right 2020. This data is licensed under the Open Government Licence v3.0.

This chapter will mention tax issues but remember this is only a guide and it is neither legal nor financial advice; it is no substitute for taking professional advice from a financial adviser or other professional adviser. Any potential tax advantages may be subject to change from future budgets and will depend upon your individual circumstances, and individual professional advice should be obtained.

Time in the market and 'timing' is everything

Over time property has increased in value but also corrects itself after periods of rapid growth. A 43 year history of UK House Price Index can yield useful help.

Average UK property price (all property types)

October 1981	**£21,452 rising**
September 1989	£60,701 period peak (before recession)
October 1991	**£57,435 dropping**
December 1992	£53,213 dropping (period low point)
October 1997	£64.604 rising
October 2001	**£97,964 rising**
October 2004	£152,050 rising
September 2007	£190,032 period peak (before banking crisis)
March 2009	£154,452 dropping (period low point)
October 2011	**£167,673 rising**
October 2017	£225,092 rising
October 2020	£243,575 rising
October 2021	**£259,708 rising**
October 2022	£288,429 (stabilising)
October 2023	£282,389 (falling)
October 2024	£292,000 (period peak)

Source: Office of National Statistics: UK House Price Index: Average price by type of property in United Kingdom. Crown copyright and database right 2020. This data is licensed under the Open Government Licence v3.0.

Time in the market is everything. If a property forms part of your net wealth you have made a good investment that has powered ahead of earnings growth and the Retail Price Index over the last few decades. It may now be able to form a key part of your retirement plans and glidepath. If you had bought the UK 'average house' in October 2001 (at £97,964) the **UK House Price Index** shows that it should have increased by about **198%** 23 years later in October 2024 (at £292,000).

House price growth has significantly outstripped **average weekly earnings annualised** over the same period which showed a **112%** increase i.e. £17,316 in October 2001 and £36,712 in October 2024.

Source: **Office of National Statistics:** Total Average weekly earnings in Great Britain, seasonally adjusted, January 2000 to October 2024

House price growth has also significantly outstripped the **retail price index** (all items) over the same period which showed a **124%** increase i.e. 174.3 in October 2001 and 390.7 in October 2024 (base year 1987 at 100).

Source: **Office of National Statistics:** Retail Price Index (all items) January 1987 to October 2024

Timing is also important. The UK House Price Index also shows that if you had bought a house in September 1989 you would have lost 12.3% by December 1992 (which was a great time to buy). My personal view of the 1988 to 1992 property crash from working in corporate recovery and insolvency at the time was a triple whammy landing together:

- A period of rapid housing demand and house price inflation (of up to 32% in the year to December 1988).
- This demand was spurred on by generous mortgage interest tax relief that was then restricted in the late 1980s.
- Mortgage interest rates of between 8% to 12% and an economic recession biting in 1989 as old industries rationalised and restructured resulting in significant affordability pressures, negative equity and repossessions.

If you had bought a house in September 2007 you would have lost 18.7% a year and a half later by March 2009 (which again was a great time to buy). This crash is probably simpler to explain - it seems to have been caused by people taking on loans they could not afford with some mortgage companies lending more than the property was worth and relying on buyers 'self-certifying' their incomes. The crash was preceded by a period of relatively high demand and price growth (circa 10% in 2007).

The downside of earnings and RPI not keeping pace with house prices means that housing is becoming unaffordable for younger first-time buyers and the supply of affordable housing is low. I also think the surge in borrowing costs that we have seen in 2023 and 2024 may mean that we have hit a point where house prices are stabilising but with some regions bucking the trend.

But the bigger picture for retirement planning is the decade upon decade growth in house prices and, if you own a property, it is likely to form one of the biggest assets in your net wealth.   So, what are the lessons for a glide-path retirement? Well, in terms of house prices we've had almost 15 years of house price growth so right-sizing or relocating to a cheaper area should generate a tax-free capital sum to help your retirement plans. If the transition also involves moving to a smaller and more modern home you will also slash your property costs which may help your financial planning. And most important of all, a property change might help you create the lifestyle that you really want.

Top tip
I think that one of the most important tips in this book for property owners is that property is probably one of the most important magic wands for delivering a positive impact to a retirement glidepath. If you get your planning right your property could help create the lifestyle you want, where you want it, releasing a tax-free capital gain and slash down your costs.

Reassess your property needs and priorities

Your home will hold many sentimental attachments and it will be a tough assignment right at the start of this book and journey but is it now time to reassess what you actually require in a home and where you want that to be? Importantly this review must consider your likely changing circumstances over your future years. With life expectancy in the UK on average at 85 years for men and 87 years for women you can start to think how you would like to live through the three phases of retirement as set out at Chapter 1. Remember it's never too soon to start planning.

Why do people 'rightsize' their home for retirement?

The common reasons for moving home in the approach to retirement or during retirement are:

- To help create the life they now want to live (perhaps in a new location?).
- To reduce costs and increase their wealth.
- To be closer to family.
- Due to actual or anticipated changes in health (bungalows/no stairs etc.).
- Due to changes in marital status.

What to consider when planning a home for the future?

There will be many **sentimental and economic factors** that will influence your decision. Everyone will come at this differently. The following questions may help you take this big question a little further on some **sentimental factors:**

- Where is the life you want to create?

- What cultural and hospitality facilities do you need nearby?

- What healthcare facilities do you need nearby?

- What size of town or city would you need 'nearby' (what is 'nearby' and what is the quality of transport links including airports)?

- What climate would you like and accept or not accept?

- What outdoor activities and clubs/associations/interests nearby would count as a bonus?

- What home and garden safety needs do you have or may need to have?

- Are there considerations for pets?

- Will you have good support networks in the area – family and friends? If not, how do you feel about developing these? Again, if there are no family or friends in the new area do your plans include having a spare room and 'space' for them to stay with you?

- What if your health and other circumstances change?

- If one person in a relationship is unhappy in a location then ultimately both of you will probably be unhappy.

The economic factors are easier. Right-sizing presents a straightforward opportunity to change the financial position and your retirement plan in two significant and positive ways.

The first positive aspect of 'right-sizing' is that the proceeds from the sale of your existing home less the purchase price of a new home (including all costs, including stamp duty) will give either a surplus or a loss. If this is your only property the surplus is called a 'gain' and is tax free (more in Chapter 4, Tax) and forms part of financing a better retirement. Briefly for now, this flows from the UK tax regime where, currently, any surplus (or 'gain' to use tax terminology) is free from tax. That is one of the reasons why people invest in extending and building up their home. With current tax rules there may also be no inheritance tax until your wealth exceeds a million pounds (for a married couple or couple in a civil partnership). Indeed, downsizing by freeing up equity in your property and having a bit more fun now may also help reduce the future 40% inheritance bill on your estate. If there is a 'loss' (for instance you are moving to a more costly house or a more expensive area) the loss needs to be funded from the finances in your retirement plans.

The second positive aspect of 'right-sizing' is the potential to move to a smaller/more modern home and reduce the ongoing cost of utility bills, council tax/rates, insurance, repairs and maintenance. Usually, **big homes** cost more to maintain and **old homes** require more upkeep unless they have been modernised with new insulation, heating, water systems and electrical systems. Smaller homes usually cost less to maintain. New homes tend to require less upkeep and are more energy efficient although garden space can be smaller and may come with a valuable warranty for, potentially, up to 10 years. New home developments that are 'packed in' means you can be significantly overlooked by neighbouring properties although this can be minimised by suitable garden planning. As with almost any property purchases there are positives and negatives so it's just a case of weighing these up and then comparing the numbers. Then assess how this can change your financial plan. Remember the multiplier effect if there is a maintenance and running costs annual saving as this runs on year after year and the amount can be significant when it spans ten or twenty years.

Releasing funds: the options of equity release, downsizing or relocating

If there is a significant gap between the retirement lifestyle you desire and the actual reality of your pension income and your investment income there are many options explored in this book that can bridge the gap. But I often find that one of the most significant is accessing the equity stored in your property by either (a) borrowing money against your property through an equity release scheme to help provide additional income, or (b) freeing up wealth by right-sizing which means downsizing or relocating. Essentially you are converting wealth that is stored up in a property into savings and then into income to spend but each route comes at a price and with pros and cons.

Staying put and using equity release

The process of equity release usually works by you being drawn into the sector by personality led advertising and other equivalent press coverage pushing the potential to 'unlock the capital in your home'. It involves you taking out a mortgage on your property whilst continuing to live there and then receiving a lump sum or drawing down funds against that mortgage. Interest then rolls up on the mortgage debt, which will be repaid when you do come to sell the house and downsize or move into alternative accommodation. The interest on the mortgage may be slightly more than on other commercial mortgages. The equity release options include:

A **lifetime mortgage** is a loan secured against your home where you can access some of the value within your property and not make payments against the mortgage. The amount released depends on your personal circumstance and usually the debt and the interest rolls up and is repaid when you pass away or move into long term care.

Home reversion is a form of equity release where you sell all or part of your home to a reversion company for a cash lump sum. You won't legally own the property any more and can live in the property rent-free for as long as you like. You'll get less than the market value for the share you sell.

Mortgage. A standard mortgage could be a cheaper alternative to a lifetime mortgage but you'll need to pass the affordability and credit checks and your home may be repossessed if you don't keep up the repayments on your mortgage.

A **retirement interest-only mortgage** is a conventional mortgage available to the over 55s where your monthly repayments cover the interest on the loan. The capital is then repaid through the sale of your property when you end the plan, right-size/ relocate, pass away or move into long term care.

The 'equity release' industry was subject to significant mis-selling in the late 1980s and early 1990s when some financial advisers persuaded elderly homeowners to re-mortgage their houses and then gamble on the stock market to try and achieve returns to beat the mortgage interest. It went spectacularly wrong for many due to some poor selling by rogue advisers, the recession, stock market turmoil and high interest rates. At the time I was personally involved in reviewing the damage across the UK as Manager of the Investigations and Recoveries Team at the Investors Compensation Scheme (the predecessor of the current UK safety net the Financial Services Compensation Scheme). Millions of pounds of compensation was paid out to disadvantaged investors and, unfortunately, many claims by investors had to be turned down as investors had strayed outside the UK safety net by not dealing with an authorised financial adviser. I provide more hints and tips around protecting your wealth at Savings and Investments, Chapter 4.

For now, if arranged properly, equity release mortgages may give you an option but these things still carry an instinctive risk due to the potential of receiving less than the value of a property, adviser and other fees and the way interest can roll up in the background on some products. So, it is vital to get trusted relatives on board to help you fully appraise any equity release scheme and look at it from all angles. A financial adviser who is registered with the Financial Conduct Authority and who is not connected with the marketing and promotion of an equity release scheme should be able to help you understand the financial implications and help you consider other property related options. More on finding a good financial adviser is set out in Savings and Investments, Chapter 4. For the equity release perspective the Equity Release Council is the industry body and it aims to facilitate the safe growth of the equity release market (www.equityreleasecouncil.com).

Some positives about equity release:

- You can stay in your home.

- You can save on stamp duty and achieve lower legal, agent and surveyor fees.

- In terms of long-term care planning equity release can be useful if you're looking to fund care and stay in your own home.

- All Equity Release Council members offer a "no negative equity guarantee" which means that, no matter what happens to the housing market, customers will never owe more than the value of their home.

Some negatives to consider about equity release:

- The compounding effect of interest as interest builds on interest. Ensure you understand how this adds up over 5 years, 10 years and 20 years (on top of the actual mortgage that was obtained).

- Your family will receive a smaller inheritance as some of the value in your home, maybe all of it if you live long enough, will go to the mortgage provider.

- The fees to arrange the equity release. Before signing anything get everything set out in writing so that you understand absolutely everything about all fees involved including: adviser's fee paid by you, valuation fee, mortgage fee, solicitor's fees and most importantly any Early Repayment Charge (ERC). Also get confirmation (in writing and beforehand, of course) of any commission payable by the lender to your adviser for you taking out an equity release product. ERC's must be understood as they can vary from 5% to 20%. No if's, no but's … just get clarity on everything, as above, <u>in writing</u> before signing anything.

- The money released may affect your state benefits.

- Borrowing may be limited to about 35% of the value of your home.

- If you wish to downsize in the future the equity remaining after repaying the mortgage and interest may limit your choice and options. Could this, instead, point to downsizing or 'right sizing' at an earlier stage to avoid double disruption and costs? More on these alternatives below.

- You retain responsibility for maintaining the property and paying the bills.

Top tip
Equity release fees and costs must be clearly set out and understood. If you do decide to consider equity release get at least two quotes from advisers and get clarity <u>in writing</u> on all fees, charges and commissions payable before you sign or agree to anything.
There should be no rushed meetings and being asked to 'just sign here' to proceed- if that's the approach run a mile. Take a time-out, reflect and discuss with relatives. Any quality adviser with be delighted to see you taking this considered approach.

If you do go ahead with equity release, think carefully about whether you need all the funds in one go or if you can draw it down in tranches. The latter is called a 'drawdown lifetime mortgage' and is usually cheaper on interest costs as you don't draw the money until you need it and, therefore, save on the interest costs on the amount deferred. This could be useful if your needs were, say, £10,000 in year one for a holiday of a lifetime, £25,000 between years three and five to help with a child/grandchild's three years of university accommodation and subsistence costs and £25,000 at some future point to help with a house deposit or wedding or such like for a child/grandchild.

Downsizing or Relocating

You should also consider if there is a 'better way'– for instance **is downsizing a better option** for some of the benefits of, potentially, a brand-new home, new view, the right size, lower property running and maintenance costs and lower council tax/rates? Add on a more manageable garden and proximity to the shops, facilities and health services which you might need for the next phase in retirement. Against this, issues such as a smaller space and new neighbourhood can be considered together with the costs of buying and selling (including solicitor's fees, estate agent fees and stamp duty). The money released may also affect your state benefits.

Another factor to consider is whether it is better to downsize/right size at the present time rather than in the future and before you get too set in your ways. Perhaps the younger the better as it may help with developing new social circles?

In addition, you could achieve a double win by not only 'right-sizing' but also look at relocating to a new area where property prices are cheaper. Or with a relocation to a cheaper area, you could still have a similar size house if 'size' is important to you but also free up significant equity. The regional variations in house prices as shown at the head of this chapter are significant especially if you are moving out of a sought-after area or high price region.

If you are considering moving to be closer to your family don't overlook the fact that everyone is now more mobile than has been the case in the past. While they may appear settled just now, new opportunities or challenges may mean that they themselves may need to move again – leaving you stranded in your new home, away from both old friends and family.

If you are thinking about moving to a new area that seems more attractive, then check it out very carefully. Don't place too much reliance on lists of so-called (over-priced?) best places to live. They may well have some attractions but you need to be sure they meet your particular requirements. Ideally, before moving it would be sensible to spend quality time in the new area (i.e. weeks and weeks and over different seasons), checking out what it is really like, whether it will meet your changing needs and whether you would be comfortable there socially. And don't forget that the social aspect is likely to be even more important to you in retirement. After a while you'll learn to trust your instincts as well and that 'feeling' that somewhere just feels right- it's a hard thing to explain so I'll just leave it at that.

Assess all those recreational and medical positives and negatives. Don't forget the hidden intelligence that is lying around on the internet, such as TripAdvisor reviews of restaurants and Facebook sites for local community groups, which can all be quite telling/reassuring. If you move from a high-cost area to a lower cost area it is difficult to unwind the decision years later due to house price inflation (and how it accumulates, and the gap widens) and paying stamp duty and other costs again. Could renting out your property and renting in the new location provide a solution to this possible issue whilst you give it a trial period? Finally, many commentators say that 'property prices always go up' but in the last four decades we have seen two significant property crashes as highlighted in the 'timing is everything' section earlier in this chapter.

Top tip
The equity release market has a high media profile and gets much attention through paid for advertising and the use of personality-based promotions. Consider it but you should also consider 'right-sizing' and whether downsizing/ relocating makes better financial and emotional sense. You may even get a super new all-mod-cons living space with a nice new view and retain a big surplus in ££££ to have fun with or pass on.

Staying put and increasing the home size

Many people who retire choose to stay put in the same area where they have lived for years rather than being tempted to move to some apparently ideal new situation. These reasons include being close to where they used to work, or near their families for whom they provide child support or help elderly relatives and staying within reach of friends and where their social networks are. Many people also find it reassuring to remain with their local medical practice and other medical facilities if ongoing or more medical support may be needed.

Even if staying put there may be adjustments to consider based on your new circumstances; if more space is required to accommodate boomerang kids (children who return to the family home after university/college - more in **Sandwich Generation, Chapter 12)** try reviewing these four options, ranging from economical to expensive.

- *Economical.* Invest in a garden room – these have boomed in quality and reduced in price in recent years and range from a glorified wooden shed to fully insulated and double-glazed structures. Some require no planning permission, and some can be built in less than a week. They can provide accommodation solutions which range from simple storage to a hobby room to living accommodation. The size of the building will influence whether or not you need any planning permission or approvals, and your local authority will be able to provide further information.

- *Fairly economical.* A garage conversion is another popular way to increase space in your home; it is reasonably simple and can be surprisingly cost-effective. If you propose to add a room above your garage, any scheme would be subject to appropriate planning permission being granted. This is needed because of the extra height and alteration to the roof line. Rooms above a detached garage make an ideal guest suite, office, study, granny annex or somewhere to carry out a noisy hobby. If you convert a garage you may worry about where you put your car but don't forget that modern cars seem quite capable of surviving without the protection of a garage. Otherwise, a cost-effective car port could be added in as part of the scheme.

- *Quite expensive.* One possibility might be to extend your existing property. If you're considering doing building works, check out both planning and building regulation controls. Some smaller extensions to the rear or side of a property can often be built without having to make a planning application, provided that the design complies with the rules for permitted development (see www.planningportal.gov.uk). But make sure you carefully check the particular rules for the area in which you live as building without the necessary approval can have serious and expensive consequences. Expect tighter rules for conservation areas and listed properties. Obtain quotes from more than one contractor and ask for references or visit their last job and learn to trust your instincts. Friends or your professional adviser can assist with recommendations before you go ahead with any works. Keep things in proportion – extra bedrooms aren't an advantage unless there are sufficient bathrooms or shower rooms and many now prefer the convenience of en-suite facilities. Remember to keep the planning paperwork and electrical certificates as these will be needed when you come to sell the house.

- *Expensive but provides radical new space and environment.* Buying the property next door: if your budget allows, becoming your own neighbour allows more space than an extension without leaving the neighbourhood. This option is neither cheap nor simple and professional advice from an architect is essential. Even if you live in a flat you might be able to buy the adjoining unit or the one above or below, then knock through or install a staircase to achieve double living space. Any construction work being undertaken must, of course, adhere strictly to planning and building regulations. Engaging a good architect will be worth the money as cutting corners will just come back to haunt you when the property is eventually sold. If you can continue to live at the property while work is progressing this can cut down costs as temporary rentals of less than six months can be hard to find; you will also be able to monitor security and work efficiency.

Top tip

Garden rooms have improved in quality and reduced in cost and may not need any planning permission – is this now the best solution to a need for more space at a relatively low cost and very quickly?

Moving abroad – full-time or part-time

If you're planning to retire abroad, the complexities and risk of a property purchase increase due to the dual factors of dealing in a foreign language and with foreign law where rights and remedies differ to the UK. Just now there are added complications and uncertainties as **the relationship between the UK and the rest of Europe has changed dramatically as a result of Brexit**. You will now pay more tax in some European countries and lower tax in others (See Chapter 5, Taxes and 'Retiring Abroad') so take advice from a tax adviser that knows the relevant tax regime. Brexit will also impact lending (mortgage deals on property abroad will be less generous), residency rights (you may need to negotiate visa rights for periods of residency beyond 90 days in a 180 day period or look into 'golden visa' for a price), health care and pensions. In the UK the State Pension increases each year and this will usually continue to apply if you move to EU countries but not in others. Once you move abroad have you considered whether you can still take 25% tax free from your pensions- the rules vary. Understand the tax treatment on savings held overseas or income received from the UK. Some countries such as Portugal, Malta, Italy and Cyprus have had low tax rates on foreign sourced pension and other income to attract ex-pats. On health care you may have to show you have enough income to support you and your family without being a burden on the new country you choose to reside in. It can be complicated but it is important so your research must be thorough and not something 'done on a whim'. If you remain unsure you may want to take advice from an appropriately qualified financial adviser- for instance for the EU it will be an EU regulated adviser. For advice or information about pensions and benefits if you live abroad or have lived abroad try .gov/uk and the 'International Pensions Centre'.

The other less obvious factor is the way things just work differently in overseas countries and this can be frustrating - just ask anyone that lives abroad. But if you're relaxed and flexible then that will help make any transition that little bit better.

Top tip

A great place for a holiday is not necessarily a good place to live permanently or part-time. The idiom 'the grass is always greener on the other side' should be remembered. A move abroad needs quality research and planning and you might just make it work brilliantly.

Some ways of protecting yourself when buying property abroad include:

- Spend an extended period in the area at high and low season before you commit yourself to a purchase and talk with local ex-pats (if they were starting again what would they do differently and how has Brexit changed things etc).

- Get a good solicitor. This is easier said than done but take recommendations from trusted friends and their network and try to identify a solicitor with offices in both the UK and the country you are buying in as this can smooth transactions (especially complex ones where there may be an extra risk factor). Get all documents translated if you are signing them and they are in a foreign language.

- Make sure the solicitor you use is independent and not involved in the sale in any way.

- Keep a very careful watch on any changes affecting those living abroad emerging from Brexit and understand the tax regime (national, regional and local) on your property in terms of acquisition taxes, rental taxes, local taxes and taxes on the sale of a property and/or on death and how your UK savings/income/pensions will be taxed.

There are many websites offering advice and information on retiring abroad. Have a browse through the following:

- www.gov.uk – Britons preparing to move or retire abroad;

- www.expatra.com- guides for overseas living;

- www.expatfocus.com – provides information and advice on a move abroad.

If you have the necessary funds (perhaps through downsizing?) another option would be to continue to live at home and buy another property abroad. If you can afford it, this might give you the best of both worlds. You would still have all the comfort and security of your home base but be able to escape to the sun from time to time as the mood takes you. To ease the financial burden you might consider letting the property out, particularly at peak times. You would, however, need to check the local rules and regulations relating to letting property and taxation – these can vary from country to country and indeed from area to area.

If you do decide that a 'home in the sun' might work as a second property the following budget planner will help you put some flesh on the likely returns to help inform your decision:

- First off, assess the structure and accommodation set-up and assess the cost of one-off adaptation work – security system, en-suites, new kitchen, fencing, roof integrity and the like.

- Income – expected weekly rental x number of weeks. Use Owners Abroad and Airbnb or equivalent sites to assess potential weekly rentals (the amounts can vary in high season), less:

- accountancy fees (you may be able to do it yourself for UK taxation but are there returns required in the foreign country?);
- advertising and marketing;
- bank charges on foreign exchange;
- cleaning and laundry between occupiers and occasional deep clean;
- electricity (higher if you have a heated pool and air conditioning);
- annual safety testing;
- gas/oil if appropriate;
- insurance – buildings and public liability (and loss of rental, i.e. utilities failure

etc);

- maintenance – house;

- maintenance – pool;

- letting agent fees;

- property service charge (flats and holiday-type villages with communal land/facilities);

- property tax of foreign country;

- local tax/rates of the area the property is in;

- gardening;

- security – annual maintenance and call-out fees;

- telephone/broadband;

- satellite or cable television;

- water rates/charges;

- administration costs (post, stationery).

- acquisition taxes, rental income taxes, local taxes and any taxes on the sale of the property or on death.

Top tip

That second home in the sun could cost a lot more than you think and can restrict other holiday getaway flexibility. But if you do the numbers first it could be a fantastic opportunity and help create a perfect retirement.

Counting the cost of a house purchase

In order to fund a house purchase assess all the key numbers and budget for costs – stamp duty alone from April 2025 could 'cost' (after a nil rate band reduced to £125,000) between 2% to 12% of the value of a new home (the higher the purchase price the higher the percentage due to Stamp Duty). For second homes the rates vary from 5% to 17%. So, add up Stamp Duty, legal fees, search fees, removal charges, survey fees, estate agent's commission and a provision for decoration and furnishings and you can refine the cost of moving. Remember agents' fees and service vary from online only offerings to traditional high-street agents. And don't pay too much for your new house. An asking price is just that – an asking price. So do your homework on websites such as Rightmove/ Zoopla which (for most of the UK) list the actual selling price of houses in the street or area for the last decade; consider additions and extensions undertaken by the seller and gain more intelligence on price. Overlaying this are the general market conditions – is it a buyers' or sellers' market? Look at the sales price divided by square feet of the accommodation – this gives a useful indicator. But overriding this and governed by the golden rule of 'location, location, location' is the fact that the truly wonderful properties are often hard to find and even harder to secure so be prepared to research, graft and undergo a bumpy journey if you set your sights really high.

When buying a new home, especially an older property, a building survey is essential before committing yourself. This costs upwards of £500 depending on the type and size of property but it may provide you with a comeback should things go wrong or help in price negotiations. Also, an early review of environmental surveys will help you avoid being sold 'a stinker' – a home built on historic landfill (check the Environment Agency website and search 'historic landfill') or a property in an area of high flood risk (search the Environment Agency website for 'flood map for planning'). Helpful to home buyers, for a small charge, the Land Registry allows members of the public to seek information directly about the 23 million or so properties held on its register via the Land Registry website: www.gov.uk/government/organisations/land-registry.

Your protection

The Property Ombudsman scheme provides an independent review service for buyers or sellers of UK residential property in the event of a complaint. It also covers lettings agents and residential leasehold management. As with most ombudsman schemes, action can be taken only against firms that are actually members of the scheme. See the Property Ombudsman website: www.tpos.co.uk.

Removals

Costs vary significantly depending on the type and size of furniture, the distance over which it is being moved and other factors, including insurance and seasonal troughs and peaks. Shop around and try a quote from just outside your local area as neighbouring removal firms are always keen to get a slice of the action in a nearby area. The British Association of Removers (BAR) lists approved member firms who work to a code of practice, see the website: www.bar.co.uk.

Home security

Your local neighbourhood watch should be able to advise you on home security arrangements. Age UK provide a helpful booklet, *Staying Safe*, which can be downloaded from www.ageuk.org.uk. Why not have a street meeting and invite your local crime prevention officer along to give a talk – it helps to be able to connect that face to a name if you really do need help.

Help with fuel bills

Winter Fuel Payment is now means tested at State Pension age and if you have deferred your State Pension you will need to claim it. It is a tax-free payment. Separately you may get a **Cold Weather Payment** if you're getting certain benefits or support for mortgage interest if the temperature in your area is recorded as, or forecast to be, zero degree Celsius or below over 7 consecutive days. You'll get £25 for each 7 day period of very cold weather between 1 November and 31 March. In Scotland it's an annual £58.75 Winter Heating Payment instead. You could also get £150 off your electricity bill for winter under the **Warm Home Discount Scheme** if you receive the guaranteed credit element of Pensions Credit or you are on a low income. The money is not paid to you - it's a one-off discount on your electricity bill, between October and March. You may be able to get the discount on your gas bill instead if your supplier provides you with both gas and electricity. Contact your supplier to find out.

Living in leasehold

An ever-increasing number of people move into a flat in retirement. If you go down this route three of the big issues to grasp are the length of the lease, your obligations to others and the size of the service fee. The general rule is that the longer the lease the more the property is worth. So, know the length of the lease and who owns the freehold of the building (maybe an investment company, a private investor, or ideally the leaseholders themselves in the form of a management company). With the advent of 'right to manage', leaseholders do not need to own the freehold but will be able to manage the building as if they were the freeholder. Leaseholders should be aware of their responsibilities, such as keeping the inside of the property in good order, paying their share of the cost of maintaining and running the building, behaving in a neighbourly manner and not contravening things as set out in the lease, such as, perhaps, subletting their flat without the freeholder's prior consent, or keeping a pet if the lease clearly states this is not permitted.

The leaseholder has the right to expect the freeholder to maintain the building and common parts. The leaseholder will be required to pay a 'service charge' to the freeholder (or their managing agent) to maintain, repair and insure the building as well as to provide other services, such as lifts, central heating or cleaners. These charges can vary massively but must be 'reasonable'. Leaseholders have a right to challenge the service charge if they feel it is 'unreasonable' via the Leasehold Valuation Tribunal (LVT) but it's better to clearly understand the service charge before you even view a potential leasehold property. see Leasehold Advisory Service (LAS), www.lease-advice.org, and Association of Retirement Housing Managers (ARHM) at arhm.org.

Park life

Park homes or caravans can be an option for retirees- either as a permanent move or part time home. At the upper end of the scale these can be large pre-fabricated bungalows. You should review the governments guidance "Buying a park home: factsheet" (available from .gov.uk) which explains "You are strongly advised to use a solicitor or some other professional in completing a purchase. There are a number of statutory procedures to follow and you, as the buyer, have a number of obligations. Professional assistance will help ensure that sales run smoothly and mistakes are avoided, which could have repercussions for you at a later stage." One key point can be that the site owner is entitled to 10% of the sale price as commission when you sell the park home. Other considerations include does the licence allow full time residential use or just holiday use? Are there restrictions on over 50's only, pets and children? Does the park owner resell you electricity, gas and water (at what cost?) or do you have your own utility contracts? In addition to the 'pitch' or rent fee what are the annual or monthly service charges and council tax charges (or rates)?

Retirement housing and sheltered accommodation

As time moves on it is inevitable that you will start to slow down and may find it increasingly difficult to maintain your existing property. At that stage, you may need to start thinking about the need to move to retirement housing or sheltered accommodation. And, of course, you also need to consider any potential changes in your partner's well-being.

The terms 'retirement housing' and 'sheltered accommodation' cover a wide variety of housing but are designed primarily to bridge the gap between the family home and residential care. There are many well-designed, high-quality private developments of 'retirement homes' on the market, for sale or rent. Generally, you have to be over 55 when you buy property of this kind. Positives include 24-hour emergency alarms or on-site wardens and built-in design features such as walk-in showers, wide doors, level access and high positioned electrical sockets. There can be a positive social community. Some 'villages' have been developed to offer on-site amenities, and some developers have identified a need for luxury-type units including a swimming pool. Negatives may include a no-pets policy, high service charges (these must be factored into any decision and, again, probably before you even view a potential property), smaller space than you are used to and a closer proximity to neighbours. Resale values should be researched as press reporting indicates some owners encounter significant reduced property resale values when the property is later sold. If there is no historic data, check similar sites. Banks normally don't lend on these properties. More information around assessing the welfare aspects of such properties is set out in the **Sandwich Generation, Chapter 12.**

The Royal Hospital Chelsea is 'home' to the **Chelsea Pensioners** famous around the world for their red coat uniforms. To be eligible for admission as a Chelsea Pensioner, a candidate (male or female) must be a former non-commissioned officer or soldier of the British Army who is over 65 years or of State Pension age (whichever is the greater, so now 66); and either in receipt of an Army Service Pension or War Disability Pension (which you would be required to surrender upon entry to the Royal Hospital). If you do not receive an Army Pension you would be required to make a weekly financial contribution towards your living costs. This contribution will be based on an assessment of affordability completed during the application process. More at

Chelsea-pensioners.co.uk.

Earning money from property

Your home doesn't have to be a drain on your finances. If you need some spare cash or a regular source of income, there are several ways beyond holiday lets as covered earlier which could make you money from your home.

- *Rent a room scheme*: This is the government's incentive that allows owner–occupiers and tenants to receive tax-free rental income if furnished accommodation is provided in the main – or only – home. The maximum amount you can earn is £7,500 per year. If you live in a suitable area, you could find a commuting lodger who only wants the room during the week and not at weekends– see websites such as Monday to Friday (www.mondaytofriday.com) or www.airbnb.co.uk. Remember you will lose some privacy and you will need to manage any risk to you and your property.

- *£1,000 tax free property allowance*: You can also earn £1,000 from letting out your home and not pay any tax via the HMRC property allowance. If you own a property jointly with others, you're each allowed the £1,000 allowance. See Gov.UK and search 'tax free allowances on property and trading income'.

- *Rent out your drive*: Some areas of the United Kingdom are chronically short of available parking for people going to work or travelling from a nearby airport. Try www.justpark.com for more information.

- *Your home in lights*: It is possible to rent out your home as a film or TV set, particularly if it is quirky or charming. You can list your home via an online agency such as Film Locations (www.filmlocations.co.uk), or Amazing Space (www.amazingspace.co.uk), although agencies will take a fee if your home is used.

- *Host students*: Offer your home as a base for a foreign language or exchange student. This pays typically £100 per week. Contact your local language schools, colleges and universities to see if they offer a pairing service for would-be lodgers and hosts.

- And finally, make money from clearing your clutter and surplus possessions that could be converted into cash. Obvious outlets are eBay and the local car boot sale and you could also try facebook marketplace.

Buy to Let

Buy to let properties have become an increasingly challenging investment. The recent 'hits' taken by this sector include increased stamp duty on second homes and restrictions on the amount of mortgage interest that you can deduct if you are a higher rate taxpayer and more red tape. The other wider economic challenge is over the affordability of housing and whether this may prompt more/other action to suppress house price increases. Up to 2025 the prospects of a capital gain has been one of the factors that property investors hoped for and, indeed, probably attained. Will this continue in the light of the reductions in the capital gains tax exemptions in in 2024/25 (see the **Chapter 5, Tax**)? For instance in the 2022 edition of this book I had said " *I believe Capital Gain Tax will change in the future and wonder if it will move to income tax rates. This would mean the tax on the profit (gain) from second home sales will move from being taxed at the Capital Gains Tax rates for a second property at 18%/28% to income tax rate rates of (presently) 20%, 40% or 45%?*" Well, it has started to change and I do still wonder if it will change further in years to come along the lines I've outlined. Time will tell. After that it comes down to the numbers and factoring in the cost of finding tenants and managing the property if you decide to outsource these tasks to an agent. Then factor in your time in 'managing' the activity. Finally factor in the risk of you ending up with a 'tenant from hell' and being left with unpaid rent, damaged property and lots of stress. At the end of the day one of the key issues is the bottom line 'yield' (income less costs as a percentage of the amount you invested in the property). How does this compare to savings deposit returns which you can earn for little or no effort? On the other hand the quantity of letting properties available on the market has reduced against a surging demand (especially in London) and landlords have found themselves able to increase their rents at figures well in excess of inflation and providing a strong yield.

Top tip
Property letting is a big area full of both opportunity and risk. Purchase the book 'Successful Property Letting' by David Lawrenson if you need help or wish to start this activity as you approach retirement.

Furnished holiday lettings

Furnished holiday lettings at home or abroad had **benefited from ample tax breaks** but there were strict rules over the number of days that the property must be available (210 days in a year) for short term lettings; the number of days actually let (105 days) and restrictions to stop certain long-term lettings. However, April 2025, the favourable tax treatment of furnished holiday lets will be abolished. From then their profits will be taxed in the same way as other rental property profits.

Commercial property and a Self-Invested Personal Pension (SIPP)

Commercial property is another option and there is the bonus of a big tax break as (currently) it can be held as part of a Self-Invested Personal Pension with the property, in turn, providing an investment and then income in retirement planning. This is significant as residential property cannot be held in a SIPP. A good Independent Financial Adviser who specialises in pensions will be able to guide you on this (more at Pensions, Chapter 3) but also note the word of caution in Chapter 3 about protection in SIPPs when things go wrong or if there is a financial crash.

Property investment funds

Finally, there are also property investment funds. When the economy is doing well there are more business tenants seeking space for their premises. If there is high demand then landlords can charge higher rents and investment funds that specialise in property tend to do well. If there is a recession the opposite happens. It is another route into property where the charges are lower and the risk is spread.

Useful reading

The Equity Release Council is the industry body of the equity release market www.equityreleasecouncil.com

Successful Property Letting by David Lawrenson

www.expatfocus.com – provides information and advice on moving abroad

Reminder: Take any action points or follow up points to Chapter 13, Your Plan For A Better Retirement.

Chapter Three
Pensions

"The question isn't what age I want to retire. It's at what income."
GEORGE FOREMAN

This chapter on pensions is always the toughest read of all the chapters in my books. Pensions are a complex subject, full of jargon and perceived as just about the dullest financial subject you could imagine. However, I know from decades of experience that pensions provide great results if you pull the right levers at the right time. The pathway has many opportunities for those who can make better choices but is also littered with risks … so read on, avoid the risks and act on the opportunities (and the earlier you start the better!).

If you have a decent final salary defined benefit pension (where the pension just keeps on paying as long as you live) which basically covers your living and leisure costs you are in a good position. Perhaps you can even skip over this chapter if you are close to retirement? For everyone else, particularly those with plenty of time until retirement with defined contribution pension schemes (where there is a pot of money for a pension and when it's gone 'it's gone'), there is much to review and some very big tips in this chapter. Some of the tips involve tax advantages that seem to be generous and may disappear in future government budgets, hence particular focus and action may be needed if the economy does not grow and the government then has to look at taxation to help with improving public services and 'welfare/care'.

Pensions give great results if you pull the right levers at the right time

This chapter features early in the **'save more'** section of my book and the knowledge you gain as part of your **'re-set'** and thinking around a glidepath retirement will hopefully help you **'plan more'** around the opportunities and risks and achieve a better retirement.

Pensions provide the main income in retirement so George Foreman's quote at the head of this chapter seems to be spot on in to-day's flexible pension environment. Chapter 1, **'plan more'** underlined the importance of determining the level of income we want to have in retirement. In 2024/25 and moving into 2025/26 in the UK we have more control than previous generations on when and how we decide to 'retire' and as we have already read we can retire more than once. This is because the world of pensions has changed radically in the UK in recent decades due to four main drivers.

The **first** is the flexibility in careers with extended and flexible working being possible in the run up to and beyond the state retirement age. It helps, of course, if you are working for a more enlightened and progressive employer who recognises the value of the talent and experience in their older workers. As part of a retirement glidepath you may retire more than once (perhaps after a late 'gap year'?) and take a top-up or part-time job that can allow you to reach the income you need depending on the phase of retirement and your needs at that time.

The **second** is the most radical change in living memory in the UK pensions world that came with pension changes introduced in 2015. This created a more flexible pension environment that, potentially, allows you to turn-off/turn-on the pension income and bring in more tax planning to work with your pension planning.

Then, **thirdly** and most importantly we have the 're-set' moment created by the Covid-19 pandemic in 2020 and 2021. This has caused many to reappraise the life they want to create and then live. The term glidepath is used throughout this book and the approach is well illustrated by looking at how pensions can be 'retuned' to help you achieve the life you now aspire to.

The **fourth** and final driver has gradually changed over the last six or seven decades. In the 1950's our grandparents faced a 10 year retirement period and probably a fixed pension. There was no planning, retirement planning books and retirement courses. It was all very easy and if you were lucky you received a carriage clock on leaving on your 'cliff-edge' retirement day. Today folk are 'retuning' into a glidepath retirement from their mid to late 50s. This involves a re-set, easing back on work and work travel pressures and commencing a glidepath through retirement that may last 30 years or more. Many continue to work with a pattern involving less hours and less stress as part of this 'glidepath'. The longer time planning horizon makes things more complex (will the money last and will you still be able to leave an inheritance?). And that's just for starters as then you add in more flexible pensions, complex pension rules, inflation, rising state pension age, frozen tax bands and lots of tax questions and you have a perfect storm of risk and opportunity. Hence this book and its efforts to give you more knowledge to help you make better choices and achieve a better retirement.

Pension planning is the biggest financial decision you will make (probably even bigger than taking on that first big mortgage) but gets little attention, is poorly understood, and is surrounded in baffling 'finance speak'. For that reason, financing your retirement through pensions is put on the back burner and too many people get a nasty shock when reality strikes at the cliff-edge of retirement. I have seen it so many times when I am brought in to run a course for an employer for their employees on preparing for retirement. The feedback is frequently *'we needed to hear this 15 years ago!'* and thankfully many of the employers I deal with are now doing this as part of their employee assistance programmes. Remember it's never too early to start your retirement planning.   As Martin Gorvett, Chartered Financial Planner of Lavender Financial Planners said in Chapter 1 of this book "The earlier you can start planning the more choices you will have. If you want to retire at 60, there is no point in starting to plan at 59....! Beginning your planning early makes things like budgeting habitual, allowing more flexibility for any bumps in the road. It can also generate surpluses that can be spent on achieving your financial goals earlier than expected – with time being the most valuable commodity, this will feel like a huge win".   It's spot on and thus worth underlining again.

Put simply I have often found that imminent pensioners are 'disappointed' that they hadn't grasped the issues, risks and opportunities around pensions at a much earlier stage. By retirement day it is often too late to do anything meaningful and make a significant impact to increase your income in retirement. At that cliff-edge 'too late' stage there are, still, some other options to work around the harsh reality of a modest pension and higher living aspirations. The first option is to work longer perhaps under a flexible work scheme that some more enlightened employers implement to help retain experience in their business. Or you could go and find an entirely new job with less hours and less stress or **start your own small business** to ramp up your income (everything you need is in **Chapter 8**). Maybe another option could include raiding your savings and investments in the early years of your retirement when you want to have more fun although this tends to create snag points later on the retirement journey and can leave little wriggle room when big one off items of expenditure arise. Then again from experience I know that **rightsizing your house or relocating** to a cheaper area to release capital in your home can radically improve your financial opportunities (as you will have read in **Chapter 2**). Or maybe it's just that great old-fashioned saying of 'cutting the cloth to suit the purse' i.e. shop or act according to your financial limitations and **reset your lifestyle and costs** and learn to live off less money (**Chapter 7** has bucketloads of tips!). All these options and more are outlined in this book to help give you some ideas to put in your plan at the end of this book. Best of all, however, **if** you have plenty of time until you start your retirement glidepath (and under the 'it's never too early to start planning ethos' of this book) is the opportunity to start making some changes now to your pension funding so you have a more tax efficient income and can glide into retirement.

Importantly, this chapter is only a guide and it is neither legal nor financial advice; it is no substitute for taking professional advice from a financial adviser or other professional adviser. Any potential UK tax advantages may be subject to change (the 2025/26 budget remains subject to approval at the time of writing this book and there may be changes following another budget) and will depend upon your individual circumstances. As always, individual professional advice should be obtained.

This chapter at a glance

- *Mind the gap.* The reality of pensions you may receive (and when) and recognising the gap in your retirement income aspirations. Pointers to possible changes in the tax regime that may influence your pensions and tax planning. Reminders to grab all the free money you can i.e. schemes where your employer matches or partially matches your contributions.

- *Information to help you understand your State Pension entitlement and any company and private pension entitlement.*

- *Pointers to the opportunities in the tax relief system around pensions* that currently exists in the UK that may help you plan your future contributions to better effect.

- *Guidance about defined contribution pension options and pension drawdown facilities that provide flexibility on planning your retirement income.* Drawdown, tax free amounts and other tax opportunities and pitfalls are explained.

- *Pointers to free guidance offered by the government's impartial service about your defined contribution pension options.* Book in your appointment via www.moneyhelper.org.uk backed by the UK government and its Pension Wise service.

- *Reminders about the importance of getting proper financial advice especially in the run up to the personal tax year end and any future budget.* Therein lies both risk and opportunity. The benefits of quality advice and options should outweigh fees that you may have to pay. No ifs, no buts ... always ensure your adviser is on the Financial Conduct Authority register at www.fca.org.uk.

- *Beware of the 'pensions predators'.* They range from crooks in suits trying to get you to move your pension before age 55 into some schemes which, in reality, could hit you with massive tax penalties to over-charging advisers who then go bust and 'disappear'. You also need to be sure of your Financial Services Compensation Scheme coverage and there could be a wake-up call in here for those relying on a SIPP.

- *Combine your pensions planning with your savings plan to finance your retirement.* But also keep half an eye on the tax implications (which can change) of both, as therein lie both opportunities and pitfalls.

The 'big picture' as we progress into 2025/26
The buck stops with you

Pensions freedom and many of us living longer means there is a greater responsibility on you to understand and plan around your pension. Whilst the buck stops with you and this chapter will give you a great start, consider engaging a financial adviser registered with the FCA where you need further help or the numbers are large. To get us started I'll deal with the two 'big picture' issues that you should grasp straightaway- 'how long am I likely to live' and 'how much roughly will I need each year'. It seems so obvious when I set it out like that but it is vital and after that we can then move onto the next pieces of the big picture. That further step will involve getting a better understanding of the pension income you are likely to receive and then some of the issues that you might be able to use to improve your retirement glidepath plan.

How long am I likely to live?

Everyone is different but no one is immortal and so I've turned again (as per the figures I quoted back in Chapter 1) to the simplicity of the Office of National Statistics ("ONS") whose 'life expectancy calculator' estimates that a male aged 66 in December 2024 has a life expectancy of 85, a 25% chance of reaching 92 and a 3.1% chance of reaching 100. A female of the same age has a life expectancy of 87, a 25% chance of reaching 94 and a 5.5% chance of reaching 100. But note that there are big variations in how long you may live depending on location, wealth, health and your lifestyle choices - sometimes by 5 years or more. I'm glad I've got that bit out of the way! You can check other ages and expectancies at ons.gov.uk and their 'life expectancy calculator'.

How much could will I be spending in retirement?

Chapter 1 'Could I retire five years earlier. Plan more' will have shown you how to develop your own financial plan and assess your own expected lifestyle, net wealth and expenditure over the three phases of retirement. In Chapter 1 I had explained that I like to use the Pensions and Lifetime Savings Association's *'Retirement Living Standards update'* to provide a starting point for thinking about the amount you may be spending in retirement. The 'standards' set the cost of three retirement lifestyles: Minimum, Moderate and Comfortable and more is explained in Chapter 1. As also explained in Chapter 1 you can then refine this with your own financial projections tailored to your projected income, your projected spending and your options for pulling various levers that could make a difference.

	2024 'cost' per annum of the living standard *
Minimum	
Single	£14,400
Couple	£22,400
Moderate	
Single	£31,000
Couple	£43,100
Comfortable	
Single	£43,100
Couple	£59,000

*IMPORTANT: the figures shown are the amounts of annual expenditure required to achieve the living standard (they are not gross income figures before tax).

The target for single retirees might seem high compared with couples, this reflects the fact that many costs – for example energy bills, broadband, media packages and insurance- remain virtually the same even if you live alone and council tax may only achieve a 25% reduction.

The buck stops with you (continued): Understand your State Pension entitlement

The State Pension is a payment made every 4 weeks by the government and is based on National Insurance contributions you have contributed. In April 2023, the State Pension went up by 10.1%- in line with the previous September's measure of inflation. In April 2024 it increased by 8.5% again in line with the September 2023 measure of inflation. **In April 2025 the full state pension is set to increase by 4.1% to just under £12,000 per annum** (the actual figure is £11,973) after September's inflation figure (1.7%) came in lower than wage growth (4.1%). More than 12 million people in the UK currently receive the State Pension and it accounts for just under half the total amount the UK government spends on benefits. Because people are living longer the state could not afford to fund the State Pension for the previous retirement ages of 65 (male) and 60 (female). Therefore, since 2010 we have seen the retirement age for women increasing and other previously laid-out plans on pension age increases being accelerated. Put simply, the funding solution was met by equalising the retirement ages of men and women and then making both wait longer to receive it. The State Pension is being paid at age 66 for both sexes in 2025, then between May 2026 and March 2028, the age at which you can claim state pension will increase to 67. This affects people born after April 1960. From 2046 the age is expected to increase further to 68. The www.gov.uk website and a search for 'State Pension calculator' will give the age at which you will receive yours. It's hard to predict the future but I do fear that the Department of Work and Pensions will bring forward the 68 age.

The State Pension and related additional elements to it have changed over the years and this has led to confusion. The last major change took place in April 2016 when a new flat-rate pension structure was brought in for those retiring after 6 April 2016. Those who retired before then remain on their old scheme.

To qualify for the **'old' State Pension** scheme and receive a full basic State Pension you required 30 years' full National Insurance (NI) contributions. In 2024/25 the full single-person basic state retirement pension was £169.50 per week **which increases**

to £176.45 in 2025/26). If you're married or have a civil partnership and both you and your partner have built up a State Pension, you'll get double this amount between you.

Some people also receive an additional State Pension (also called the State Second Pension or, before 2002, it was called SERPS), which is the government's earnings-related additional pension. How much additional State Pension you get is complicated and depends on your National Insurance contributions and whether or not you 'contracted out'. You will have been contracted out if you opted for National Insurance contributions to be diverted to a work or personal pension. There is then a range of further options including: deferring your pension (by deferring it you can have a bigger pension when it starts); adult dependency increases (for a husband, wife or someone who is looking after your children); Pension Credit (an income-related benefit); payments to an overseas address; provisions for married women and widows; divorce, death and disputes; and the Christmas bonus. More detailed information can be found at the independent UK Government backed moneyhelper.org.uk (0800 138 3944). It provides tips and tools on pensions and retirement planning as well as a wide range of topics including day-to day money management. Moneyhelper's support is always impartial and free.

Then we have the **'simpler' state pension regime** for those retiring after 6 April 2016 which pays £221.20 per week for 2024/25 giving about £11,502 per annum which increases to **£230.25 for 2025/26 (or £11,973 per annum)** if you have the 'full' 35 years of national insurance contributions.

You will get a reduced amount of state pension providing you have at least 10 qualifying years on your National Insurance record. You will receive a proportionate amount if you have between 10 and 34 qualifying years and you may receive more if you have accrued SERPs or State Second Pension. But don't worry too much as the simple and easy step is to get a State Pension forecast as shown on the next page.

The triple lock on your State Pension

The 'triple lock' system provides that the UK State Pension increases each April in line with whichever of these three measures is highest:

- inflation, as measured by the Consumer Prices Index in the September of the previous year
- the average increase in wages across the UK
- or 2.5%

The triple lock was introduced by the Conservative-Liberal Democrat coalition government in 2010.

Early retirement and your State Pension

Because some people retire early they can mistakenly assume it is possible to get an early State Pension. While the information may be correct for some employers' schemes it does not apply to the basic State Pension.

Deferring your State Pension

You don't have to take the State Pension when you reach the relevant age and can instead defer it and receive a larger pension in the future. Whether it is wise to do this or, instead, reinvest surplus pensionable earnings into a pension and take the state pension when it becomes due is a complex issue. More information at gov.uk and 'deferring state pension.

Next steps – getting that State Pension forecast

You can request a pension statement estimating your State Pension based on your current National Insurance record. You can apply online at www.gov.uk/check-state-pension, by telephone on 0800 731 0175, by text phone on 0800 731 0176 or by post sending form BR19 to:

The Pension Service 9
Mail Handling Site A
Wolverhampton
WV98 1LU

> **Top tip**
> **Nearly half the population is not prepared for retirement. Spend 10 minutes getting your State Pension forecast and keep a record of this.**

If you are on the new system of State Pension and don't have full 35 years of national insurance records you may be able to buy missing years from the HMRC. This is usually a sensible option if you don't have sufficient years until your state retirement age to make up missing years and are in good health. You have until 5 April 2025 to buy back and missing national insurance years from 2006 to 2016.

> **Top tip**
> **Currently (December 2024) the deadline for buying back missing years between 2006 and 2016 is 5 April 2025. Don't miss the boat... get an estimate for buying missing years from The Pension Service and do the numbers and make a choice.**

The buck stops (continued): Understand and control your other private pension income

Private (or personal) defined contribution pensions and 'drawdown'

Gather in details of all your pension plans and understand what you have. If you have a pension it will either be:

A defined benefit 'final salary' pension	A defined contribution 'money purchase' pension
You pay fixed contributions and the employer pays variable contributions.	You pay fixed contributions and the employer pays fixed contributions.
The amount you are paid is based on how many years you've worked for the employer and the salary you earned.	A retirement pot of money builds up from your and your employer's contributions plus investment returns and any tax relief.
Pays out a secure or 'defined' pension income for life.	The income you receive depends on the size of the pot and the choices you make as it builds up and then when you retire.
It usually continues to pay a pension to your spouse, civil partner or dependents when you die	

Private (or personal) defined contribution pension schemes are a pension 'pot' from which future pension income payable to you will depend on the investment growth of your contributions. **These contrast massively with defined benefit schemes** which are often known as 'final salary' pension schemes and were the norm until the mid 1990s (more below). Defined contribution pensions are now the norm.

The 2014 Budget brought in 'pensions liberation' in April 2015. In the 'old world' most people bought an annuity with their defined contribution pension pot on retirement. The annuity then provided a fixed income for life. The 'old world' system attracted criticism as it was perceived as representing poor value and some annuities were miss-sold to those in ill health or were unsuitable as they may have resulted in no or limited financial protection for dependents on the death of the annuity holder.

The 'new world' of **pensions liberalisation** resulted in a dramatic change and since April 2015 everyone now has a right to access their defined contribution pension pots from age 55 (which increases to 57 in April 2028) and no one is forced to buy an annuity. Instead, we have the new concept of 'drawdown' and this is just financial speak for taking money out of your pension as an income. You'll have 25% tax free and then pay income tax on the rest depending on your tax band. **The risk, however, is that you may outlive your pension pot and exhaust your funds** as there is not the same certainty that annuities provided (albeit you could purchase one if this proved more suitable). **The other risk is the fact that financial markets fluctuate.** Over the longer-term stock markets appear resilient and grow. But what happens if the markets collapse just as you are about to start drawing on your funds or need to but an annuity? Some readers may remember the Japanese asset price bubble of the early 1990's (Nikkei 225 at 13,000 in December 1985, rising to 39,000 4 years later in December 1989 before crashing to 14,400 in August 1992) and a decade of despair that followed for Japanese investors. Or some others will remember the US bear market of 2007 to 2009 (between October 2007 and June 2009 the Dow Jones Industrial Average, Nasdaq Composite and S&P 500 all fell 20% from their peaks in 2007). More recently we had a collapse in many worldwide financial markets in March and April 2020 as a result of the Covid-19 pandemic and then the subsequent full recovery to levels above the pre-Covid times. But where will the markets now head? Fluctuations vary according to the risk that you have selected for your funds. The bigger the risk the bigger the potential fluctuation for a gain or loss so I think my main recommendation is for you to invest quality time in understanding fully the level of risk that you have selected for your pension funds (where you have a choice) and ensure you understand and accept it as the buck stops with you.

> **Top tip**
> **If you have significant funds in defined contribution
> pensions you must, therefore, understand and accept
> your risk levels. Ultimately the buck stops with you but
> quality advice and assistance from an adviser can help so
> arrange a review if you have not had one in the last year.
> Make a planned and considered approach to the
> management of your funds going forward.**

Related to this is another risk and that is one of complacency. Most people just accept the charges proposed by an adviser/ pension provider and do not shop around. However, plans are hard to compare in terms of risk, reward and fees and other charges. Martin Gorvett, a Chartered Financial Planner, of Lavender Financial Planners Ltd, explains the fee structure on advice and what to look out for in fees, charges and costs when considering defined contributions and 'drawdown':

"More often than not people are tempted to avoid professional fees in favour of directly accessing retirement products. If you have the knowledge, all well and good. Just look out for the 'unknown, unknowns'. Professional fees do vary and have historically been hidden. However, the modern financial planning advice market is designed to provide a service based on value, not a toll gate to products. Regulated Financial Planners will charge a fee relevant to the work expected of them. This will either be fee or percentage based. Average costs in the industry have dropped from 5% to around 3% over recent years. Some advisers will take this further to somewhere between 1-2%. Don't be afraid to challenge the fee being charged. A good Financial Planner will be able to justify their fees. Thankfully the modern pension market is designed to be portable. Very few modern financial contracts harbour surrender penalties. If there are they will be disclosed at the outset. Again, don't be afraid to ask for clarification. Typically, you would expect to pay fees as a percentage of your fund, although some pension contracts operate in £'s. There are three layers of cost to an advised product:

Advice – typically between 0.5% and 1%
Product – typically between 0.25% and 0.35%

Investment – typically between 0.2% (for a passive solution) and 1.8% (for an actively managed solution)

As with other industries, going direct to a provider could end up costing you more, as the retail price of direct offerings may be higher. During the course of 2024 (implemented on 31st July 2024) all firms in the financial services industry underwent a good practice review called 'Consumer Duty', led by the FCA. One outcome for consumers is that if your financial adviser is charging you a fee, they must be providing you with a service – as described in their 'Terms of Business', or 'Fair Value Statement'. So if you haven't seen your financial adviser for over 12 months, and they are continuing to charge you a fee, do ask for them to account for themselves, and perhaps even pursue a refund....you wouldn't let a car garage bill you for an engine service that they haven't carried out for you, would you?"

The fee band range above could be a total range of fees from 0.95% to 3.15%. On a £300,000 pension pot that equates to a staggering spread of 2.2% or £6,600 a year. Over 20 years that amounts to £132,000 and a fee review that takes an hour could add (effectively) tens of thousands of pounds to your pensions' pot so a fee review would be time very well spent. Watch out also for any 'tie-ins' – these are exit fees that are payable if you wish to move advisers/providers. From my own experience over the last two decades I would add one important extra factor beyond the fee side of things. It's the quality of dialogue you have with your financial adviser and the 'quality' of their annual review and their 'written' advice and recommendations each year. Importantly, how well do they link in with your other advisers (for instance any accountant/tax adviser) as this is just as important. In summary do you feel they really know you and any partner, where you are in life and where you intend to go with your 'retirement glidepath'. Then there are the returns offered and then actually attained by the adviser. These 'quality factors' could shift the value of your pension pot by tens of thousands of pounds (either up or down!). The quality factor is difficult to weigh up but if you have not spoken with your financial adviser in the last year in a way that is tailored to you then that probably tells its own story and it's time for that review and perhaps a change?

Top tip
The key issue on adviser and pension firm fees is the quality of interaction with you, pension performance and

> **fees. Get absolute clarity on all fees and precision on any exit fees and review the fees you are paying. Then review the quality of the financial advice you are receiving. Is there a better service/ fee structure for <u>you</u> out there for 2025 and going forward?**

In drawdown you can take as little or as much as you need and therefore income levels can be varied to take advantage of other income you may be earning (perhaps from a new part-time job, or having started a small business) or whilst waiting for the State Pension to kick in. This might make your tax affairs more efficient and could save you money and, as I said above, you should ensure your financial adviser is working effectively with any tax adviser you have retained to try and leverage these benefits for your ultimate benefit. The point is that you can then manage your income more easily to take advantage of the zero rate and basic rate tax bands more efficiently and this may save you tax and provide more of an income (as flagged up earlier in a top tip). Importantly, the new regime ensures that currently you can pass on your pension on death to a loved one more tax efficiently up to the age of 75 because up to that age defined contribution pension pots do not form part of someone's estate for Inheritance Tax purposes. Under previous rules there used to be a 55 per cent Pensions Death Tax. Now, if you die before 75 there is no tax to pay on funds passing from defined contribution schemes. A death after the 75th birthday will be subject to your pension beneficiaries' marginal rate of Income Tax. BUT and it is a BIG BUT all is set to change from April 2027 unspent pension pots will be included in IHT liability calculations at death, unless passed to a spouse (spousal exemption) provided the legislation announced in the October 2024 budget proceeds as expected. Most pension experts agree that pensions liberation is a good thing but also add a note of caution about the IHT changes announced in the October 2024 budget. Martin Gorvett advises:

> *"Modern pension flexibilities have helped enormously in making my clients' retirement strategies more efficient. For those with other savings, pensions have become an efficient way of handing your wealth on to those whom you leave behind. But with these freedoms comes temptation and a lot of new responsibility. At the other end of the spectrum, there's a danger that some pension savers will draw their pension savings and fritter it all away without*

*any constraints to hold them back. Most pension providers are acting as a
second line of defence for savers looking to draw pension benefits under flexi-
access. They will ensure that professional advice has been considered and that
savers aren't being scammed."*

Top tip

**If pensions were part of your Inheritance Tax planning
then monitor the progress of the October 2024 budget
announcements on pensions and IHT and if concerns
remains or amounts are significant consult with a
financial adviser on your options and plans.**

Pension access ages and 25% tax free

The minimum age you can take money from a pension is currently 55. It rises to 57 in
2028 albeit some schemes that were marketed to specifically allow retirement at age
55 'may' be given protection to still allow access at 55. If you move schemes you may
lose that protection. Employer pension schemes are able to set their own rules on
accessing pensions so the access age could be higher. Generally speaking most defined
contribution schemes (explained below) let you access the money at 55 (or 57 from
2028) and employer schemes may have a higher age.

You may be able to withdraw up to 25% of your pension tax free up to £268,275
and this limit remains capped. This is fairly simple for defined contribution schemes
but final salary schemes (again explained below) are a little more complicated and a
calculation involving a 'commutation' works out a reduced final salary in lieu of taking
25% of your pension tax free. Often financial advisers see this as coming out at around
3 years worth of pension but each scheme will vary according to it's own rules so this
is just a rough guide.

Tax and related pension issues

Tax and pensions go hand in hand due to significant differences in the tax rates you pay under income tax. For many years I have seen much press speculation before each budget about the government potentially taking action to reduce tax reliefs on pension payments but the threat has only been partially addressed by amending some allowances some of which were then subsequently relaxed. More in Chapter 5, Tax and in the section 'Playing the tax bands ... while you can' that follows below. There are several other useful pointers to help your plan below that involve the interaction between pensions and tax (now that's two complex issues merging together ... so I hope the following helps you).

The tax perk most parents don't know about

Did you know that pension contributions paid by parents to their children's pensions come with tax relief- even if the child is grown-up and earning a salary of their own? You can save up to a maximum £3,600 a year into a pension from the day they are born (i.e. cash paid in of £2,880 to which the government add £720 as a credit in the form of a 20% tax break bonus from HMRC). Mothers and fathers who have taken care of their own retirement and see children dealing with student debt and the cost of living crisis are looking to this opportunity to lend a hand. It may also help avoid inheritance tax issues that could be looming ahead for the parents if they are, for instance, gifting away surplus income. It's a little known feature of the pensions system which means that the contribution by the parent is treated as if it was made by the child so it gets the tax relief credit. If your child is a higher rate taxpayer they are entitled to 40 % relief and can claim the extra 20% back from HMRC when completing their annual self-assessment. As pensions count towards reducing income for child benefit entitlement purposes there could also be a further benefit if your child's income is just over £50,000.

The Pensions Advice Allowance

The **Pension Advice Allowance** allows you to withdraw £500 tax-free from your pension pot on three separate occasions (but not more than once in a tax year), to help pay for advice from a regulated adviser. It only applies to defined contribution pension schemes but not all pension providers offer this.

Small pension pots- clean up?

Job switching in your career may have left you with a number of small pension pots. Another little known rule may give you an opportunity to tidy these up and receive some early cash without falling into one of the pension traps that limit future pension planning. '**Small pots**' can be paid out as a lump sum to you as long as the schemes are valued at £10,000 or less and you are aged 55 or above (rising to 57 in 2028). You must take the whole value from one pot at once and will receive 25% tax free with the remainder taxed at as income in the year. You will want to check that the payment does not push your income into a higher tax bracket. Another method of cleaning up pensions worth £30,000 or less is under the rules of '**trivial commutation**'. More information on both is available from the Low Incomes Tax Reform Group at litg.org.uk and search 'how do I cash in my small pension'.

Playing the UK tax bands … while you can

This is potentially a big opportunity for many readers of this book – especially if they are higher rate tax payers who have quite a few years before starting their 'retirement glidepath'. One way of increasing your income in retirement is by playing the tax bands in the years when you are earning. This has particularly good impact if you are earning above the higher rate tax band. In England, Wales and Northern Ireland this band starts at £50,270 in 2024/25 and 2025/26 and the threshold remains frozen up to 2028. This 'freezing' creates a form of stealth tax which I outline in **Chapter 5, Tax** as more tax payers fall into the higher rate tax band each year as earnings rise and they pay a greater proportion of their earnings in tax. In Scotland the higher rate tax band starts at £43,663 for 2024/25 and 2025/26. There may be an even more powerful impact if your earnings are in the tax 'kill zone' of £100,000 to £125,140. The tax 'kill zone' is described further in **Chapter 5, Tax**. Pension planning can, potentially, shift income from being taxed at 40% or 45% (or 42%, 45% and even 48% in Scotland) to being taxed at 20% if you get your planning right and make some good choices (and then it gets even better as a quarter of your pension pot may be able to be extracted free which could bring the effective rate down to 15%). It might even, potentially, shift tax from being taxed at 60% or 68% in the 'kill zone' to 15% (deriving from extracting pension at 20% but with a quarter of the money shifted being tax free). Phew - it is complicated but worth digging into and any future change of government or budget may include changes to the rules so don't miss the boat on the opportunity. For the moment (December 2024) there is still an opportunity to shift more earnings into a pension and because of the relatively high opportunities and also risks if you get it wrong after taking independent professional advice.

> **Top tip**
> Get to a better understanding of your income now and
> what it will be in retirement and look at ways of shifting
> income from being taxed at a higher rate now to a lower
> rate later when you draw your pension (subject to reliefs
> and allowances outlined below and, of course, your
> current spending commitments). This offers big
> opportunities at present but those could tighten or close
> as part of any new UK budget. Planning ahead would
> seem a significant 'opportunity'.

The pensions expectation and 'mind the gap'

The Office of National Statistics measures the average total weekly UK pay
(including bonuses and before tax) and in October 2024 it was £706 a week or
£36,712 per annum. As a very rough rule of thumb a reasonable retirement goal is
to expect an income in retirement of between 40 and 75 per cent of your employed
earnings. Three examples detailed below may help you see how the 'gap' can be
surprisingly big. The examples may prompt more planning on how much extra you
may need to be putting away into pensions to bridge the gap between State Pension
and your retirement income ambitions in **2025/26 where the full state pension will
bring in £11,973** (compared to £11,502 in 2024/25). I find that many people are
surprised at how much you need to build up in your pension pots to achieve the
sort of lifestyle you wish to create and especially if you now plan a longer 'glidepath'
retirement lasting maybe 30 years. **Note** the size of the pots in the 3 examples
below and how much income they may provide and for how long. **Note** also what
happens to the different pensions and what happens when the pots run out. All
three examples are based on individuals who are at the state pension retirement
age of 66 (it increases to 67 in 2026). They also assume that no 'spare' significant
savings or investments have been built up (or any savings are already ear-marked
for one-off planned expenditure) and that retirement income is being financed only

by state and other pension income.

Case study 1. Sarah is single, aged 66, has worked in the retail industry, is on average earnings of about £36,700 per annum and her pension aspiration is to be able to spend around £20,000 a year to achieve somewhere between a minimum and moderate retirement. Sarah owns a 2 bedroom flat and has paid off the mortgage. Sarah has no defined benefit pension so it will depend on how she has built up her other pension pots and the numbers will work like this. [The term 'defined benefit' pension is explained earlier in this chapter but basically it means a great form of pension income as it pays a percentage of your salary and just keeps on paying year after year no matter how long you live.]

Sarah can probably expect to get a State Pension of about £11,973 in 2025/26. This means she would need a pension pot of about £280,000 to generate a 25% lump sum of about £70,000 and then further pension income of about £10,500 each year for about 20 years. This gives Sarah a total income in retirement before tax of about the desired £22,473 for about 20 years and after paying tax of about £1,980 she is left with £20,493 to spend and achieve her retirement spending goals. At around 86 (after 20 years) Sarah's pension pot will have probably run out and she will then live off the state pension or consider whether she can use her property to improve her pension income prospects at that point.

[In today's money subject to any investment growth or loss etc for an estimated 20 years i.e. state pension of £11,973 and pension income of about £10,500 less income tax at 20% which will be about £1,980 on the £9,903 received above the tax free personal allowance of £12,570].

The tax free lump sum is assumed to be allocated to 'one-off' expenditure - perhaps a new, kitchen or long haul holidays.

Case study 2. Let's next look at **Tom** a high earner in a civil partnership, aged 66 with his own tech consulting business bringing in around £100,000 per annum (from salary and dividend income). He also has an old employer defined benefit pension scheme from the 1980's which will pay about £15,000 per annum from age 66. His partner, also aged 66, will only receive a full state pension. They own their home and the mortgage is paid off. Their retirement goal from 2025 is be able to **spend around £59,000** a year so they can achieve a **comfortable** retirement. Their numbers will work like this.

Tom and his partner will each receive a full State Pension of about £11,973 each. Tom will also receive £15,000 per annum from his defined benefit pension scheme (after taking a 25% tax free lump sum of around £100,000). He will have needed to build up a further personal pension pot of around £700,000 to generate a further 25% tax free lump sum of about £175,000 (which he adds to the tax-free lump sum of £100,000 from his defined benefit pension and which, in total, they have earmarked for a holiday home abroad in Spain). The pension pot will then pay further pension income of around £26,250 per annum (for around 20 years). Their combined income will be £65,196. Tom will pay about £8,700 tax and his partner will pay no tax leaving them with about £56,500 to spend on their comfortable retirement. Not quite the £59,000 they hoped for, but they can reduce costs here and there and Tom may even do a bit of ad hoc consulting after taking a year out initially (you can retire more than once!) so things will work out fine for Tom and his partner. One of the key things he did to build up such a big pension pot was to contribute most of the excess of his earnings above £50,000 into pensions for the 10 years leading up retirement and after he had repaid his mortgage.

[In today's money subject to any investment growth or loss etc for an estimated 20 years i.e. two state pensions between the couple bringing in £23,946, Tom's defined benefit pension of about £15,000 and income from Tom's personal pension of £26,250. A total income of around £65,196 on which tax of about £8,700 will be paid leaving £56,500 to spend].

The state pension should have risen by the usual Government triple lock rules (which could be subject to change of course) and the defined benefit pension should have normally risen by approximately RPI to protect its equivalent purchasing power. Tom and his partner can then expect to gear down their spending as they move into passive retirement when Tom's personal pension pot may run out at about the age of 86. They then live on just their State Pensions and Tom's defined benefit salary pension. Maybe around that time or just before they sell their second home abroad to provide a fund for luxury cruises. At that stage maintaining an overseas property that starts to 'age' may have become a burden and visits may becoming less frequent and could be satisfied by an alternative airbnb?

Case study 3. Next is **Muhammad,** aged 66 in 2025 who is a civil servant earning £50,000 per annum. He retires in 2025 and has a retirement aspiration to spend about £36,000 a year placing him in the midpoint of the moderate to comfortable living standard. He is single and has a public service defined benefit salary pension of about £25,000 per annum before tax and after commutation which could have provided him a tax-free lump sum of approximately £166,666. He also has a State Pension of about £11,973 per year. The lump sum is earmarked for luxury holidays for the next twenty years. Muhammad's income in retirement of about £36,500 before tax will just run and run for as long as he lives with the same sort of growth expectations as indicated above for Tom.

So, could you retire 5 years earlier?

The above examples are at a high level and serve to illustrate some of the numbers and how this could, in turn, relate to you. The focus is to help you identify potential gaps in pension expectations and how some pensions 'run out' and thus the importance of knowing what you are likely to receive and for how long. The key next step for you is to do some preparation work and get to grips with your own pension position and then consider options if you find a gap. The younger you are reading this chapter the better as **with more knowledge and some well laid plans you could knock 5 years off your retirement age**. This could be good news for a younger woman who envies her mother who received the state pension at age 60 in 2009. She now faces a state retirement age of 68, will live longer and may have taken career breaks to start a family. The trick for younger readers is easier than you think:

- Draw up your plan.
- Join your workforce pension scheme or set up your own pension and make sure you understand the maximum 'free money' the employer will provide and try and leverage that to your benefit.
- Play the tax bands while you can.

Martin Gorvett, a Chartered Financial Planner, of Lavender Financial Planners Ltd, has helped hundreds of individuals understand and bridge the gap. Martin advises:

"For many the kick-starter for funding a pension comes from our first job. In our early years we may accumulate several small pension pots as our career progresses. It's important to keep track of what you have and ensure that inertia doesn't creep in. Whilst in the early years you may only be able to afford to contribute a little towards your pension, every pound is important. The more you can fund in the early years the longer it has to grow (the effect known as "pound cost averaging"). Those starting later in their life face a daunting reality. The rule of thumb is that you should take your age, half it and that is the percentage of earnings that you should then start to contribute. For example, someone who starts at 50 should contribute 25% of their earnings to a pension to have any chance of having a decent retirement. Whereas someone who starts at 20, should contribute 10%."

Annuities - shop around!

Annuities are potentially very complicated and could take up a whole chapter and maybe even a whole book. Most folk understand the concept of life insurance where your money is covering the risk of you dying too young as it provides a lump sum to your dependents. If I strip it right back, I think annuities could be seen as covering the risk of you living too long. This may not be a risk for those with **defined benefit** pensions where the pension just keeps paying and paying until you are 100 years old and beyond. But for others with **defined contribution** pensions your pension pot could run out leaving you with just the state pension. Is this a risk you want to take and, for instance, give yourself a guaranteed amount so you can then gift away surplus money as part of an inheritance strategy so dependents get the money when they need it (i.e.at a younger age)? The 'light bulb' moment may just have happened around annuities. Annuities are also like a bet on your life- if you die soon after taking one out you or your dependents may not see any more of the money you put in (although there are some types of annuity that can cover this risk as you'll read below). If your financial adviser earns their fees from the % of your wealth and pension funds that they manage they could see annuities as the competition but really should consider these as part of the options available to you, your circumstances and objectives.

In very simple terms, therefore, an annuity is a sort of bet on your life expectancy. An annuity does not form part of your estate. It is money invested in exchange for an income for a period of time until your death. Since April 2015 and pensions flexibility you are no longer compelled to buy an annuity if you have a defined contribution pension to fund your pension. The concept of annuities needs some explanation as the option of purchasing an annuity still remains. When you buy an annuity you hand over a lump sum (your pension fund after taking out 25 per cent of it as a tax-free lump sum) to an insurance company in return for a regular, guaranteed income for the rest of your life called an 'annuity' and the income is subject to income tax. Under the current rules the earliest age you can do this is 55 (increases to 57 in 2028). Once you have bought your annuity, the income you receive is effectively free of investment risk. The risk has been transferred to your provider. There is little danger of running out of money, as your provider has to pay you for as long as you live.

When you approach retirement your pension company will contact you about purchasing an annuity and provide you with a quotation, which will tell you the amount of money you have in your 'pension pot', the amount of tax-free lump sum you are entitled to take and the level of income you will receive each month (should you convert your pension fund to an annuity with them) and will explain the options available to you including flexible drawdown. Too many savers just take the annuity or draw-down plan offered by their pension company rather than comparing rivals who may offer better rates.

Top Tip

Worried about outliving your pension pot- annuities could be the answer? You don't have to buy your existing provider's annuity. Shop around for better annuity and drawdown pension deals with a financial adviser registered with the Financial Conduct Authority ("FCA") or after taking free help from the government funded www.moneyhelper.org.uk. Beware of pension predators as set out further a bit later in this chapter.

Types of annuities

There are several different kinds of annuity and some, at first glance, look superbly attractive but there may be a catch in terms of amounts offered and related conditions. The most basic is a *level annuity*. This pays you a fixed income for the rest of your life. If you die, the income usually stops. And – crucially – it will not change if prices rise. So, in an inflationary world, your annuity will lose real value every year.

To avoid this you could buy an *increasing annuity*. Here, the amount of income you receive will rise in line with inflation each year, or by a set percentage. And if you are worried about your insurance company keeping a large chunk of your pension fund should you die after only a few years of retirement, you could buy a *guaranteed annuity*. So, if you bought a five-year guarantee, and you died after two years, your nominated beneficiary (your spouse perhaps) would receive annuity income for another three years.

Another option is a *joint-life annuity* where your partner can receive some or all of your pension income if you die before them. If you want to take a bit more of a risk, you could choose an *investment-linked annuity*. Here you start with an initial level of income while your fund is invested in an insurance company's with-profits fund. If the fund makes a profit, your income goes up. If it loses money, however, your income goes down.

Your health can also have a significant impact. If you are a smoker or have an illness, you may be eligible for an **enhanced annuity** or **impaired-life annuity**. These pay a higher annual income than a standard annuity. In short, the annuity provider is betting that you won't live as long, so it can afford to pay you more.

Other annuity options

If you don't want to buy an annuity because of low rates, there are a number of strategies you can use. One is known as **phased retirement**. This is where you set up a series of annuities and drawdowns with 25 per cent tax-free lump sums. You will get a lower starting income but if you think annuity rates are going to rise it might be worth considering.

Another possible option is **fixed-term annuities**. Here you set up an annuity for a fixed period (say 5 or 10 years). You get paid an income for the fixed term but at the end of the period you have a guaranteed pot of money to reinvest again. As with phased retirement, your income will be lower than from a standard annuity.

Finally, remember that due to pensions flexibility you can now avoid buying an annuity and, instead, manage your own defined contribution pension under flexible drawdown.

Self-invested personal pensions (SIPPs)

If you want to use a pension to save for your retirement, you don't have to give your money to a fund manager in a personal pension provider. This might be an alternative if you have the knowledge, interest and confidence to manage your own retirement fund with a self-invested personal pension (SIPP). You can buy a range of asset classes, from stocks to bonds to gold bullion (though you can't buy fine wines or residential property). Monthly contributions can be as low as £50 or as much as 100 per cent of your annual salary (subject to the tax restrictions set out further below). These were designed for people who wanted to play a more active part in their investment strategy. The investments that can be held in the SIPP are quite wide and can even include commercial property, and for this reason some owners of small businesses may look at holding their commercial property within their SIPP to, potentially, good end effect. A specialist pension adviser should be able to assist further. Martin Gorvett, Chartered Financial Planner advises:

"Specialist pension products, SIPPs, are becoming a lot more mainstream but be warned a product bearing this title doesn't always promise full functionality. If you are venturing away from the more traditional investment routes, especially buying commercial property, it is important to ensure that a 'pure' SIPP is used where you are a co-trustee of the SIPP and hence a co-landlord of the property. Just be careful that if you don't need a 'pure' SIPP, you aren't inadvertently paying for one. 'SIPPs' have become somewhat of a buzz word for pension wrappers. Ensure that the functionality of the product meets your needs (and nothing else). A SIPP can be anything from a drawdown providing open architecture personal pension, to a full-blooded personalised pension trust that has the capacity for esoteric investments. Just check the label first."

If you are someone who finds the idea of investing your own money daunting, a SIPP may not be for you and I also set out a major wake-up call on SIPPs in the section below in this chapter 'Protection when things go wrong or if there is a financial crash'.

How much should you pay in?

The more precise number should flow from your own plan but as an indicator (and maybe a shock?) Martin Gorvett provided a basic rule of thumb earlier in this chapter saying you 'should take the age you start your pension and halve it. Put this percentage of your pre-tax profits (or before tax salary perhaps via salary sacrifice after speaking with your employer) aside each year until you retire.' So, for a 45 year old with no real pension provision it would be 22.5 per cent of your profits/salary for the next 23 years (until aged 68) and they may attain a reasonable retirement pension income. For those who own their own business, pension contributions are an efficient method of profit extraction and usually deductible for corporation tax if you get the paperwork right.

Yet again this just reinforces one of the key messages in this book that **it is never too early to start your retirement planning** so you have a better chance of achieving the retirement you want to create.

Restricting tax relief on pensions

You can save as much as you like towards your UK pension but (and it is a BIG BUT) there is a limit on the amount of tax relief you can get. For that reason, linking savings together with pensions can be wise for your retirement planning and especially for higher earners. The rules on how much you can contribute and still receive tax relief have been changed over recent years and the **'annual allowance'** is currently **£60,000** for 2025/26, 2024/25 and 2023/24 and £40,000 for the previous year. There are provisions to use three previous years' unused annual allowance and if this becomes a potential issue the sums involved would usually justify paying for specific professional advice as the opportunity may be significant and equally the risk of getting it wrong and incurring tax penalties should not be underestimated. Another restriction, called the **'tapered reduction'**, hits big earners as it reduces the amount of tax relief that can be obtained on pension contributions for taxpayers with **'adjusted income'** (which includes employers pension contributions) in excess of £260,000 (back in 2020/21 this was £240,000 so care is needed when utilising the three years back provision outlined just above). Where an individual is subject to the taper, their annual allowance will be reduced by £1 for every £2 by which their income exceeds £260,000 subject to a maximum reduction of £50,000 (£36,000 earlier years). A reduced annual allowance of £10,000 will, therefore, currently apply to taxpayers with adjusted income of £360,000 or more. The reduction does not apply to individuals who have a **'threshold income'** of no more than £200,000. The key difference between adjusted income and tapered income is that threshold income excludes personal pension contributions. Unfortunately HMRC's definitions of adjusted income and threshold income can cause confusion but I usually find at this level of earnings the individual navigating the issue has an Independent Financial Adviser navigating the issue for them.

Another big restriction on the tax relief available on pension contributions has changed recently. The 'restriction' was called the **'lifetime allowance'** which used to limit the maximum amount that can be paid into pensions to a total 'ceiling' which was set at **£1,073,000**. The Conservative Chancellor Jeremy Hunt announced in March 2023 that the cap on the lifetime allowance of £1,073,000 would be removed. The then Labour opposition stated it would be restored and then reversed their strategy and it was removed . This, at first, indicated that some individuals with large pension pots (rising to over £1m) could store more in a tax-advantageous environment for inheritance tax and other tax purposes. However, Labour's October 2024 budget announced changes to inheritance tax which mean that, from April 2027, unspent pension pots will be included in IHT liability calculations at death, unless the spousal exemption applies, provided the legislation proceeds as Expected (witing at December 2024). Specialist advice should be taken from an appropriately qualified IFA if this is an issue. Martin Gorvett , Chartered Financial Planner advises

"For many years, financial planning for even the moderately well off has involved an increasing focus on using pensions as a tax planning tool to transfer wealth without an inheritance tax charge. The Chancellor's announcement forcibly brings the focus back to considering pensions for their original intended purpose - of funding retirement only.

The pre consultation briefing was typically very light weight, and presently leaves many questions unanswered. What it does show is not only the need to have flexibility in your planning; because life events and legislation can never be predetermined, but also the need to maintain an ongoing relationship with your professional advisers; because wider planning may be needed."

By way of further background the lifetime allowance 'ceiling' has been slashed significantly since 2011/12 when it had then stood at £1,800,000. There were HMRC protection schemes which preserved, for instance, £1,250,000 of lifetime allowances existing at 5 April 2016 – more at www.gov.uk and search for 'pension schemes protect your lifetime allowance.' Where pensions contributions in a year exceed the available allowance tax charges will be payable through your self-assessment. These tax penalty rates could see up to 55% being levied as a tax charge – hence the 'risk' I mentioned earlier in this section and the need, I believe, for advice and recommendations from an IFA specialising in pensions at this level of opportunity.

As presently envisaged, there will continue to be a limit on the maximum an individual can claim as a Pension Commencement (Tax Free) Lump Sum to 25% of the current Lifetime Allowance (£268,275 i.e. 25% of £1,073,000) except where previous protections apply. Feeling confused? I don't blame you! Just to triple underline the point, at this level of pension and tax planning specialist advice is usually needed from a financial adviser registered with the FCA who is a pensions specialist.

Top Tip

The cap on the lifetime allowance of £1,073,000 has been removed. The lifetime allowance had represented an iceberg lying ahead for anyone approaching this limit. This is especially the case if they have multiple pension schemes with potentially more than a £million and where establishing valuations was difficult and interpretating how future growth could impact planning strategies. The removal of the limit may mean that some individuals can

store more in a tax-advantageous environment for inheritance tax or other tax purposes and specialist advice should be taken from an appropriately qualified IFA. The IHT advantage could end in April 2027 and if this causes concern specialist advice would usually be needed from a financial adviser registered with the FCA who is a pensions specialist.

Timing of withdrawals – don't shoot yourself in the foot

Receiving tax relief on £60,000 of contributions in 2025/26 and the back-dating provisions of unused relief from £60,000/£40,000 in the relevant years is a valuable planning tool for tax efficiency. This is especially the case for the small business owner who may face volatile income streams and variable spending patterns or those facing redundancy (for any payments beyond the initial £30,000 relief from income tax). **Once you start withdrawing taxable income from your defined contribution pension pot a barrier comes down.** After that date tax relief on contributions into a pension will be limited to that available from £10,000 contributions per year in 2025/26, 2024/25 and 2023/24 (rising from £4,000 as existed in 2022/23) – this is known as the 'Money Purchase Annual Allowance'. This along with some other measures are partly to prevent the 're-laundering' of pension income back into pensions to try and get double tax relief on the tax-free element of a withdrawal.

There are some exemptions to this rule for small pension pots where withdrawals can be taken without being subject to the reduced allowance. If in any doubt check it out with a financial adviser who is a pensions specialist and carefully consider your future income and anticipated pension contributions before starting to draw down on your pension. This action could restrict the future tax efficiency of contributions. Indeed, it must be considered very carefully where you are considering a glidepath retirement and continuing to work and save into pensions as a tax saving strategy. **'Don't shoot yourself in the foot'** by taking an income from a defined benefit pension when instead you may have been better off, for instance, living off savings and investments or a tax-free lump sum for a few years. The rules may not be so harsh if you have started to draw on a defined benefit pension this just illustrates the risks and opportunities in planning and the need to take advice before acting if you are unsure.

"Don't shoot yourself in the foot"

Top tip
Tax rules and tax reliefs can and do change and their exact value depends on each individual's circumstances. As the numbers increase so does the tax efficiency opportunities and risk (subject to allowance caps as outlined) and planning at higher levels really should be undertaken with a financial adviser registered with the Financial Conduct Authority ("FCA"). On 6 April a new tax year opens up and further planning could be considered for implementation from that day if appropriate.

Employer pension schemes

Types of employer pension schemes

The pension that your employer offers may be 'contributory' (you and your employer pay into it) or 'non-contributory', which means that only your employer does. There are four main types of employer pension:

- a final salary pension scheme (a **defined benefit** scheme and often considered to be the 'king' of pensions for those lucky enough to have one and who had promotions late in their careers);
- another **defined benefit** pension scheme called a 'career average' pension scheme;
- a **defined contribution** money purchase pension scheme; and
- a **defined contribution** group or personal pension scheme.

Final salary pension scheme

Final salary pension schemes are known as a type of defined benefit scheme. You build up a pension at a certain rate – one-sixtieth or one eightieth are quite common – so for each year you've been a scheme member, you receive one-sixtieth/ one eightieth of your final salary as a pension. The pension benefit keeps paying for as long as you live and, therefore, the cost and risk of funding the pension sits with the employer. This is, potentially, a very big win for employees given extending life expectancy rates. Many private sector employers have exited this sort of arrangement as the cost of funding them has become just too onerous. The biggest winners of all are those employees who secure big salary increases towards the end of their employment.

If you work for one of the few remaining employers with a final salary scheme you would need a compelling reason not to join it. Again, you would probably need a compelling reason to shift the benefits to another scheme after you leave the employer. Whilst this holds true some large employers have been offering increasingly large sums to buy leavers out of their scheme. Some considerations may make this a worthwhile option to review with an independent financial adviser registered with the FCA. Perhaps the prompt could be that the amount offered seems 'too good to be true'. On review factors such as health concerns of the future pensioner and/or the spouse pension being low may make the option more viable. One other factor that used to be considered was the inheritance tax breaks which applied to defined pension contribution pots as these did not apply to final salary scheme payments on the death of the pensioner. However, as I have explained already (but it is so crucial it needs underlining) Labour's October 2024 budget announced changes to inheritance tax which mean that, from April 2027, unspent pension pots will be included in IHT liability calculations at death, unless the spousal exemption applies, provided the legislation proceeds as Expected (writing at December 2024). So from April 2027 and if under 75 the inheritance tax breaks may no longer apply which previously could be tax free money for the non spouse recipient. It is vital to remember that any such review would need to be undertaken by an Independent Financial Adviser, regulated by the Financial Conduct Authority. Martin Gorvett, Chartered Financial Planner, provides some guidance on this:

> *"Final salary pension schemes are usually the 'golden goose' of the pensions world as these schemes just keep paying, which will be a nice win if you live to over 100. Only in the rarest of exceptions would there ever be a need to shift out of a final salary pension scheme – if you are unmarried or fear decreased mortality due to health concerns you may wish to seek advice on this topic. If you are tempted to move your final salary benefit to a defined contribution scheme just make sure that the temptation isn't driven by the ability to invest into an unregulated investment vehicle that promises the earth as happened with some British Steel workers. Also, there is only modest risk, as if a salary-related occupational scheme or the sponsoring employer gets into financial trouble, the Pension Protection Fund can provide some protection - normally of up to 90 per cent of your expected pension, subject to a cap (more at www.pensionprotectionfund.org.uk)."*

Career average pension scheme

This is another type of defined benefit scheme and differs from the final salary pension scheme outlined above as the benefit (your pension) is worked out using an average of your earnings in the time that you're a member of the scheme, rather than the final salary.

Money purchase pension scheme

These are defined contribution schemes, as described earlier and therefore provide additional benefits through flexible access options and inheritance tax breaks (up to age 75- but this is subject to change as I have outlined from April 2027). The money paid in by you and your employer is invested and builds up a fund that buys you an income when you retire; significantly, the funding risk sits with the employee (in contrast to the defined benefit alternatives above where the funding risk sits with the employer). The fund is invested, usually in stocks and shares and other investments, with the aim of growing it over the years before you retire.

You can usually choose from a range of funds to invest in. The Pensions Advisory Service has an online investment choices planner to help you decide how to invest your contributions (see www.pensionsadvisoryservice.org.uk and go to 'choosing investment funds').

Group/personal pension scheme

These are also money-purchase schemes and a defined contribution scheme so, again, the funding risk sits with the employee but there are additional benefits through flexible access options and inheritance tax breaks (up to age 75 but this is subject to change as I have outlined from April 2027). Typically, your employer offers access to a personal pension plan, which you own, and can take with you if you get a new job. Your employer will choose the scheme provider, deduct the contributions you make from your salary and pay these to the provider, along with their employer contributions. In the November 2023 budget the government announced that it hopes to introduce one pension 'pot for life' to help solve the problem of workers having numerous pensions throughout their career. Don't expect any major changes to happen soon as this will take some time to consider, consult and work through.

Automatic enrolment

This was introduced in 2012 because people in the UK were living longer but were not saving enough to finance their increasing retirement. Auto-enrolment (as it is called) was designed to help shift the responsibility away from the state and towards the individual and their employer. It now covers all employees.

To be eligible an individual must live in the UK, be between 22 and State Pensionable age and earn more than £10,000 a year. Some employers may offer schemes which better the auto-enrolment rates but for all other employers each individual will pay 5 per cent of their pre-tax income between £6,240 and £50,270 (split 4% employee and 1% from the government). Their employers will pay a minimum of 3 per cent. Many employers use the National Employment Savings Trust ("NEST") as their pension scheme for auto-enrolment purposes. This is a national defined contribution workplace pension scheme established by the government to support auto-enrolment. It is transportable between employers and has relatively low charges. More at www.nestpensions.org.uk. Other auto-enrolment schemes are available.

Questions on your employer pension scheme

If you have a query about your company pension they (or their delegated representative) should be able to assist with the usual questions that arise such as: Could you have a refund of contributions if you were to leave shortly after joining? What happens if you become ill or die before pension age? What are the arrangements if you want to retire early? What will your pension be on your present salary? What spouse's pension will be paid on the death of the pensioner? Can a pension be paid to other dependents? What happens if you continue working with the organisation after retirement age?

Top tip

With all forms of employer pension scheme check the answer to this question. "What is the maximum amount or percentage the employer will match or contribute?" Then review if you are missing out on free money to help boost your retirement. I only say this a few times in this book but this is an urgent and vital step- as free money does not happen often in life!

Other pension opportunities and issues

Lifetime Individual Savings Account - a different pension?

The lifetime ISA (LISA) has been available since April 2017 for adults provided they were aged under 40 when they opened the account. There is an annual contribution limit of £4,000 and savers will receive a 25 per cent government bonus. The intention is to encourage individuals to save towards their first home or for retirement once aged 60. The LISA could be an early step in a new approach to pension funding where taxed money goes in and is tax-free on the way out (with the 25 per cent government bonus being a welcome addition). This switches the traditional pensions world on its head. The difficulty for many imminent retirees is that it is currently only available to the under-40s and lack of availability as not many of the traditional ISA providers have introduced the product. In addition, better tax relief can currently be obtained by higher and additional rate tax payers using traditional pensions.

Individual Savings Account – tax sheltered savings for a top up 'income' or a 'big one-offs' savings reserve

ISAs provide significant tax breaks as you do not pay any tax on the interest or the income (dividends) you make and there is no Capital Gains Tax if shares in your ISA soar. They are not, however, tax free on death and could be subject to the 40% Inheritance Tax charge if the Estate is above tax exempt levels.

You can currently put up to £20,000 into an ISA so that is £40,000 between yourself and your partner. There is no age restriction as found with the Lifetime ISA as outlined immediately above. Whilst pensions win for overall tax efficiency ISAs are a great second option for any savings or investments that are not tax sheltered already and for any free money that you receive (lottery, gaming or inheritance) or excess income received that you wish to 'put away' if you have used up your pension lifetime allowance or beyond the pension annual allowance.

Minimum retirement age

The minimum age at which you are allowed to take early retirement and draw your pension is 55 and rises to 57 in 2028 maintaining a 10-year gap from the State Pension age. It may be possible to draw retirement benefits earlier if you are in poor health and unable to work.

Other help in retirement - benefits

Pension Credit is an income-related benefit. It's an extra payment that guarantees most people over 66 a minimum income of £221.86 in 2025/26 (an 1.7% increase from £218.15 in 2024/25) for single people. For couples the minimum income guarantee is £338.61 in 2025/26 again a 1.7% increase from £332.95 in 2024/25. You might get more if you're a carer or disabled. You must live in England, Wales or Scotland (there are separate rules for Northern Ireland where the 2024/25 rates equalled those in GB) and you won't get pension credit if you move abroad permanently. For more information visit gov.uk and 'Pension Credit'.

Death and divorce

What happens on death will depend on the type of pension you have and the options you have chosen. The state pension will stop being paid when someone dies but their spouse or civil partner might inherit some or all of it, depending on their state pension ages and the date of their marriage/civil partnership. Contact the pension service to check your state pension entitlement. Private pensions will usually follow the 'expression of wish' form detailing the intended recipient. Occupational defined benefit schemes will usually pay any tax-free lump sum remaining and then any income forms part of the survivor's taxable income. Labour's October 2024 budget announced changes to inheritance tax which mean that, from April 2027, unspent pension pots will be included in IHT liability calculations at death, unless the spousal exemption applies, provided the legislation proceeds as Expected (writing at December 2024). So from April 2027 and if under 75 the inheritance tax breaks may no longer apply which previously could be tax free money for the non-spouse recipient.

Top tip
Review your expression of wish forms held with your pension schemes. Do they still meet your wishes? They can be amended easily via your current provider. Consider it as a Will for your pension.

Divorce can see pensions split in a number of ways and what can be divided also depends on where you live in the UK. Most pensions can be split but many divorce settlements still leave one partner worse off in retirement which can be rectified, potentially, as part of the divorce settlement negotiations and then agreement. This seems to be due to a lack of understanding into the incredible value of pensions and then a lack of an awareness of rights to a spouse's pension on divorce. The options may include offsetting (where one person keeps their pension and another keeps another asset for instance the home); sharing (where the pension is shared between two parties and this can be now or deferred) or by informal agreement which is then documented and formalised. There is substantial free trusted advice and assistance available from the four organisations referenced at the end of this chapter at 'free trusted advice' and therefore further analysis is not detailed here. These organisations together with any legal advice that may obtained may also assist couples separating.

Property versus pension

You may hear people say *'my property is my pension'*. It could work but it is a path that has many trip points for the unwary but also opportunities. These centre on the ups of the property market but sometimes omit the historically less frequent property crashes - timing is everything! There is then tax and the taxation of property which is a complex area so it is important to seek advice on the tax treatment of property transactions in advance.

If this pricks your interest I'd start by revisiting Chapter 1, Property which explains more about your property in the context of retirement planning and then **Chapter 5, Tax** and the section on Capital Gains Tax and the tax traps for the unwary. Financial advice from a financial adviser registered with the Financial Conduct Authority and a tax adviser will help you work through the following considerations which are just for a starter.

Property	Pensions
Significant amount required for deposit to get started.	You can invest small amounts and get an early start.
Provides opportunity for capital growth (or loss). Less susceptible to short term shocks in the stock market. Income stream through rent.	Provides opportunity for capital growth (or loss) and income stream through investment income (interest and dividends).
Agent's fees, solicitor's fees, surveyor fees and initial and then ongoing maintenance and repair.	Financial adviser fees, fund manager fees.
Paying stamp duty.	Your employer may add 'free' extra contributions.
Down-sizing, right sizing, or relocating your main residence can provide a tax-free windfall.	25% tax free at retirement (up to £268,275 unless earlier protection applied) and opportunities around

playing the tax bands and reducing income tax rates.

You can access cash at any age but with slow timescales to sell the property and then access the cash.	Can't access until age 55 (57 from 2028).
Capital gains tax on second homes is attractive and you may be able to plan around timing for tax reasons and get more of the gain taxed at (currently) 18% rather than the higher rate of 24%.	Once you are beyond age 55 (57 from 2028) there is fast and flexible access to your funds.
Take care if you make frequent property transactions. HMRC may interpret that you are potentially undertaking a property trade and liable to tax at higher income tax rates (rather than lower capital gains tax rates).	More opportunity to diversify risk by spreading your investment types and geographical spread.
Agents fees, insurance, services, other costs and income tax on rentals.	Real time information on valuations and portfolios and 'cockpit style' tools to help you monitor investment performance and adjust risk.
Stress of buying/selling and potential other stresses of property blight and 'tenant from hell' issues if renting.	For certain pensions up to a certain age there are opportunities to shelter your pension pot from inheritance tax.
Increasing red tape on rental properties.	
It's not an either/or- maybe you can consider both.	It's not an either/or- maybe you can consider both.

Protection when things go wrong or if there is a financial crash

You would normally approach **the Pensions Ombudsman** if the pension scheme manager (or trustees) and the Pensions Advisory Service are unable to help. The Pensions Ombudsman is a non-departmental public body funded by the Department of Work and Pensions and can investigate complaints of maladministration by the trustees, managers or administrators of a pension scheme or by an employer. The ombudsman will assist with disputes of fact or law with the trustees, managers or an employer. The ombudsman does not, however, investigate complaints about mis-selling of pension schemes, a complaint that is already subject to court proceedings, or those that are about a state social security benefit. In 2023/24 around 39% of determinations by a Pensions Ombudsman were upheld or partially upheld compared to 51% in 2022/23 (i.e. helping the pensioner) and most complaints were again about contributions, administration, transfers, retirement benefits, transfers and misquote/misinformation. An interesting case spotlighted in their 2023/24 annual report was where the Pensions Ombudsman found a pension scheme administrator negligent in cyber fraud. The applicant who approached the Pension Ombudsman for help complained that the pension scheme administrator had accepted fraudulent email instructions to withdraw £20,000 and he incurred a financial loss as a result (this helps show the scammers are everywhere and gives me a chance to signpost the help I set out in **Chapter 7** on scams and protecting yourself and the Investor Protection content as **Chapter 5**).

The Pensions Ombudsman has also taken on the role of Pension Protection Fund Ombudsman, which helps final salary pension scheme members who are at risk of losing their pension benefits owing to their employer's insolvency. Members below the scheme's normal retirement age will receive 90 per cent of the Pension Protection Fund level of compensation plus annual increases, subject to a cap and the standard fund rules. More at www.pensions-ombudsman.org.uk.

Some aspects of complaints about pensions can be investigated by the **Financial**

Ombudsman Service (FOS), such as complaints about the suitability of advice to start a personal pension arrangement (perhaps they would have been better off being advised to join, remain or top up their employer's company pension scheme). More at www.financial-ombudsman.org.uk. The interaction between the FOS and the Pensions Ombudsman can seem confusing but don't worry too much as they have good arrangements to point you in the right direction if you end up with the wrong ombudsman.

The financial turmoil that has arisen in recent years and with the UK entering a recession it could be the shock needed to reassess our pensions 'exposure' under the current UK safety net arrangements. Unlike occupational pension schemes where the Pension Protection Fund can provide some protection there are different protections on personal pensions and SIPPs. For a salary-related occupational scheme if the sponsoring employer gets into financial trouble, the Pension Protection Fund can normally (under current arrangements) provide a pension of up to 90 per cent of your expected pension (and there is more above on employer pension schemes).

In marked contrast the protection on annuities, personal pensions and SIPPs is currently through the UK financial services safety net of the **Financial Services Compensation Scheme ("FSCS"** and see fscs.org.uk for further information). Cover varies and if you are unsure you should ask your financial adviser to review your position and advise if any changes are required to optimise your compensation protection.

1   Pensions that are provided by UK-regulated insurers that are **'contracts of long-term insurance'**. This could be a fund in a personal pension or an annuity. Where FSCS can pay compensation, they will cover the pension at 100% with no upper cap. FSCS cannot confirm whether individual plans with specific providers would be classed as 'contracts of long-term insurance' or not – you would need to speak to your provider directly or check with your financial adviser.

2   A share in your SIPP goes bust akin to Northern Rock in 2008. There is no FSCS cover as **FSCS does not protect investment losses** arising from shares falling in value or becoming worthless.

3   A fund goes bust or a series of funds go bust that are not 'contracts of long term insurance'. There is no FSCS cover as **FSCS does not protect investment losses arising from poor investment performance**.

4   The bank or banks which hold the SIPP or personal pensions cash goes bust. Usually the FSCS would expect the cash deposit to be held by the

SIPP/personal pension (not the member) and would look through the SIPP/personal pension to regard the member as the eligible claimant for up to £85,000. **This may leave some exposure where the member holds cash in excess of the £85,000 per bank.**

5   Where the SIPP/personal pension provider is negligent in advising on or arranging investments or scheme assets and the customer has suffered loss the customer may have a claim under the FSCS's rules up to £85,000.

6   Where the SIPP/personal pension provider goes bust. This could be a complex area but where a regulated firm owes a civil liability to a customer in connection with a regulated activity (e.g. for negligent advice/due diligence), and the customer has suffered loss, the customer may have a claim under FSCS compensation rules up to £85,000. If a SIPP provider has failed but there is no shortfall in SIPP assets (which should have been ring-fenced from the provider's own assets) and the SIPP provider does not otherwise owe a civil liability to customers (e.g. for negligent advice/due diligence), customers would not have an FSCS claim.

Top tip

If you have a SIPP in any format or a personal pension that is not a 'contract of long term insurance' review (with your independent financial adviser) and assess your holdings against FSCS compensation limits that may apply if there is a financial crash and consider adjusting your holdings accordingly based on the advice you receive from your IFA.

Beware of predators stalking your pension

Beware of anyone claiming that they can help to cash in a pension early and before you are 55 (it rises to 57 from 2028 albeit some schemes may allow protection at 55 beyond 2028 where the scheme specifically marketed this as I mentioned earlier in this Chapter). Whilst initially attractive, the sting in the tail is that you could face a tax bill of more than half your pension savings. The main warning signs are unsolicited text messages and phone calls, a transfer overseas and seeking to access a pension fund before the age of

55; the crooks also try to create some false urgency.

To counter this you must always check that any financial adviser is registered with the Financial Conduct Authority; always obtain a written statement about any tax charges; never allow yourself to be rushed into agreeing to a pension transfer; and create a 'time out' to check things out. The benefit of dealing with a financial adviser who is registered with the Financial Conduct Authority is the safety net if things go wrong – in the form of the Financial Ombudsman Service – and, if the firm fails and is insolvent the protection offered by the Financial Services Compensation Scheme.

Six must-do steps in 2024/25 and 2025/26

Martin Gorvett, Chartered Financial Planner, of Lavender Financial Planners Ltd, helps you get to grips with financing your retirement with his six 'must do' steps to help you firm up on your preparations. Perhaps some of these should feature in your own plan?

1. *Keeping track of your retirement goals*. Retirement is not uniform. Everyone has different expectations. Start by understanding your likely expenditure by splitting your spending into three categories:

    —   *must-have*: day-to-day living costs such as food and heating etc. (see the budget planner set out in Chapter 1);

    —   *like-to-have*: a holiday twice a year;

    —   *nice-to-have*: a new car, a new kitchen or a legacy for the children.

    Consider how these categories will change during the phases of retirement. Then you can start to consider the income you need to meet your personal retirement goals.

2. *Don't rely on the state*. The State Pension is certainly no substitute for private pension provision and other savings but it does provide a secure guaranteed baseline income on which to build. Ensure you understand what you will be entitled to and when from the State Pension.

3. *Retirement isn't just a pension*. You may need professional help to think differently about your goals for later life and how you want to finance them. The traditional view is that your pension provides income, and other investments are viewed as 'rainy day' funds.

4. *Understand just how long retirement could last and the effect of inflation*. A 66-year-old can now typically expect to live for another 22 years, and in all likelihood may well live a lot longer. Any income that will finance your

retirement that is not inflation proofed will reduce in value over time. Getting the investment strategy right may sustain the funds for longer and may provide the desired investment returns while also limiting volatility.

5. *Pensions are still the most tax-privileged savings.* Pensions still offer the best tax breaks for mainstream savings. Where else can you get tax relief on contributions, tax-free investment returns and take 25 per cent out tax-free? Treat the pension annual allowance of £60,000 like your ISA allowance of £20,000 and save, save, save.

6. *Your pension is now perhaps the most efficient device for sheltering part of your wealth (the pension fund) from Inheritance Tax (IHT) if you are under 75.* Look upon this as part of your savings armoury and, potentially, save 40 per cent for those you leave behind by carefully planning how you create your savings and pensions and which you draw from first.

Martin also explains that modern pensions allow much more flexibility than ever before. 'Flexi-Access' – modern pension freedoms – which can allow you to 'mould' your pension income (and tax-free cash) into any shape you wish.

> *"With expenditure typically higher in the early years, planning can ensure value is extracted from your pension savings when you need it most. Retirement income doesn't have to come from the pension alone. Having a variety of different savings and investments can achieve the optimum tax-efficient income. Do take professional advice – the benefits arising usually justify any cost."*

Other help and advice
Lost previous pensions

In addition to understanding your current pension scheme, you may also need to chase up any previous schemes that you can't seem to track down due to takeovers and mergers. The Association of British Insurers report that people typically move house 8 times in a lifetime but that few remember to tell their pension schemes about their change of address and **over time £26.6 billion of pension pots has gone unclaimed for around 1.6 million people.** That's nearly £17,000 per pension pot. For free help tracking down a pension go to www.gov.uk and then to 'Pension Tracing Service' or call them on 0800 731 0193.

> **Top tip**
> **1.6 million people have lost a pension. Track down your missing pension with the help from www.gov.uk and then to 'Pension Tracing Service'. This could be worth an action point at Chapter 13.**

Trustees or managers of your pension scheme

These are the first people to contact if you do not properly understand your benefit entitlements or if you are unhappy about some point to do with your pension.

Useful reading

Book a free appointment with **Pension Wise** (now part of Money Helper, see immediately below) from the age of 50 to understand more about your pensions and access free and quality help at pensionwise.gov.uk.

Money Helper which provides general information and guidance on pension matters and assists individuals with disputes about pensions. It can also help you find missing pensions schemes. More at moneyhelper.org.uk.

Low Incomes Tax Reform Group at litg.org.uk and 'pensioners'.

In addition **citizensadvice.org.uk** has good free information on pensions.

The Service Personnel and Veterans Agency: www.gov.uk/government/organisations/veterans-uk.

> **Reminder: Take any action points or follow up points to Chapter 13, Your Plan For A Better Retirement**

Chapter Four
Savings and investments

"An investment in knowledge pays the best interest"
BENJAMIN FRANKLIN

Just like pensions the world of savings and investments is poorly understood and filled with 'financial jargon'. As part of your 're-set' and glidepath into and through retirement this chapter will help you invest in more knowledge on savings and investments as Benjamin Franklin's famous tip urges immediately above. It's a superb quote and the cornerstone of my approach. You will 'save more' and may even save a fortune armed with better knowledge of the UK's financial safety net and staying within that safety net.

This chapter follows close on the heels of the chapter on pensions as the two subjects are interlinked. They often work well together in the 'active' phase of retirement when expenditure tends to be much higher. The three phases of retirement are important and were outlined in Chapter 1. The active retirement phase is when you may be spending more of your retirement funds: either those held in your savings and investments; or perhaps, drawing on more of your pension where this is allowed if you have pensions flexibility (as per Chapter 3, Pensions). In the active retirement phase you still have the appetite and energy to devour all those things set out in the 'live better' chapters of this book and many of the activities come at a financial cost. The '**save more**' and second essential step of my retirement planning approach is therefore taking another big step forward in this chapter. With an improved knowledge on savings and investments you will make better 'choices' (remember Aristotle from Chapter 1) '**save more**' and you will achieve a better retirement.

This chapter at a glance

- *How to find a good financial adviser and the importance of getting proper financial advice.* The benefits obtained from good financial advice should more than outweigh the fees that you may have to pay. Always ensure your adviser is on the Financial Conduct Authority register at www.fca.org.uk and receive written advice and recommendations tailored to your circumstances .

- *Understanding risk and reward and just as importantly understand the UK financial safety net and your Financial Services Compensation Scheme protection limits.*

- *How to '**save more**' by combining your pensions planning with your savings plan to finance your retirement.*

- *Be alert to the tax implications (which can change) as therein lie both opportunities and pitfalls.* Dividend tax free amounts have been slashed down and down in recent years and remain at just £500 in 2024/25 and into 2025/26. Tax efficient savings and investment products include ISAs and LISAs. Premium Bonds also offer a tax free opportunity.

Importantly, this chapter is only a guide and it is neither legal nor financial advice; it is no substitute for taking professional advice from a financial adviser or other professional adviser. Any potential UK tax advantages may be subject to change (and the 2025/26 budget remains subject to approval) and will depend upon your individual circumstances, and individual professional advice should be obtained.

How do I find a good financial adviser and why should I have one?

Two easy questions to ask but not so easy to answer. You are free to manage your own savings and investments and this may interest you especially if you have a good knowledge of the financial markets. Financial advisers offer an alternative for a fee and their knowledge and skills may remove the work from you and, potentially, improve returns over the long term. Another alternative is a financial services company which sells funds, shares, related products and provides you with information through its website to assist you in making decisions. They make money from dealing and transaction fees which will usually be less than a financial adviser's overall fees.

One of the biggest wealth warnings in this book is to **always ensure your adviser is on the Financial Conduct Authority** register at www.fca.org.uk - if not you are left outside the impressive UK financial services safety net if things go wrong. If a financial adviser gets things wrong you will usually have a remedy against them and their professional indemnity insurance or can escalate matters to the Financial Ombudsman Service. If the financial adviser goes bust, there may be compensation payable by the Financial Services Compensation Scheme ('FSCS' more below - see section on 'protection'). In short, stay inside the UK financial services' safety net.

My tips on finding a good financial adviser would be:

- **Always trust your instincts** – if in doubt walk away and find another adviser.
- Look for recommendations from trusted family, friends or other professional advisers and then **talk to at least two financial advisers before deciding**.
- Look very closely at the attention your adviser gives to fully understanding where you and any partner and any dependents are in life, where you want to get to and when you may need to access your savings and investments.
- Confirm you will receive, at least annually, a **meeting** to review of your changing finances and circumstances. Confirm you will then receive **written advice and recommendations**, time to reflect and consult with any other advisers (tax advice) and then a further meeting to implement recommendations well before the end of each tax year (5 April).
- **Consider all relevant costs and get these set out in writing** before you agree to anything so that you can understand the actual net return over a year to you. The financial adviser's costs are either paid by fees from the return they make for you (perhaps an hourly rate) or they may charge a percentage of the funds they manage. In addition, there may be charges levied by the fund management company itself. These should all be set out

for you in writing before proceeding.

Stay within the UK financial services safety net

- A good financial adviser will gain a complete understanding of both you and your partner's wealth and in the event that one of you is incapacitated or dies the financial adviser's knowledge and advice will be invaluable to the person remaining (especially if they were not the one used to the finances). **So both of you need to be happy** with the financial adviser if you have a partner.

- The adviser's assessment of your **appetite for risk** should help the adviser recommend more suitable products- make sure you understand <u>and</u> accept the different categories of risk and the adviser's assessment of your appetite for risk each year. The higher your appetite for risk the higher the variation in returns. For instance, a high risk investor may expect returns that could rise by 10% to 20% per annum during a surge of optimism. Equally they would not be surprised by a fall of 10% to 20% or maybe more during an investment shock as happened around most of the world in the first quarter of 2020 as a result of the Covid-19 pandemic. For instance, the index of the UK's 100 biggest companies the FTSE 100 fell by 32% between 17 January 2020 (7,645) and 20 March 2020 (5,191). By 5 June 2020 it had risen 25% to 6,484 and now on 13 December 2024 it is well beyond its pre-covid peak at 8,300. A 'no risk' investor will expect no downside risk and may accept returns of 2% - 3% per annum with all savings and investments managed within FSCS limits. They may be prepared to lose out on their buying power as inflation outstrips returns albeit inflation as I write (December 2024) seems to be reducing to a level which more closely matches low risk returns. An investor's appetite for risk can change over time and it is not uncommon to see risk reduce as the retirement years approach.

- A good financial adviser should be keen to **link up with and work with your other professional advisers** including solicitor and any accountant/tax adviser to assist your overall tax efficiency.

Paying for financial advice - understand the fees. Then review and renegotiate the fees.

Charges vary widely and should be set out clearly on any proposal letter provided to you <u>before</u> you decide to engage a financial adviser. Check that everything fee and charge wise is understood before you sign up including adviser fees, product provider fees, any hourly rates, annual management fees and any fee charged if you move advisers (exit fees). Check that the letter specifies you are going to get a one to one 'review' at least annually and that the outcome of this review will be confirmed to you in writing together with the adviser's recommendations. The following may assist you in understanding the types of financial adviser, the types of cost and the range of fees. You can then make a more informed decision and don't be afraid to negotiate on fees as the percentage is usually negotiable at the start and can even be revisited further down the line.

Restricted or Independent Financial Adviser

The distinction is important because it lets you know whether you are dealing with an adviser who can offer you solutions from a restricted pool of providers /solutions (restricted) or an adviser who can offer products/solutions from across the market (independent).

Likely fee components

There may be an **initial advice fee** to assess your circumstances and assess what you can invest in. This could be 0.5% to 3% of the sum invested or hourly rates of £100 to £400. Further fees can involve the following approximate amounts:

Ongoing advice fee 0.5% to 1% per annum on the amount invested for the financial adviser.

Fund charges 0.2% to 1.9% per annum for the funds you are invested in.

Platform charge 0.1% to 0.45% for the financial organisation that the financial adviser selects to manage your investments.

There may also be **exit fees** if you change advisers or platforms. Sometimes VAT of 20% is added to some of the fees.

Top tip
Obtain clarity on the type of adviser you are dealing with and double check they are registered with the FCA. Obtain written details of the entire proposed fee structure and

ensure this includes annual reviews, written advice and recommendations. Don't be afraid to negotiate if selecting an adviser for the first time or renegotiate with an existing adviser. Any saving secured will mount up to a very tidy sum if you take, say, a twenty-year horizon.

Savings and investing

Money in **'savings'** and deposit accounts at banks was earning minimal interest in 2021/22 (maybe 1% if you were lucky) but rates increased to around 5% in December 2023 and now in December 2024 rates of around 3.5% to 4.5% are achievable. With inflation at around 3.5% the gap between interest and inflation is virtually resolved helping those on a 'retirement glidepath' keep up with cost of living increases.

Then we have **'investing'** into the shares of a company, or funds, bonds and other investments which has never been easier. This chapter will help shine a light on the risks and rewards of savings and/or investing and the vital role of knowledge, quality financial advice and an improved knowledge of the **UK safety net** if things go wrong.

Remember also the Individual Savings Account (ISA) annual limit is £20,000. This allows savers to protect part of their wealth from Income Tax and Capital Gains Tax. Between a couple and over several years that can equate to a powerful tax-free fund that can help in retirement. Also, the first £1,000 (£500 for higher-rate taxpayers and £nil for additional rate tax payers- all of these terms are explained in Chapter 5, Tax) of savings interest received in a tax year and the first £500 in dividends will not be subject to Income Tax in 2024/25 and 2025/26. For those who are interested in saving and investing for retirement, and for the long term, the principles remain the same. Martin Gorvett, Chartered Financial Planner of Lavender Financial Planners Ltd explains the golden rules:

"Keep the costs down; shelter as much money from the tax office as you can; buy assets when they are cheap and sell when they are expensive (albeit that few people have the financial knowledge or crystal ball to really make a success of this but the motto, generally, is worth remembering). To be a successful investor you have to be disciplined. You need to decide on a strategy, allocate your money to your investment accordingly, then stick with that through the ups and downs that the markets will inevitably bring. Remember once a market has fallen, the stock it

contains are 'on sale'. Equally when markets are at an all-time high, it could be overpriced (although markets should always continue to increase in value over the long term)."

There's a big difference between 'saving' and 'investing'. Investing is for the long term. It is money you can put away for your retirement, and in the long run it should grow more rapidly than in a savings account. If you are saving for a shorter-term goal, perhaps in less than five years, then you're looking to get the most interest paid on your money. Martin Gorvett provides more valuable insights and tips:

1. *Buy what is right for you and don't believe everything you read or hear.* Just because an investment works well for someone else doesn't necessarily mean it will be right for you. Social media promotions can be misleading. Ensure that the investment provider is regulated by the FCA; you don't have to wander off the beaten track just to avoid the herd.

2. *Remember that the Financial Services Compensation Scheme* does not protect investment losses arising from poor investment performance or if the company you have bought shares in goes bust.

3. *Diversify and don't put all your eggs in one basket.* Consider spreading your risk by diversifying across a mixture of asset classes, industry sectors and geographical areas. When the value of one asset is falling, another might be rising so could help to compensate.

4. *Invest for the long term.* Adopt a strategy and stick with it. Investing isn't a matter of 'timing the market', it is about 'time in the market'. Similarly, try not to get emotionally attached to your investments. Review and rebalance your portfolio regularly to ensure you haven't strayed from the original strategy.

5. *Take professional advice.* Investing is not free. Every avenue to market has a cost. Professional advisers will have a tried-and-tested process, often accessing institutional prices, rather than retail classes available to direct investors.

6. Lastly, *don't risk investing money that you can't afford to lose.* Investments carry a huge caveat – you may get out less than you put in. So don't overstretch, stick within your means and know when to walk away.

Since everyone has different financial aims, there is no 'one-size-fits-all' approach to investing. In very simple terms, there are four different types of saving or investment that you could consider:

1. *Cash savings*. Made into a bank account or cash ISA. These are generally short-term and offer easy access to your money and lower risk, so the potential returns are much less than other types of investment.

2. *Bonds and gilts*. Effectively, an IOU from the government or big companies. When you buy one you are lending money that earns an agreed fixed rate of interest. Government bonds (called gilts) are backed by the state and hopefully are as good as guaranteed in the UK. Corporate bonds carry greater risk if the issuing company goes bust or cannot afford to repay you and because of this element of risk they offer the possibility of improved returns.

3. *Shares*. Sometimes referred to as 'equities', this basically means putting money on the stock market. You can do this by buying shares in individual companies or by investing through a professionally managed investment fund, such as a unit trust.

4. *Investing in property*. Directly as a buy-to-let investor or indirectly through certain investment funds. Property prices go down as well as up, and it can take time to sell property and get your cash back. This is dealt with at Your Home and Property, Chapter 1.

Top tip

"Investing should be more like watching paint dry or watching grass grow. If you want excitement, take $800 and go to Las Vegas"

**Paul Samuelson, Nobel prize winner in economics.
He is saying that if you think investing is gambling then you are doing it wrong.**

Sources of investable funds

These are the common sources where you will usually find funds to invest:

- *Long term savings built up out of excess income over expenditure.*

- *Commuted lump sum / 25% tax free from your pension*: One-quarter of your pension can usually be taken as a tax-free lump sum. The remainder will then be paid out subject to the ordinary rates of Income Tax.

- *Insurance policies (such as endowment policies)*: Designed to mature on or near your date of retirement. These are normally tax-free.

- *Profits on your home*: If you sell it and right-size to less expensive accommodation (more at Chapter 1). Provided this is your main home, there is no Capital Gains Tax to pay.

- *Redundancy money, golden handshake or other farewell gift from your employer*: Currently you are usually allowed £30,000 redundancy money free of tax.

- *Sale of SAYE and other share option schemes from an employer*: The tax rules vary according to the type of scheme and the rules are liable to change with each Budget statement.

- *Inheritance or a big lottery/premium bond win*: Self-explanatory and tax-free for the recipient!

Some key saving and investment products

Investments differ in their aims, their tax treatment and your tax objectives and the amount of risk involved. Your investments should be tailored to provide either income to supplement your pension or capital appreciation to build up over time for the longer term or a mix of both depending on your needs and the products you are likely to encounter are outlined below.

National Savings and Investments (NS&I)

Most banks only guarantee your savings up to £85,000. NS&I are the only provider that secures 100% of your savings, however much you invest. This is one of the main reasons for saving with National Savings and Investments - they are secure as they are backed by HM Treasury in the UK and if that institution goes bust we may as well all pack up. More information is at nsandi.com about their products which currently (December 2024) include:

- *Guaranteed Income Bonds*. One of British Savings Bonds announced by the Chancellor in the Spring 2024 budget. Useful if you need a monthly income but not for you if you want access to your money during the term. The minimum investment is £500 and the maximum is £1 million per issue, per person. Gross income is taxable and is currently at 3.44% (3 year fixed) 3.54% (2 year fixed).

- *Guaranteed Growth Bonds.* Another of the British Savings Bonds announced by the Chancellor in the Spring 2024 budget. Useful if you want a guaranteed interest rate for a fixed term but not for you if you want access to your money during the term. The minimum investment is £500 and the maximum is £1 million per issue, per person. Gross income is currently taxable and is currently at 3.5% (3 year fixed) 3.6% (2 year fixed).

- *Direct saver.* Save from £1 to £2 million with no notice, no penalty. Gross income is taxable and the interest rate is variable and is currently at 3.5%.

- *Direct ISA.* Invest from £1 to £20,000 each tax year. Interest is tax-free and is variable and is currently at 3%.

- *Junior ISA (for children).* Invest from £1 to £9,000 each tax year. Interest is tax-free and is variable and is currently at 4%.

- *Green Savings Bonds.* Invest from £100 to £100,000 for three years. You cannot take money out until the Bond reaches the end of its term. Interest is taxable and is fixed and currently at 2.95%.

- *Premium Bonds.* The maximum amount that can be saved into Premium Bonds is £50,000. Prizes range from £25 per month to £1 million. Prizes are paid out tax-free every month. The rate used to calculate the prize fund is currently (December 2024) 4%. The 'fun' of investing up to £50,000 per person in premium bonds provides a tax-free 'average' return that matches many routine savings accounts (but you may do better in ISAs and if you shop around); and you can get access to your money quickly if you need to- a matter of days only. The odds of winning a prize each month are currently 22,000 to 1 (for every £1 bond).

Top tip
For those with very large savings that exceed the £85,000 limit (£170,000 for a couple) for Financial Services Compensation Scheme protection ('FSCS' – more below) NS&I is attractive for 'safety' as it is backed by HM

Treasury.

Variable interest accounts

The accounts include instant access accounts, high interest accounts and fixed-term savings accounts. For 2024/25 and 2025/26 the first £1,000 of interest earned is tax-free, reducing to £500 for higher-rate taxpayers and £0 for additional-rate taxpayers. If you only have State Pension income and bank interest you don't pay income tax until you have more than about £6.600 in savings interest. This is estimated by adding the personal allowance at £12,570, the £5,000 starting savings allowance and the personal savings allowance at £1,000 to give a total of £18,570. Then deduct the State Pension in 2025/26 of £11,970 which gives £6,600. If you largely rely on your savings income and believe you are or have been paying excess tax you can reclaim this from HMRC using form R40 or reclaim it through self-assessment.

Top tip
If your funds are not with NS&I (see above) and should the bank or building society get into serious financial difficulty up to £85,000 (double that if in joint names) of your money will be protected under the Financial Services Compensation Scheme. The cover can increase for up to 6 months to £1 million for certain life events (for instance moving home). More on the FSCS at the end of this chapter and at fscs.org.uk where you can also check out banks and their different brands (some of which combine under one limit so be careful in your selection).

Gilt-edged securities

Gilts, or gilt-edged securities, are bonds issued by the UK government that offer the investor a fixed interest rate for a predetermined set time, rather than a rate that goes up or down with inflation. You can either retain them until their maturity date, in which case the government will return the capital in full, or sell them on the London Stock

Exchange at market value. Index-linked gilts are government-issued bonds – glorified IOUs – that you can buy to obtain a guaranteed rate of return over inflation. Gilt interest is paid gross (before tax). No Capital Gains Tax is charged on any profit you may have made, but equally no relief is allowed for any loss. Importantly, the government guarantees the payment of interest and the repayment of the capital sum.

Permanent interest-bearing shares (PIBS)

These are a form of investment offered by some building societies to financial institutions and private investors as a means of raising share capital. They have several features in common with gilts including a fixed rate of interest that is set at the date of issue. The interest is usually paid twice yearly; there is no Stamp Duty to pay or Capital Gains Tax on profits. Even though PIBS are issued by building societies, they are very different from normal building society investments.

Unit trusts and Open Ended Investment Companies ('OEICs')

Unit trusts and OEICs are forms of shared investments, or funds, which allow you to pool your money with thousands of other people and invest in world stock markets. They are simple to understand, you get professional management, there are no day-to-day decisions to make and they invest in a broader spread of shares so that your risk is reduced. The minimum investment in some of the more popular funds can be as little as £25 per month or a £500 lump sum. Investors' contributions to the fund are divided into 'units' (and the term is changed to 'shares' in OEICs) in proportion to the amount invested. As with ordinary shares, you can sell all or some of your investment. The key differences between the two are:

1. *Pricing*: When investing in unit trusts, you buy units at the 'offer price' and sell at the lower 'bid price'. The difference in the two prices is known as the spread. An OEIC fund, contrastingly, has a single price, directly linked to the value of the fund's underlying investments. All shares are bought and sold at this single price.

2. *Flexibility*: An OEIC fund offers different types of share or sub-fund to suit different types of investor. The expertise of different fund management teams can be combined to benefit both large and small investors. There is less paperwork as each OEIC will produce one report and accounts for all sub-funds.

3. *Complexity*: Unit trusts are more complex, which is one of the reasons for their rapid conversion to OEICs. Unit trusts allow an investor to participate in the assets of the trust without actually owning any. Investors in an OEIC buy shares in that investment company.

4. *Management*: With unit trusts, the fund's assets are protected by an independent trustee and managed by a fund manager. OEICs are protected by an independent depository and managed by an authorised corporate director.

5. *Charges*: Unit trusts and OEICs usually have an upfront buying charge, typically 3–5 per cent, and an annual management fee of between 0.5 and 1.5 per cent. It is possible to reduce these charges by investing through a discount broker or fund supermarket, but this means acting without financial advice. Charges on OEICs are relatively transparent, shown as a separate item on your transaction statement.

Investment trusts

One of the benefits that investment trusts offer is to income investors. While open-ended funds must pay out all the income they receive, investment trusts can hold some back in reserve. This can allow them to offer a smoother and more certain return. There are three major advantages that an investment trust has over a unit trust or OEIC:

- *Cost*: The initial charges on unit trusts are usually lower.

- *Gearing/ borrowing*: Investment trusts can borrow for investment purposes. Unit trusts, however, are usually restricted by regulation. When markets are rising, and the trust is run well, gearing should deliver better returns.

- *Size*: Investment trusts tend to be smaller than unit trusts and more focused on their investment objectives.

Tracker funds and exchange-traded funds

Tracker funds and exchange-traded funds ('EFTs') are investments that seek to mirror the performance of a market index. As they track the market or index they can go down as well as up. EFTs are listed on a stock exchange and provide minute by minute pricing during trading hours.

Ordinary shares listed on the London Stock Exchange

Top tip

An important wealth warning on shares – the financial pages of the Sunday newspapers carry regular stories about investors who have been scammed into buying worthless shares traded on some obscure stock exchange. Just as many column inches are devoted every year to investors who have bought some sort of bond offering glamorous interest rates but which is not covered by the Financial Services Compensation Scheme (FSCS). Don't be caught out by the scammers – read the advice in the Cut Costs, Complaints and Scams, Chapter 7 and check if FSCS cover applies and get the answer in writing.

Public companies issue shares as a way of raising money. When you buy shares and become a shareholder in a company, you own a small part of the business and are entitled to participate in its profits through a dividend, which is paid annually or a few times a year. It is possible that in a bad year no dividends at all will be paid. The money you invest is unsecured. This is vital and means that, quite apart from any dividends, your capital could be reduced in value – or if the company goes bust you could lose the lot. The value of large 'quoted' public company's shares are decided by the stock market. The price of a share fluctuates daily. Stockbrokers will buy or sell the shares on your behalf and you will be charged commission (which can be as low as £6 a trade) and Stamp Duty (the latter is currently 0.5 per cent).

An individual can receive £500 of dividend income tax free in 2024/25 and 2025/26. The reductions in tax free dividend amounts have been tough on investors over the last decade. If you go back to 2016 the dividend tax free allowance was £5,000; it was then reduced to £2,000 from April 2018 where it remained through to 2022/23. A special income tax rate of 8.75 per cent is payable through your self-assessment if further dividend income takes you beyond £13,050 of income in 2024/25 (personal allowance of £12,570 and dividend allowance of £500). Just so you can see the 'tax pain' on investors in recent years the special rate of income tax increased by 1.25% in April 2022 from 7.5% to the current 8.75%. If part of your pension planning relied in dividend income you can understand if you are feeling frustrated by the combination of stealth taxes seen in this one small area over the last decade- the tax free amounts have been slashed and the tax rate has gone up. High earners suffer dramatically higher levels of special dividend tax. This dividend income tax rate increases to 33.75 per cent if it falls in the higher rate tax band and then increases further to 39.35 per cent if it falls in the additional rate tax band (both had increased by 1.25% in April 2022).

Top tip

If you are married or in a civil partnership review carefully who holds shares if one of you is a high rate or additional rate tax payer and the other is a basic rate tax payer. Even better could be building shares up in an ISA and a tax-free shelter (more on ISAs below).

Free money- your company share scheme

Many employers with shares on a stock exchange offer share-save schemes which you can save into on beneficial arrangements. These arrangements can include a fixed share price that you can exercise and buy at a future date or, if the share price goes down, you can just take your savings back so it's like 'no lose' share investing. There may also be discounts on the share price and there may be tax breaks. They can be incredibly good for savers and should be checked out where available. Most employers will have guidance and information to help you decide and then monitor the share price. Other schemes may be available where you can buy shares at a bigger discount or you may be given options to buy shares at a future date at a, potentially, low price. The latter can be very lucrative if the share price soars but come with tax twists when you come to sell (i.e. with a tax twist on buying out the option in the form of income tax which might push you into the 60% tax kill zone, again see Chapter 5, Tax). There may be a further twist on the eventual share sale and potential capital gains. As it's potentially lucrative but complex you may need a financial adviser registered with the Financial Conduct Authority to help with your share options. Share options are also called 'long term incentives' (or LTIs) and the clue is in the name- they are designed as a pair of golden handcuffs to retain you with the employer. You may lose your rights to all or some of your options when you resign (but that is not usually the case when you retire or are made redundant). On approaching retirement a planned approach to your LTI portfolio is advisable.

Top tip
Company share save schemes can offer you free money and should be seriously considered. Options and long-term incentives are even better but come with tax twists and there may also be a sting if you resign rather than retire.

Tax advantaged investing

Individual Savings Account (ISA)

An Individual Savings Accounts ("ISA") is a 'tax wrapper' that holds cash or investments and the effect of the 'wrapper' is to provide significant tax breaks. It shields the cash and investments so you do not pay any income tax on the interest or capital gains tax on the profits you make. They are not, however, tax free on death and could be subject to the 40% Inheritance Tax charge if the Estate is above tax-exempt levels. Shop around for the best rates and take full advantage of your annual allowance. You can currently put up to £20,000 into an ISA. Some ISAs are 'flexible' which allow you to replace money that you take out of your ISA, without eroding your £20,000 allowance – only if you do so within the same tax year. On death your spouse will inherit an Additional Permitted Subscription (APS) allowance equal to the value of your ISA. This may help your tax-free funds remain so for your spouse. The APS does not apply to ISAs passed to children/others on death.

Business Property Relief, Agricultural Property Relief and AIM shares

Business Property Relief, Agricultural Property Relief and AIM share relief are reliefs from Inheritance Tax (IHT) which apply on the transfer of 'relevant business property' and AIM shares. Tax relief is given at either 100% or 50%. Significant changes were announced to these reliefs at the 2024 Autumn Budget and more at Chapter 5, Tax.

Top tip

If inheritance tax ("IHT") planning is driving your ISA investment decisions you may be able to avoid your ISA savings being subject to IHT on your death by investing in Alternative Investment Market ("AIM") shares within your ISA that specifically meet a niche tax exemption called Business Property Relief ("BPR"). This is about as complex as this chapter gets but it illustrates a point as shares that qualify for BPR fell outside of the scope of inheritance tax as long as the shares have been held for at least two years, and are still held at the time of death. But it is all changing. This is a bit niche and is a higher-risk investment but it offers a window to leave ISA funds to beneficiaries free from IHT (albeit remember that funds passing on death to a spouse are exempt from IHT - more in the Tax chapter).

Lifetime Individual Savings Account (LISA)

A Lifetime ISA ("LISA") is another 'tax wrapper' which became available from April 2017 and offers those under 40 a pensions or house purchase savings device where interest is tax free and there is no capital gains tax on the growth of investments. Provided you start a LISA before 40 years old you can then keep saving into it until you hit 50. The big reason to take out a LISA is the government will give you up to £1,000 of free cash every year but there are significant restrictions on what you can spend the LISA funds on. Here is how it works. You can save up to £4,000 a year either by a lump sum or saving regular amounts and the government will then add 25% as free cash into the fund. The restrictions are fairly simple as the LISA can only be used for either a pension after age 60 or savings towards a first home. Significantly the property can cost up to

£450,000 across the UK so there is no outside London cap of £250,000 as found in the Help-To-Buy ISA.

If one of the two events does not happen and you draw out the funds you will lose the free cash and may receive less than you initially invested although there are allowances to retain the bonus if you die or are terminally ill. You are free to transfer it to another provider and you are allowed to split the overall ISA limit of £20,000 between an ISA and a LISA (LISA up to £4,000). You can have a LISA and a Help to Buy ISA but you can't get the first-time buyer's bonus on both but you could, for instance, use the Help to Buy ISA on a home and then retain the LISA for a pension and retirement.

As outlined in the pensions chapter a downside on pensions planning through a LISA is that better tax relief can currently be obtained by higher and additional rate taxpayers using traditional pensions. At present only a small number of companies sell this product.

LISAs can also be used to assist in purchasing your first home and can be withdrawn tax free if all the following apply (or retirement at age 60):

- the property costs £450,000 or less
- you buy the property at least 12 months after you open the Lifetime ISA
- you use a conveyancer or solicitor to act for you in the purchase - the LISA provider will pay the funds directly to them
- you're buying with a mortgage.

If you withdraw cash or assets for any other reason you will pay a withdrawal charge of 25% which recovers the government bonus you received on your original savings.

Top tip

LISA's seem attractive at first glance for the under 40s looking to plan their retirement but better tax relief can currently be obtained by higher and additional rate tax payers using traditional pensions.

Enterprise Investment Scheme, Seed Enterprise Investment Scheme, Venture Capital Trusts and Social Investment

This may be a bit niche but is important to flag up as these schemes are often used by entrepreneurs and high or additional rate tax payers to save tax in return for taking a risk. Unquoted companies (i.e. those whose shares are not traded on a recognised stock exchange) can face problems when trying to raise finance. The Enterprise Investment Scheme (EIS) offers tax relief at 30% for amounts up to £1,000,000 (increased to £2,000,000 if anything above £1,000,000 is invested in knowledge-intensive companies). The Seed Enterprise Investment Scheme (SEIS) offers tax relief at 50% on up to £200,000 if the shares are held for three years. The risk level of such investments is high and specialist advice and recommendations should be secured before venturing down this path, albeit the tax breaks prove enticing to some with the appropriate risk attitude and, perhaps, with specialist knowledge of the business concerned (perhaps through family or other connections).

Another variant is venture capital trusts (VCT), where tax relief can be secured at 30% on new shares up to £200,000 in any tax year providing the shares are held for five years.

A final variant is Social Investment tax relief which helps social enterprises raise finance by offering tax relief to investors. These can be set up by community interest companies and charities and offer investors 30% tax relief and capital gains tax breaks. Martin Gorvett, Chartered Financial Planner explains more:

"With restrictions on the amount of tax relief available to investors through pensions (£ 40,000 per annum) and ISAs (£ 20,000), the use of EIS/VCTs/SEISs has become more mainstream for higher rate and additional rate taxpayers. These products should be approached with your eyes very much wide open. You are getting tax relief for a reason. They are high risk investments by their very nature and should be approached on their risk merits, rather than the tax relief available.

SEISs carry the highest of risk. That's why you get 50% relief. Next EIS's with 30% after three years. Finally VCTs offer 30% relief but over 5 years. Taking more time to achieve profit status. Once the tax relief period has expired, ditch them or reinvest for more relief. Don't let inertia sink in. Some products reduce risk by the investment choices they make, such as Solar Power, renewable energy and 'peer to peer' lending. They are worth researching.

How do you tell which will succeed and which will fail? In short you can't. Expect a third of your investment to fail, one third to do nothing and one third to do well. It's the latter third that makes up the return you achieve. Alternatively seek the use of EIS/VCT/SEIS platforms where significant due diligence has already been completed. Don't be tempted by online crowd funding type operations, these 'opportunities' tend to be the ones the professionals have already discounted. Tread carefully, take advice and invest within your means."

Business asset disposal relief

Further tax breaks are also available under Business Asset Disposal Relief (which used to be called Entrepreneurs Relief) which in 2024/25 enables a low 10% Capital Gains Tax rate on selling shares in, for instance, a family company. The rate increases to 14% in April 2025 and then again to 18% in April 2026. The relief has been reduced to £1,000,000 which potentially saves £100,000 on a disposal that could have been charged at 20% Capital Gains tax. In last years Retirement Planning Expert 2024 book I had said *"I think this relief may be further reduced in future budgets as part of a review of Capital Gains Tax where we have seen some cuts in tax reliefs in recent years"*. The increase in the rate from 10% in 2024/25 to 14% in 2025/26 and then again to 18% in 2026/27 may pave the way for a further increase. Martin Gorvett also has some thoughts on Business Asset Disposal Relief:

> *"As a business owner Business Asset Disposal Relief is your new best friend. It allows you to sell a trading business and avoid high taxes on the value you extract. Just don't leave the decision too late. Shares in an unlisted business are also Inheritance efficient if held for more than two years. Make sure you remember to at least consider re-entering the arena in later life."*

Investing for your child/grandchild

Children without any other form of income don't pay income until they earn more than £18,570 in savings interest. This is the personal allowance at £12,570, the £5,000 starting savings allowance and the personal savings allowance at £1,000 all added together. To deter parents from giving away cash to children to reduce the parent's income tax on savings there is a basic tax rule where money given by a parent or stepparent that generates more than £100 per year in interest is taxed at the parent's tax rate. The interest on money deposited by grandparents isn't caught by this rule and parents saving into a Junior ISA avoid this potential tax trap as it is tax free.

Children's Savings Accounts: All you need to set this up is the child's birth certificate. Interest rates are currently as high as 5% (per moneysaving expert, December 2023) if you shop around as the banks and building societies are keen to sign up new potential customers as early as possible.

Junior ISA (JISA): You can currently save up to £9,000 a year into a JISA. The child can take control of the account at 16 but can't access the fund until 18 when it is usually converted to an adult ISA. There is both a cash variant and a stocks and shares variant of the Junior ISA and both can share the one annual limit. The interest is tax free so the £100 parent's tax rate rule does not apply.

Child Trust Funds (CTF): All babies born between September 2002 and 2 January 2011 got £500 or more free from the government to save in a CTF. Children born after December 2010 are not eligible for a child trust fund. However, accounts set up for eligible children will continue to benefit from tax-free investment growth and you can still add £9,000 a year tax-free. Withdrawals will not be possible until the child reaches 18. These are now a defunct product and with less competition the interest rates tend not to be as good as a JISA (which you can switch to).

Child's pension: For really long-term saving, pay into a pension. Your child/grandchild takes control at 18, but can only access the money aged 55. Tax relief currently applies so the government will top up a payment of £2,880 to the limit of £3,600. Martin Gorvett says:

"What better way to teach your child about the value of long-term savings. If you start a pension for them early enough, the effect of compound growth will give them a huge step up the retirement savings ladder when they themselves begin to focus on their own financial future."

Help to Buy ISA: These accounts were available from banks and building societies but were closed to new accounts on 30 November 2019. If one was opened before then you can keep saving into your account until 30 November 2029 when accounts will be closed to additional contributions. As they are 'old' style accounts the interest rates tend to be less competitive which are in a 'tax wrapper' so the interest is tax free but it may be worthwhile seeing if you can switch them into a LISA without losing the built up benefits within. Help-to-Buy ISAs were available to prospective first-time buyers purchasing properties in the United Kingdom and are only paid when purchasing the first home (on purchases up to £250,000 outside London and £450,000 in London- note the 'better' LISAs are £450,000 throughout the UK). Deposits can then be made of up to £1,200 when the account is opened followed by deposits up to £200 each month and you can continue saving until November 2029. The big benefit of help to buy ISA's is that the government boosts the young person's savings by 25 per cent, i.e. £50 for every £200 saved. So, 'free cash' which always gets the attention. The maximum free cash bonus is £3,000 on £12,000 of savings. **You can transfer from the Help-to-Buy ISA to the LISA providing you meet the LISA conditions** (aged 18 to 40) and you are also free to transfer it to another provider.

LISA: This is explained in more detail above so this is just a prompt that once children are 18 think about setting up a Lifetime Individual Savings Account to access the generous bonus paid, which can be put towards a first house or retirement.

Long-term lock-ups

Certain types of investment, mostly offered by insurance companies, provide fairly high guaranteed growth in exchange for your undertaking to leave a lump sum with them or to pay regular premiums for a fixed period, usually five years or longer.

Bonds

Bonds generally offer less opportunity for capital growth but they tend to be lower risk as they are less exposed to stock market volatility, and they have the advantage of producing a regular guaranteed income. The two main types of bonds are:

- *Gilts*: They are secured by the government, which guarantees both the interest payable and the return of your capital in full if you hold them until their maturity.

- *Corporate bonds*: These are fairly similar to gilts except that you are lending to a large company rather than owning a piece of it, as you do with an equity. The company has to repay the loan at some point, known as the bond's redemption date. If the company goes bust you may lose the lot.

Investment bonds

Investment Bonds are tax wrappers rather than specific investment instruments. They are a method of investing a lump sum with an insurance company over the long term. Available in both onshore and offshore variants, both offer life assurance cover as part of the deal, although this is usually only 101% of the fund value at time of death. The underlying investment of any type of investment bond will be retail unit trusts and

OEICs – similar to those available under ISA or SIPP wrappers.

There has been much interest in offshore bonds from high earners looking for an alternative to pensions for their retirement savings. These can provide significant tax savings or tax deferrals but ongoing charges for offshore bonds are high – typically an extra 0.4% per annum in addition to usual investment costs. Professional adviser charges on top mean that bonds are generally best for investments greater than £100,000. Chartered Financial Planner Martin Gorvett says:

> "Investment bonds may seem friendly on the outside but they can pack a tax punch if not regularly reviewed by a professional adviser. Don't let investment inertia settle in. They are not tax-free (but are often promoted as such), they are tax-deferred. Returns in your hands are net of special rate of Corporation Tax. It may be that when other income ceases, freeing up your Personal and Basic Rate Allowances, investment returns 'live' to tax may offer greater 'net' returns."

Structured products

A structured product is a fixed-term investment where the payout depends on the performance of something else, typically a stock market index (eg. FTSE 100 or S&P 500). They are complex and can carry hidden risk because they can appear on the surface to be an alternative to cash. The use of the word 'guaranteed' in the literature does not mean what you may first think! It means you are 'guaranteed' to get the returns stated *only* if the stock market index performs as required in the product's terms and conditions – noting that fees and charges may ultimately mean you get back less than you put in. Professional advice would be recommended for anyone seeking to make this type of investment. Martin Gorvett, Chartered Financial planner advises:

> "There are plenty of allowances for you to utilise to create 'tax-free' income in retirement. Indeed, these can be doubled if you involve your spouse in the planning phase. You each have a Personal Allowance of £12,570, a savings allowance of £1,000 (£500), the dividend allowance of £500 in 2024/25 and 2025/26 and a Capital Gains Tax Allowance of £3,000 in 2024/25 and 2025/26. That's potentially £17,070 each in 2024/25 and 2025/26 tax free if planned correctly between two people. When you add in the tax-free element of your pension (25 per cent of the fund value), investment bond withdrawals of 5 per cent (or original capital) and income from your ISA (tax-free), the payment of tax in retirement could be a preventable obligation with an investment in knowledge and planning."

Protection products

Protection products in financial services have been designed to pay out in the event of death, serious illness or accident. Different products have different names and costs and eligibility criteria and a knowledge of the main ones may help you shore up your protection.

Life assurance policies and endowments

Life assurance can provide you with one of two main benefits: it can either provide your successors with money when you die or it can be used as a savings plan to provide you with a lump sum (or income) on a fixed date. There are three basic types of life assurance: whole-life policies, term policies and endowment policies.

1. *Whole-life policies* are designed to pay out on your death. You pay a premium every year and, when you die, your beneficiaries receive the money.

2. *Term policies* involve a definite commitment. If you die during this period, your family will be paid the agreed sum in full. If you die after the end of the term (when you have stopped making payments) your family will normally receive nothing.

3. *Endowment policies* are savings products with some life cover. You pay regular premiums over a number of years and in exchange receive a lump sum on a specific date. If you wish to surrender an endowment policy before the date of the agreement you can request a 'surrender value' from the product provider but shop around as you may be able sell the policy for a sum that is higher than its surrender value. See the Association of Policy Market Makers website: www.apmm.org.

The size of premium varies depending on the type of policy you choose, the amount of cover you want and any health underwriting that may be required (medical checks may be involved). Under current legislation, the proceeds of a qualifying policy – whether taken as a lump sum or in regular income payments – are free of all tax.

Top tip
If you have assets above £325,000 and potentially another £175,000 if you have a house being left to a child

you may be able to avoid significant Inheritance Tax by having your life insurance policy or endowment written into a trust so that the payment falls outside your estate on death. Instead payment will be made to the trustees to distribute to the beneficiaries of the trust. Your solicitor or financial adviser should be able to arrange this for very little cost.

Income protection and critical illness benefit

These can assist if you are still earning and do not have sick pay from your employer as they will pay a monthly income (income protection) or lump sum (critical illness benefit) if you suffer a serious illness and/or can't work due to this. There may be age restrictions although cover can last to 75 with some providers and medical screening questions will be required. If you have a challenging health history the premiums will increase. In return for regular monthly premiums it may provide added peace of mind. If you stop paying the premiums the cover stops. The payments you receive are normally tax free under the current rules.

Simple accident protection

This cover usually is very restricted in the events it will pay out for but it can give some peace of mind in the event of an accidental injury. It is fairly cheap, can be arranged with immediate effect and you may find insurers who will cover you up to 81 years of age. It does not require you to attend a medical and no medical questions are asked although UK providers do usually require your main place of residence to be in the UK. It is often overlooked but in the event of an accident and injury or death it could provide you or your partner with vital funds at a time of need.

Investor protection

Most financial transactions involving banks, investments, pensions and insurance take place without any problems but sometimes things go wrong. This is where the UK's regulatory regime steps in.

The **Financial Conduct Authority (FCA)** is accountable to the Treasury and aims to make sure the UK financial markets work well so that consumers get a fair deal. It registers individuals and companies that are suitable to work in the industry, checks that they are doing their job properly and fines them if they do a bad job. The FCA has a range of helpful guides and factsheets. More at www.fca.org.uk.

The **Financial Ombudsman Service (FOS)** is a free service set up by law with the power to sort out problems between consumers and registered financial businesses. It is an impartial service and will investigate your complaint if you have been unable to resolve matters with the registered individual or company. More at www.financial-ombudsman.org.uk.

The **Financial Services Compensation Scheme (FSCS)** is the body that can pay you compensation if your financial services provider goes bust. The FSCS is independent and free to access. The financial services industry funds the FSCS and the compensation it pays. There are limits on how much compensation it pays and these are different for different types of financial products. To be eligible for compensation the person or company must have been registered with the FCA. The FSCS website outlines some key limits and criteria and more information is available at www.fscs.org.uk.

- Should the bank or building society get into serious financial difficulty up to £85,000 (double that if in joint names) of your money will be protected under the FSCS and the cover can increase for up to 6 months to £1 million for certain life events (for instance moving home).
- If a company that you own shares in goes bust there is no FSCS cover as FSCS does not protect investment losses arising from poor investment performance.

In addition, the £85,000 per person limit also applies to the following:
- If your claim is about negligent advice, the advice must have been given on or after 18 August 1988, the firm must have been authorised at the time, and you must have lost money after acting on the advice you were given.
- If a firm fails holding client money or assets in connection with a regulated activity that FSCS can cover, they can compensate if there is a shortfall in your client money/assets. The activity and product must have been regulated and you must be an eligible claimant. Generally, individuals and small businesses are eligible.

Top tip
Check how the UK safety net The Financial Services Compensation Scheme applies to your savings and investments.

Useful reading

- Martin Lewis's website www.moneysavingexpert.com

- The consumer section and register of the Financial Conduct Authority ('FCA') website at www.fca.org.uk

- The Financial Services Compensation Scheme at www.fscs.org.uk

- The Financial Ombudsman, www.financial-ombudsman.org.uk for free help and financial dispute resolution that's fair and impartial

- The government funded service offering free impartial information on saving and investing www.moneyhelper.org.uk

---

Reminder: Take any action points or follow up points to Chapter 13, Your Plan For A Better Retirement

---

Chapter Five
Tax

"I like to pay taxes. With them I buy civilization."

OLIVER WENDELL HOLMES JR

There are significant opportunities to improve your retirement with a better knowledge around tax and some planning. Some tax opportunities are fairly easy like boosting your ISA held savings and investments and not wasting your Capital Gains Tax position and exemptions. Others carry both opportunities and risk and flow from an overly complicated UK tax system. Maybe it is reducing your taxable estate or topping up your pension pot while the current allowances remain, reviewing your taxable income or giving younger generations a head start when they need it the most. It is time for the complex but absolutely necessary tax chapter to identify opportunities (and avoid the related risks) to 'save more' and achieve a better retirement.

The Prime Minister Kier Starmer said "it's time for tough decisions" after Labour won the 2024 election. Rachel Reeves in October 2024 then announced the biggest tax raising budget since 1993 that brought significant changes to the tax that would be collected from business owners, investors and on some pensions wealth. For glidepath retirement planners I think it's time for better tax-based decisions and some of these could radically transform your life ahead. With tax I like to go straight to the really big picture about taxation which is summed up by two quotes. Benjamin Franklin said *"the only things certain in life are death and taxes"* and underlines that we'll always have taxes and just need to learn how to deal with them. For the second one I'm going to the USA again. Oliver Wendell Holmes Jr (one of the most widely cited US Supreme Court Justices and quoted at the head of this chapter) famously said *'I like to pay taxes. With them I buy civilization'*. Surely very few would want to disown the NHS, schooling, roads, security and rescue services that our taxes pay for (in one way or another)? The problem (if that's the right word?) is that the taxation system is just too complex in the UK with twists and turns and side alleys that are almost impossible to navigate. But after over 30 years dealing with UK taxation I'll give it a good go and try and help you with some better decisions and to create a better plan. So let's get down to it.

We are now moving into tax year **2025/26 after a general election year** and in addition to the big tax raising measures announced in October 2024 we still have the 'stealth taxes' imposed through the freezing of various tax allowances and thresholds until 2028. These will push more people into higher tax bands causing those affected to pay more of their earning in tax as we progress through the next 4 years (unless changes are made in a future budget). But most significant of all, the UK tax system is far too complicated and, therefore, it is a tough job finding the opportunities and avoiding the risks. You therefore need a plan! I've been red flagging this for over ten years in my books and pleading for the UK government to make the really tough decision and create a simpler UK tax system. Given the system we've got in the UK I find that most people need to improve their knowledge and then plan around taxes as both the proportion of income that is taxed in total and the proportion that is taxed at the higher rate increase. So you are not alone if you find tax both confusing and challenging and I hope that this the chapter helps you move forward with better tax information and, as a result, you can make some better choices.

Firstly let's get the **'elephant in the room'** of the UK economy into focus – how to properly fund health and social care. Maybe that's the toughest decision of all? I've lost count of the number of governments that make grand noises about tackling the 'elephant in the room' but little follows in a way that solves a sector that is creaking under the patently obvious and mounting pressures of an older 'retired' population, with increasing demand and limited funding and massive staff costs. Speak to just about anyone about finding and then funding care facilities for our elderly or the state of our health care and benefit system to gauge the temperature around this 'hot topic'.

UK tax System: Far too complicated. Plan needed!

We'll probably see some review ordered by the Government that takes years to complete and is then kicked into the long grass and forgotten only to be repeated 5 years later. The problem comes back to an 'impossible equation': improved health and social care costs billions and billions which probably comes from taxation if there is insufficient economic growth. No Government wins votes by promising to increase taxes so that brings me back to my opening sentence in this chapter and echoing the Prime Minister's words 'it's time for tough decisions' as I can't see the economic growth coming through on my radar in December 2024.

Readers who work their way through this chapter will find that I shine a light on the complexities and then try and break things down into digestible content that will help you improve your tax knowledge and then make better plans with that knowledge. I provide tips and pointers on retirement and tax planning.

This knowledge will give you an advantage and you will, as part of the second essential step of retirement planning set out in this book, **'save more'** and achieve a better retirement. There may still be time to leverage something meaningful in tax year 2024/25 but the good news is that I also cover off 2025/26 albeit things may change in any new budget - especially if economic growth falters and tax rises are needed to fund improved public services.

Let's start with the **four basics** when looking at your retirement planning and tax in 2024/25 and into 2025/26.

Firstly, **taxes are necessary** and seem likely to increase. Remember Oliver Wendell Holmes Jr quote *'I like to pay taxes. With them I buy civilization'*. I'd expect further 'tax pain' beyond the frozen thresholds and allowances if the government comes under intense pressure to improve public services and economic growth does not flow through in the UK.

Secondly we no longer have a low-interest-rate environment. **So review how you can shelter your savings interest from tax.** Tax relief on interest and dividends has been introduced for most people, however, the dividend exemption has been slashed from £2,000 in 2022/23 to £1,000 in 2023/24 and then again to £500 in 2024/25 where it remains for 2025/26; the tax-free limit on ISAs is £20,000 per annum and there is the Lifetime ISA for adults aged under 40. Premium bond winnings are also tax free. There is also some useful tax free money for those earning £1,000 or less from small business income or property letting.

Thirdly one of the biggest tax opportunities for future retirees lies in the world of pensions and **flattening your tax bands** by deferring income received today to some point in the future. Too many people just miss this point or find out too late. This opportunity may be removed or reduced as part of the Government's measures to increase taxation and therefore time may be running out to act on this.

Fourthly changes in inheritance tax means the winners from the October 2024 budget could be the children of the wealthy as earlier gifting of wealth takes a greater priority. Perhaps no bad thing as the children are more likely to receive the money when they really need it (help with buying unaffordable housing, help with childcare, college fees or a wedding, or even their pensions).

The UK has one of the longest tax books in the world and, therefore, tax knowledge and **planning can save you money**. This is not 'dodgy' – it is simply knowing the rules and applying them and having a plan. The problem is not in this planning activity; it is in the long and complicated rule book. It is not the effect; it is the cause that is the real problem. I'm repeating myself from above now but surely there is a better way by massively simplifying taxation in the UK?

Related to this is the split between tax planning, tax avoidance and then tax evasion. **Tax evasion** is the easiest to define and remember because E is for evasion, which is 'E-legal'. That is the work of the tradesperson who takes cash above the £1,000 income exception per year and does not declare it to the taxman. It is also the UK resident who deliberately hides wealth in some offshore tax jurisdiction to try to evade tax on the interest they were earning or trade they are undertaking. HM Revenue and Customs' ('HMRC') own definition of tax evasion is: '*When people or businesses deliberately do not pay the taxes that they owe*' (source: www.gov.uk). Then there is **'tax avoidance'** and this is HMRC's own definition:

> *"Bending the rules of the tax system to gain a tax advantage that Parliament never intended. It often involves contrived, artificial transactions that serve little or no purpose other than to produce tax advantage. It involves operating within the letter – but not the spirit – of the law."*

It is, for example, the person who mostly resides in the UK and takes an income and routes it and themselves around the world, writes it off through loans and puts it in and out of trusts and (somehow?) ends up spending the very same money in the UK and pays little or no tax. Hey presto, there is a rich lifestyle and no tax paid. The individual concerned would probably dismiss Oliver Wendell Holmes Jr's quote at the head of this chapter while still enjoying the free benefits their society provides. HMRC are targeting this sort of person with increased resources and commitment (and powers) – more later.

On the other hand, **tax planning** is taking a planned route through the UK's overly complicated tax regime with your wealth and paying less tax. Quite simply you've been able to work your way through the overly complex rules (or paid someone to help you do this) and taken one route (rather an another) and paid less tax. A simple and very basic example could be a husband and wife (or civil partners) deciding that one person holds the most savings and investments.

Importantly, this chapter is only a guide and the opinions are intended for general information purposes only and should not be used as a substitute for tailored professional advice. Any potential UK tax advantages may be subject to change (and the 2025/26 budget remains subject to Parliamentary review and then Royal Assent in 2025). There may also be changes following another budget and your own choices will depend upon your individual circumstances and individual professional advice should be obtained. The information outlined in this chapter may, however, assist you in understanding some of the issues you may face and the terminology used. Taking further professional advice or doing your own follow up (flagging this as you go along at the back of this book, Chapter 13, Your Plan) should help you **'save more'** and achieve a better retirement.

This chapter at a glance

- **The main income tax bands** for zero, basic rate 20%, higher rate (40%) and upper rate (45%) are explained (as are the differences and additional tax bands in Scotland). National insurance, inheritance tax and capital gains tax are explained and the way they interact is outlined. This will help you get a broad understanding of the main taxes and the potential impact of tax planning for retirement.
- Potential opportunities are outlined to help you understand and then consider with professional help the use of your **pension allowances** to contribute to your pension pot and receive extra Income Tax relief. These may change in the future as flagged up in Chapter 3, Pensions and thus could deserve attention in 2024/25 and going into 2025/26.
- **Highlighting the damage of inflation** and noting how, in contrast, many vital tax break thresholds are being frozen until April 2028. This stealth tax might claw away a bigger proportion of your income over the next three years.
- A reminder on being careful about drawing down your pension pot too early as once you access the defined benefit pension pot taxable income the **Money Purchase**

Annual Allowance rules may restrict future tax relief to only £10,000 gross of pension contributions a year. This is to stop people recycling pension withdrawals and getting double tax relief.

- Reminders that you usually **can't access pension pots before the age of 55** (it rises to 57 from April 2028) without incurring massive tax penalties so beware of anyone who says you can. Ensure any adviser is registered with the Financial Conduct Authority ("FCA") and call FCA to check that they are, indeed, registered.

- For 'big earners' the loss of your tax-free Personal Allowance is explained if your income is between £100,000 and £125,140. This is what I call the **tax 'kill zone'** where income is effectively taxed at 60 per cent (higher in Scotland) due to the gradual loss of the personal allowance. But did you know that you might be able to shift the tax to being taxed at less than 20% if you make the appropriate pension contributions?

- If you do not use your **£20,000 ISA allowance** by 5 April each year the tax shelter for that amount will be lost forever. If you have a spouse or civil partner the amount doubles.

- Highlighting the higher taxes for investors with increased **capital gains tax rates and reducing capital gains tax breaks.** In another hit for entrepreneurs the tax after Business Asset Disposal Relief increases.

- Reduce your **Inheritance Tax** liability by gifting using the reliefs set out in this chapter. Larger gifts are normally inheritance tax-free if the giver survives a further seven years. Watch out for capital gains tax on the giver if they have made a large gain at the date they give the asset away (over its original cost or value at 31 March 1982). Inheritance Tax rules can allow the IHT limit to increase from £650,000 to £1 million when a house is involved and money is left to your children.

- The October 2024 budget appears to have turned **pensions and IHT planning** on is head. The announcement appears to bring pensions into inheritance tax from April 2027. The wealthier will be considering their options if the proposals are implemented.

- Highlighting the October 2024 budget proposals involving caps on reliefs for IHT on those with farms and business assets and AIM traded shares where, again, the wealthier will be considering their options with a new focus.

- **Tax reliefs** allow you £500 of **dividend** Income tax-free for 2024/25 (and 2025/26) and £1,000 of interest tax-free (for basic rate taxpayers and for higher rate taxpayers the amount reduces to £500 and nil for upper rate tax payers). If married or in a civil partnership should you consider how best to structure who holds investments and bank deposits?

- If you are both basic rate taxpayers you may be able to **transfer part of your Personal Allowance** to make you jointly more 'tax efficient' if you are a married couple or in a civil partnership.
- Tables of the **main tax rates** and allowances are set out as an annex at the end of this chapter.

Help! It's all so complicated – and I can't afford a tax adviser

The Retirement Planning Expert 2025 will try to help you cope with the challenges of the over-complicated UK tax system and the main taxes and related issues are set out below step by step. I admit it's not a light read but I have tried to boil down a complex system into digestible chunks with a focus around some of the main retirement related issues where some knowledge and some plans might just help. If someone cannot follow the information in this chapter and cannot afford to pay for professional advice they are not alone. Here is the pick of free further help for those who may be elderly, recently bereaved (losing vital help and support) and find tax challenging.

Top Tip
Share information about these three organisations with older or vulnerable friends and relatives that may need <u>free</u> help with tax.

- *Tax Help for Older People* (TOP) is a charity that provides independent, free tax advice for vulnerable and unrepresented people over 60 on low incomes (less than £20,000)– www.taxvol.org.uk.

- *Tax Aid* is a charity that advises only those people on low incomes (less than £20,000) whose problems cannot be resolved by HMRC – www.taxaid.org.uk.

- *Citizens Advice* is very useful if someone does not meet the 'low income' criteria of the above two recommendations. It has a very useful website to help you understand tax and how it is collected and what to do if you have a tax problem. They can also provide face-to-face and telephone support.

www.citizensadvice.org.uk.

Self-assessment

Self-assessment is the system HMRC uses to collect tax from individuals. Income tax is usually deducted automatically from wages and occupational and private pensions (but, significantly, not from the State Pension). Those people with other taxable income and capital gains must report it on the self-assessment return once a year. The tax you have to pay depends on allowances you have and the Income Tax band you're in; there are also different rates for Capital Gains Tax ('CGT') and Inheritance Tax ('IHT').

Self-assessment notices to complete the form are sent out in April each year. The details you need to enter on the form you receive in April are those relating to the period 6 April of the current year to 5 April the following year. Not everyone has to complete a self-assessment form but one is required from the self-employed who earn more than £1,000 and a partner in a business partnership. You may also need to send one to HMRC if you are a company director; have income from savings and investments of £10,000 or more; have taxable income of more than £150,000 or have Capital Gains Tax to pay (if you have sold or 'disposed of' something that increased in value or have foreign income or receive money from renting out a property). You may also choose to fill in a tax return to claim some income tax reliefs. If you don't receive a self-assessment request but owe tax to HMRC you are required to notify HMRC. Do this initially by writing to HMRC at: Self-Assessment, HM Revenue & Customs, BX9 1AX.

All taxpayers have an obligation to keep records of all their different sources of income and capital gains. These include:

- details of earnings plus any bonus, expenses and benefits in kind received;
- bank and building society interest;
- dividend vouchers and/or other documentation showing gains from investments;
- pension payments (state and occupational or private pensions);
- income and costs of any trading or other business activity;
- rental income from letting a property and associated costs;
- taxable social security benefits (for instance Jobseeker's Allowance and Carer's

Allowance);

- gains or losses made on selling investments or a second home;

- payments against which tax relief can be claimed (e.g. charitable donations or contributions to a personal pension).

If you don't voluntarily disclose the fact that you may owe tax and HMRC finds out about untaxed income and launches an investigation into your tax affairs you could face stiff penalties as well as paying any tax due and interest (more on this later). Ignorance is no defence.

Income Tax

This is calculated on all (or nearly all) of your income, after deduction of your tax allowances. The reason for saying 'nearly all' is that some income you may receive is tax-free (a list of the main ones appears further on in this chapter).

The tax year runs from 6 April to the following 5 April so the amount of tax you pay in any one year is calculated on the income you receive between these two dates. The tax bands in England, Wales and Northern Ireland are as follows:

- The point at which most people start paying Income Tax will be after the **Personal Allowance** of £12,570 for 2024/25 and 2025/26 and this will be frozen at that level until April 2028 (subject to any new budget or changes). With inflation the overall 'value' of the personal allowance is being reduced when it does not keep in step with the cost of living.

- **The 20 per cent basic rate** of income tax is payable on income beyond the Personal Allowance up to £50,270. The tax-payer who pays a top rate of tax in this band is a *'basic rate taxpayer'.* Again, the Chancellor when announcing the threshold said it will be frozen at that level until April 2028.

- **The 40 per cent higher rate** Income Tax threshold therefore starts at £50,271. The tax-payer who pays a top rate of tax in this band is a *'higher rate taxpayer'* but remember you only pay tax at 40% on the taxable income above £50,271. With rising inflation and some pay rises but a capped higher rate threshold, more individuals will start paying some higher rate tax on a part of their income.

- **The very top rate of 45 per cent rate** is levied on incomes in excess of £125,140. This person is called an *'additional rate taxpayer'.*

The rates are different in Scotland where there is a slightly lower 'starter' tax rate of 19% Income Tax for income in 2024/25 between £12,571 and £14,876 (the latter increases to £15,397 in 2025/26); the 20% 'basic' rate applies to income £14,733 to £26,561 (and £15,398 to £27,491 in 2025/26) and then there is a 21% 'intermediate' rate from £26,562 (£27,492 in 2025/26) to £43,662. The rates then step up to 42% between £43,663 to £75,000 for 2024/25 and 2025/26. In 2024/25 a new band was introduced with income between £75,001 and £125,140 taxed at 45% which remains for 2025/26. Finally, over £125,140 is taxed at 48% in 2024/25 and 2025/26. The cumulative effect of the changes seen in Scotland is to help lower earners pay a bit less tax and higher earners pay more tax to balance the Scottish government's books.

Wales has the ability to alter its income tax rates but they currently remain the same as England and Northern Ireland.

All of the rates are set out in tax tables at the end of this Chapter. A knowledge of the bands starts to highlight the complexities of the UK tax systems. It is vital to understand these as they are at the heart of many of the tax planning opportunities that lie ahead and which could help you **'save more'** and **'live better'** in retirement. So far so good? If so, you're ready for the next vital piece of knowledge.

Tax allowances

Personal Allowance and tax codes on your payslip

The Personal Allowance is £12,570 and will remain fixed until 2028 (subject to any new budget). This is the amount of money you are allowed to retain before Income Tax becomes applicable. If you receive the full personal allowance you will see it as a **tax code** on your payslip as **1257L** (one digit is dropped off the personal allowance of £12,570 to arrive at this 'code'- tax codes are as simple as that). Sometimes this basic tax code is amended by HMRC for various reasons and if appropriate the reasons will be set out on the tax code notice you receive from HMRC. An individual's personal allowance may be **reduced** if they have savings, rental profits or dividends above their annual allowances. On the other hand, an individual's tax code may **increase** on their main PAYE source of income if they have allowable expenses or a higher tax relief on charitable donations or personal pension contributions.

If an individual has a secondary source of income (maybe a second job or pension income) these will usually be allocated to a basic rate tax code, indicated by the letters

BR, meaning the person will pay 20% basic rate tax on this income. The letters **D0** will mean the person will pay 40% higher rate tax on the income and **D1** means they will pay 45% additional rate tax. A **K** code is when a person has a negative allowance applied to their income (for instance a pensioner who receives the state pension and income from private pensions). Finally the codes **W1, M1 or X** at the end are emergency tax codes and usually appear following a change of employment which HMRC update when your employer gives them all required information.

You should check any tax code notices you receive and if something seems incorrect call HMRC self-assessment who will explain things and adjust any errors they have made. For big earners there is one big snag with the Personal Allowance as it is reduced by £1 for every £2 of income over £100,000. The Personal Allowance will therefore disappear completely if your income is above £125,140.

    For 2024/25 and 2025/26 'big earners' you may still be able to preserve part or all of your Personal Allowance if your income is between £100,000 and £125,140 by making pension contributions as such contributions (subject to certain allowance limits) can, effectively, preserve the personal allowance. This can extend the £100,000 income 'barrier' and is worth considering as income in this tax '**kill zone**' is taxed, effectively, at 60%. The effect can be positive as income deferred into a pension may then be accessed more tax efficiently and, if you get your planning right, it may be 25% tax free and the remainder taxed at 20% basic rate. So put in very stark terms it's either tax of 60% or about 15% on that slice of £25,140 and the difference is just a bit of knowledge and then some planning. I regularly encounter new clients and attendees on my seminars who are shocked to discover the simplicity and effectiveness of this piece of tax planning so it's time for a top tip and maybe another entry on your own planning chapter 13. There is more on this in **Chapter 3, Pensions** and the section 'Playing the UK tax bands – while you can'.

Top tip

'Big earners' may still be able to preserve part or all of your Personal Allowance if your income is between £100,000 and £125,140 or beyond by making pension contributions if your pension allowances allow this.

In much the same way individuals that end up as additional and higher rate taxpayers can also make pension contributions to shift income from being taxed at 45% or 40% to, potentially, receiving 25% tax free and the remainder taxed at the 20% basic rate if you get your planning right.

Top tip
Shifting income so that it is taxed at a lower rate can form a big part of retirement planning. All this may change in a future budget or after the general election so act sooner rather than later and revisit again each year (more in Chapter 3, Pensions).

The other main tax allowances include:

- **Married Couple's Allowance** of £11,270 (2024/25 £11,080) is available if at least one partner was born before 6 April 1935. Tax relief is restricted to 10 per cent of this amount which is reduced by £1 for every £2 over £37,700 until you reach £4,360 (2024/25 (£37,000 and £4,280).

- A widowed partner, where the couple at the time of death were entitled to Married Couple's Allowance, can claim any unused portion of the allowance in the year he or she became widowed.

- Registered blind people can claim an allowance (the **Blind Person's Allowance**) of £3,130 (2024/25 £3,070). If both husband and wife are registered as blind, they can each claim the allowance.

- **Marriage Allowance**. Transferable tax allowances between married couples and civil partners could reduce your tax where you have a basic rate tax payer that is married or in a civil partnership to someone who does not use up all of their tax-free Personal Allowance. This is called the Marriage Allowance and works by the partner who is not earning above £12,570 transferring £1,260 of their Personal Allowance to their partner. It is the non-taxpayer that must apply and you do this online at www.gov.uk (go to 'marriage allowance') or call HMRC on 0300 200 3300. It is possible to backdate your claim for up to 4 years. This reduces the recipient's tax bill by up to £252 a year so a back claim could save you over £1,000 in tax. One final thing – you both must have been born on or after 6 April 1935. If you were born before that date your own extra tax break is found at the Married Couple's Allowance, as above.

Same-sex partners

Same-sex couples in a civil partnership are treated the same as married couples for tax purposes.

Tax-free income

Not all income is taxable and the following list indicates some of the more common sources of income that are free of tax:

- Attendance Allowance.
- Child Benefit: there is a partial tax clawback if one parent earns above £60,000 or repayable if one parent earns £80,000 or more.
- Child Tax Credit.
- Disability Living Allowance and Personal Independence Payment.
- Housing Benefit.
- Industrial Injuries Disablement Pension.
- Income-related Employment and Support Allowance.
- Personal Independence Payment (PIP)
- Pensions paid to war widows (plus any additions for children).
- Certain disablement pensions from the armed forces, police, fire brigade and merchant navy.
- The Winter Fuel Payment (paid to pensioners).
- Working Tax Credit.
- National Savings Premium Bond prizes.
- Winnings on the National Lottery and other forms of betting.
- Income received from certain insurance policies (mortgage payment protection, permanent health insurance, creditor insurance for loans and utility bills, various approved long-term care policies) if the recipient is sick, disabled or unemployed at the time the benefits become payable.

- Income and dividends received from savings in an ISA.

- The bonus on contributions to a LISA.

- Dividend income from investments in Venture Capital Trusts (see Chapter 4, Savings and Investments).

- Virtually all gifts (in certain circumstances you could have to pay tax if the gift is above £3,000 or if, as may occasionally be the case, the money from the donor has not been previously taxed).

- Certain redundancy payments up to the value of £30,000.

- A lump sum commuted from a pension.

- A matured endowment policy.

Top tip

If you are in doubt about whether income is taxable take professional advice on any 'unusual' income that you receive. For free information see Citizens Advice website: www.citizensadvice.org.uk – taxable and non-taxable income.

Income Tax on savings and investments

Savings

Most people can earn some interest from their savings without paying tax due to the **Personal Savings Allowance** of £1,000 for basic rate taxpayers (£500 for higher rate taxpayers). There is no allowance for additional (45 per cent) rate taxpayers.

So far so good, but it then gets complicated. Some individuals can also get a £5,000 tax-free (0 per cent) savings income band on top of the Personal Allowance so if you earn less than £18,570 a year in income plus savings interest you won't have to pay tax on the interest. It is not available if taxable non-savings income (employment etc) exceeds £5,000. This comes from the £12,570 Personal Allowance (increases a bit if you have Blind Person's Allowance or Married Couple's Allowance), £5,000 savings income band and then the £1,000 Personal Savings Allowance.

> **Top tip**
> There is a tax-planning opportunity for a husband and wife (or partners in a civil partnership) on different tax bands (i.e. zero rate, basic rate, higher rate or additional rate). Review who holds the money and earns the interest and who can therefore benefit the most from the personal savings allowance.

Investments

There is a £500 dividend allowance in 2024/25 which remains for 2025/26 which allows dividends up to this value to be taken 'tax-free'. Dividends are basically a return of income each year from the profits made by a company that you have invested in. Dividend taxes would then be levied on amounts above £500. Dividend taxes have increased over recent years) to the following % based on the band the income falls into:

8.75% if it is income within the band £12,572 to £50,270 (basic rate)

33.75% if it is income in the band £50,271 to £125,140 (higher rate)

39.35% it is income above £125,140 (additional rate)

> **Top tip**
> Review how you hold your investments and consider the advantages of tax-free dividends against the costs of running an ISA.
> There is also a tax-planning opportunity for a husband and wife (or partners in a civil partnership) on different tax bands (i.e. zero rate, basic rate, higher rate or additional rate). Review who holds the shares and, therefore, who earns the dividends and who can benefit the most from the lower dividend rates.

Top tip
Check out any opportunities to invest in your employer.
Shares acquired under share incentive plans or sharesave
schemes usually provide price discounts and tax breaks
for taking part. Most schemes have 'plain English' FAQs
that will help build your tax knowledge around this
opportunity. If available through your employer find out
more. Think about and plan your annual contribution
limits so that there could be a steady flow of share sales
in the future.

Reclaiming tax on savings income

You can reclaim tax paid on savings interest within four years of the end of the relevant
tax year by filling in form R40 and sending it to HMRC. It normally takes about six weeks
to get the tax back.

Mistakes by HMRC

HMRC does sometimes make mistakes. Normally, if it has charged you insufficient tax
and later discovers the error, it will send you a supplementary demand requesting the
balance owing. However, a provision previously known as the 'Official Error
Concession' and now labelled 'Extra Statutory Concession A19' provides that, if the
mistake was due to HMRC's failure 'to make proper and timely use' of information it
received, it is possible that you may be excused the arrears.

Undercharging is not the only type of error. It is equally possible that you may
have been overcharged and either do not owe as much as has been stated or, not
having spotted the mistake, have paid more than you needed to previously. If you
think there has been a mistake, write to HMRC explaining why you think the amount
is too high. If a large sum is involved it could well be worth asking an accountant to

help you. If HMRC has acted incorrectly you may also be able to claim repayment of some or all of the accountant's fees (your accountant will be able to advise you on this).

As part of the Taxpayers' Charter, HMRC has appointed an independent adjudicator to examine taxpayers' complaints about their dealings with HMRC and, if considered valid, to determine what action would be fair. Complaints appropriate to the adjudicator are mainly limited to the way that HMRC has handled someone's tax affairs (perhaps undue delays, errors and discourtesy). Before approaching the adjudicator, taxpayers are expected to have tried to resolve the matter with HMRC directly and the Charter contains details of how complaints can be raised with HMRC .

Important dates to remember

The deadline for filing paper self-assessment forms for the tax year is 31 October. Those filing online will have until 31 January. The penalty for breaching these deadlines is £100. There are penalties for both the late submission of the self-assessment and the late payment of the tax due- these can rack up quite substantially.

If your return is more than three months late an automatic penalty from 1 May of £10 per day commences up to a maximum of £900 in addition to the initial £100 penalty. If your return is still outstanding after a year another penalty arises based on the greater of £300 or 5 per cent of the tax due. In serious cases of delay a higher penalty of up to 100% of the tax due can be imposed. You have 30 days to lodge an appeal with HMRC against a penalty if you believe have a reasonable excuse and if you remain dissatisfied with HMRC's review of its decision you can ask a tax tribunal to hear your appeal.

In addition, if the **payment** is 30 days late from 31 January following the end of the tax year there is a further penalty of 5% of the tax due and then a further 5% if 6 months late and a further 5% if 12 months late.

If you are in financial difficulties engage with HMRC and request a formal 'time to pay agreement'. The late payment penalty is suspended but the taxpayer will become liable to the penalty if the agreement is broken. If it is your first instance of requesting a 'time to pay agreement' you should find that HMRC are approachable albeit they will want to know how you got into the situation and something about your assets and debts.

One final key date – you can amend your self-assessment at any time in the 12-month period after the latest 31 January deadline if you find you need to rectify a mistake.

Top tip

Submit a 'best efforts' self-assessment tax return rather than a late one. Explain any figures that are provisional in the additional notes section, apologise and explain that you will rectify matters as a priority (and do so!).

The late payment penalties can be worse than the late filing penalties. If you can't pay your tax do contact HMRC and see if you can enter into a 'time to pay agreement'- and then stick to the agreement.

Tax rebates

When you retire, you may be due a tax rebate because tax has been collected using PAYE assuming you will earn your salary for a whole year. Rebates can often arise for summer or autumn retirees. The tax overpayment would normally be resolved automatically, especially if you are getting a pension from your last employer or move into part-time employment. The P45 (tax form for leavers) should be used by the pension payer or new employer and, normally, the tax sorts itself out. If not, and the potential reclaim is for a previous tax year, HMRC may be ahead of you as they may spot it (usually by the end of July following the tax year) and send you a P800 tax calculation if they know you have paid too much tax. You will then get your refund automatically within 14 days of the P800.

If you have not received a P800 or can't wait to the end of the tax year you may make a claim to HMRC for any of the four previous tax years. You will need to know your National Insurance number and have your P45 if you have one and details of the jobs or state benefits you were getting at the time. HMRC will process the payment or explain what further information they need. Use this address for all Income Tax correspondence: Pay As You Earn and Self-Assessment, HM Revenue & Customs, BX9 1AS.

National Insurance

You pay National Insurance contributions ("NIC") on your salary (or profits, if self employed) to qualify for certain benefits and the State Pension. They are paid if you are over 16 and are either an employee earning more than £242 per week from one job or self employed making a profit of more than £12,500 a year. You usually do not pay National Insurance, but may still qualify for certain benefits and State Pension, if you are an employee earning £123 to £242 a week from one job or if self employed your profits are £6,725 or more per year. If you are employed you stop paying class 1 National Insurance when you reach State Pension age and if you are self employed you stop paying Class 4 National Insurance from 6 April after you reach State Pension age. NIC rates are detailed in the tax tables at the end of this chapter but, for now, the main ones are:

	2024/25	2025/26
Class 1 (employed)		
Employee		
Earnings per week		
Up to £241	Nil	Nil
£242- £967 (upper earnings limit) * applies from 1 January 2024	8%	8%
Over £967	2%	2%
Employer		
Earnings per week		
Up to £175	Nil	
Over £175	13.8%	
Up to £96		Nil
Over £96		15%
Class 4 (self employed)		
Below £12,750	0%	0%
£12,570 to £50,270	6% on profits	6% on profits
Over £50,270	2% on profits	2% on profits

The October 2024 budget introduced two significant changes to national insurance. The big tax increase was a 1.2% increase to employers' national insurance and lowering the threshold at which businesses start to pay the levy from £9,000 to £5,000. At the time the government sought to underline that this was a tax on business rather than the "working people" its manifesto promised to protect. But its hard to see how this tax won't be passed through to lower wages and higher prices.

Corporation and business taxes

Refer to the Chapter 7, Starting Your Own Business.

Capital Gains Tax

You may have to pay Capital Gains Tax (CGT) if you make a profit (or, to use the proper term, 'gain') on the sale, exchange or other disposal of an asset and this can include giving it away. The usual assets are a second home, a valuable painting or a share investment that soars in price. CGT applies only to the actual gain you make after deducting a tax break known as the annual exemption from CGT. This was slashed from £12,300 to £6,000 for 2023/24 and reduces again to £3,000 in 2024/25 and remains for 2025/26. This means that a married couple or a couple in a civil partnership can make gains of up to £6,000 in 2024/25 and 2025/26. It is not possible to use the losses of one spouse to cover the gains of the other. On the other hand, transfers of shares or assets between husband and wife or civil partners usually remain tax-free so should you be rethinking how your investments are held in this situation so that future gains are spread between the two of you or advanced and crystalised in 2024/25 if they are building up and likely to be needed again in 2025/26?

Last year in Retirement Planning Expert 2024 I had said in this section *"The CGT rates of tax still appear generous when compared to rates of income tax and, therefore, may be subject to change as part of any future budget or changes following a general election. Could the Chancellor, for instance, decide that gains should be charged instead at income tax rates to increase the tax receipts of the government and go towards the national debt arising from the Covid-19 pandemic and subsequent economic trauma and inflation shock?"* CGT rates were increased significantly in the October 2024 budget with the chancellor announcing that from 30 October 2024 any gains you make are taxed at 18% (previously 10%) for basic rate taxpayers and 24% (previously 20%) for higher rate and additional rate taxpayers; however, sales of a second interest in a residential property (mainly aimed at people with second homes) remain at older rates of 18 per cent for basic rate taxpayers and 24% for higher rate and additional rate taxpayers. Taxpayers realising a taxable gain on the sale of residential property need to make an electronic tax return and tax payment to HMRC within 60 days of the sale, a significant acceleration compared to all other capital gains which are reported on the normal end of year tax return. Non-UK residents are subject to similar obligations and deadlines but on the disposal of **all** types of UK land and property.

Following the same logic as immediately above, remember, transfers between husband and wife or civil partners usually remain tax-free so should you also be rethinking how your investments are held in this situation so that more of any future gains (after the annual exemption) are taxed as a basic rate rather than higher/additional rate taxpayer? If your husband, wife or civil partner later sells or otherwise disposes of the asset, they will have to pay the tax on any gain made over the total period of ownership (after 31 March 1982, see below for more on this 'special' CGT date). The following assets are generally not subject to CGT but you should be aware that anti-avoidance HMRC rules could be triggered in some examples (for instance in selling part of your garden under certain circumstances) which could result in any profit being subject to income tax. Getting professional advice, particularly where the sums involved are significant and the issues unclear, as early as possible will help you plan more effectively:

- your main home (see below);

- selling part of your garden on properties up to 1.2 acres- sometimes larger than this (unless, for instance, you purchased the property with a view to realising a profit on the sale of the land);

- most private use cars;

- personal belongings up to the value of £6,000 each, such as jewellery, paintings or antiques;

- proceeds of a life assurance policy (in most circumstances);

- gains from assets held in an ISA (and older PEPs);

- Premium Bond winnings: the maximum holding is £50,000 per person aged over 16 and under that age they may be by parents or guardians;

- betting and lottery winnings;
- gifts to registered charities;
- usually small part-disposals of land (limited to 5 per cent of the total holding, with a maximum value of £20,000 (but the amount you receive is taken off your cost for any future disposal);
- gains on the disposal of qualifying shares in a Venture Capital Trust or within the Enterprise Investment Scheme and Seed Enterprise Investment Scheme provided these have been held for the necessary holding period. These are complex and tax-efficient investment schemes and they carry risk and are outside the scope of this book so professional advice should be sought. Find further information at www.gov.uk and go to 'enterprise investment scheme' and 'venture capital trusts'.

You work out the profit on disposal of an asset by comparing the sale proceeds with the original cost of the asset. If it was bought before 31 March 1982 you use the market value at that date. If you dispose of an asset left to you by the will of a relative you use the market value on the date of death of the relative. If you give away an asset to a child or other close relative you use the market value on the date of the gift as the proceeds instead of any amount received. To bring clarity to potential complex situations you can agree the valuation with HMRC before you submit your tax return by completing form CG 34 and, again, professional advice as early as possible may prove beneficial.

You can add other allowable costs that were incurred when acquiring the asset- such as stamp duty, solicitor's costs and valuation fees on a second home. You add these to the original cost so remember to keep the receipts or go and dig them out now and keep them in a safe place. Improvement costs, such as adding a conservatory or converting a garage also can be added to the cost on, say, a second property that may be subject to CGT but not, for example, maintenance costs such as decorating and repairs.

Property and capital gains tax

Your main home is usually exempt from CGT and for that reason individuals who buy small and extend tend to be tax efficient in using their funds to build up a tax-free asset. They down-size (or 'right-size' as I explore further in Chapter 2, Your Home and

Property) if it remains their main residence and release a tax-free windfall to enjoy in retirement. Perhaps the strategy of buying the smallest and most run-down property in an up-and-coming area makes sense now! Many people, in fact, say 'my property is my pension' due to the power of the greatest tax exemptions you will probably come across in your life- it's called the principal private property relief and means the profit (or 'gain') you make when you sell your main residence is usually tax free. Again, this is explored further in Chapter 3, Pensions under 'property versus pension'.

There are a few trip points. One is if you convert part of your home into a dedicated office with, for instance, a separate entrance. Or into separate self-contained accommodation on which you charge rent. Both examples show how you may taint part of the CGT exemption for the relevant portion of the house over the relevant period and some CGT may be payable when you come to sell it.

If you leave your home to someone else who retains it for a while (as a property speculation or to rent out) and then later decides to sell it then they may be liable for CGT when the property is sold (although only on the gain since the date on which they acquired it). If you own two homes, only one of them is exempt from CGT, namely the one you designate as your 'main residence'. There may be some overlap opportunities and, providing a dwelling home has been your only or main home for a period, the final period of ownership that qualifies for relief can be useful as can periods of absence under 24 months and extensions when moving to a care home. The final period of ownership of a private residence that potentially could qualify for relief is currently, for most cases, 9 months. More information at HMRC's helpsheet HS283, 'Private residence relief' at www.gov.uk.

Top tip

Understand how to untap the profits in your main residence. If you can relocate or right-size your main residence it can yield one of the biggest tax efficient windfalls that you will encounter and it will dramatically change your retirement plans.

Top tip

If you have two homes and have lived in both consider taking professional advice on which could work better as your main residence. One of the tests used by HMRC when considering the availability of such reliefs is the actual period of residence and the quality rather than quantity of that residence.

Selling or liquidating a business

CGT is payable if you are selling a business and is 24 per cent for higher rate and additional rate taxpayers, but at a reduced level of 18 per cent for basic rate taxpayers. There are a number of CGT reduction opportunities or deferral reliefs available including the potential to attain **business asset disposal relief** ('BADR'- this used to be called entrepreneurs' relief) which could produce a tax rate of 10 per cent in 2024/25. I tell my clients that this is one of the lowest extraction tax cost routes that they will encounter and could be seen as a once in a lifetime opportunity. The October 2024 budget announced that the BADR rate will increase to 14 per cent for 2025/26 on 6 April 2025 and then 18 per cent from 6 April 2026. This has a lifetime limit of £1 million and is targeted at directors and employees who own at least 5% of the ordinary share capital of a company. This, however, is a complex area and timing could be vital, so well before either retiring or selling your business or shares you should seek professional advice. You will want to do so anyway as the buyer will probably be getting professional advice and you could find yourself down on the deal pretty quickly if you are not receiving good professional advice (irrespective of any tax advantages). If you are considering liquidating your business as part of your retirement and are intending to wind it down to a position where there are the last few customers and a lot of cash on the balance sheet an early discussion with an Insolvency Practitioner about a Members Voluntary Liquidation ('MVL') is vital. An MVL can take a few months to work through so action this early if you plan to receive the distribution and qualify for 10% BADR before 5 April 2025 or then 14% BADR by 5 April 2026. BADR then increases again to 18% at the start of the next tax year on the next day 6 April 2026.

Top tip
Was your 2025 New Year's resolution to pack up your business and retire? Is so you will need to get your skates on if you wish to do a Members Voluntary Liquidation and

> **obtain 10% Business Asset Disposal Relief as the process can take several months. Consult an Insolvency Practitioner.**

A higher lifetime limit of £10 million applies to the separate **investors' relief** for gains on disposals made prior to 30 October 2024. From 30 October 2024 onwards, the lifetime limit for investors' relief is £1 million (as announced in the October 2024 budget). The main beneficiaries of this relief are investors in unquoted trading companies who have newly subscribed shares but are not employees.

Inheritance Tax

Inheritance tax ('IHT') is the tax paid on assets (the estate) that are left when someone dies. It is at a high rate of 40% and applies to the value of assets on death (property, bank funds, investments, cars and payouts from life insurance companies) but there are many important exemptions and reliefs which may mean that no tax is payable on the estate. No one knows precisely what is around the corner so this should be talked about sooner rather than later to help manage, wherever possible, Inheritance Tax to be paid on your 'estate'. Above all else there is the straightforward wish of not wanting ambiguity about what should happen after you die. So, time to take a deep breath and read on and then promise to talk to those that matter to you or put a large circle around the above sub-heading 'Inheritance Tax' and pass this book to them with two words 'let's talk'.

The tax threshold (the level at which you'll need to pay tax) is currently set at £325,000. The threshold amount for married couples and civil partners is twice this, so £650,000, and this can be stretched to £1 million with the Main Residence Nil Rate Band (more below). The value of estates over and above this sum are taxed at 40 per cent. So the starting point is for you and your partner to sit down and make a list of your assets and then deduct all outstanding liabilities.

> **Top tip**
> **Many people underestimate how much they are worth and forget assets like pensions in a defined contribution pension pot - that is why this is a two-person job as it is**

easy to overlook assets acquired over a long time.

Some people mistakenly think that giving away your wealth gets around IHT. This is where the clouds of confusion sometimes arise from casual conversations with friends. Yes, there are some points where this can be true, such as gifts for the national benefit. There are also other exemptions that have been brought into the debate, which are correct, such as servicemen dying on active service being exempt from IHT. There are then grey areas such as war service hastening a veteran's death, which found, upon challenge, that the estate could be exempt from IHT.

However, the root of the confusion referred to above is because there is no immediate inheritance tax on lifetime gifts between individuals – it is only deferred. The gifts can then become wholly exempt if the donor survives for seven years. So, when the donor dies, any gifts made within the previous seven years become chargeable as their value is added to the estate for IHT reasons. For this reason, in the seven-year period they are known as 'potentially exempt transfers' or PETs for short. Where gifts exceed the nil rate band there is a tapering relief which begins to soften any resulting tax charge, on a sliding scale between years three and seven following the gift. Gifts with strings attached are treated as if they did not happen so if you try to 'give away' your house to the kids but still live in it without paying a marketing value rent to the kids the 'gift' probably won't be a gift in the eyes of HMRC so it falls back into your assets pot with IHT due. The basic rule is that gifts 'with strings attached' probably won't work. Extreme care must be taken here, as not only might you fail to secure the desired IHT saving, you might also inadvertently create a CGT liability which would otherwise not have existed. Linked to 'give away' tactics are various schemes that seek to lock away the home in some form of a trust.

Trusts

A trust is a relationship between persons and property under which property is vested in persons known as trustees, who hold the property for the benefit of other persons known as beneficiaries. The settlor is the person who provides the property to be held on trust. The golden rule is that the terms of the trust must be certain and to be valid. There must be three certainties: certainty of what was intended; certainty of what was going into the trust; and certainty of the beneficiaries (who they were). Trusts are complex and are usually created by family solicitors who are experienced in the relevant jurisdiction and can help with potential complexities such as conflicts of interest between generations and care around the settlor retaining sufficient assets to continue to live on to a standard that is acceptable. The jurisdiction point reflects England and Wales having a common system; minor differences in Northern Ireland and other differences in Scotland.

Certainly, some very old and established trusts have sheltered significant family estates from IHT as the occupier never actually owns the property; they are merely allowed to live there subject to conditions. This sort of thing was used by the wealthy to stop their children and subsequent grandchildren disposing of the main assets within a family estate and, instead, simply being allowed to live in or use the asset and receive some income. Trusts were also used to keep the family money within the bloodline (in the case of divorce and remarriage). This allowed the big family estate to be passed down intact from generation to generation.

In recent years, some firms have tried to market tax saving schemes to 'protect your assets from the taxman' or schemes to shelter assets from 'claims for care home fees' based loosely on schemes involving trusts. These may include fancy seminars with free coffee and biscuits and smiling salesmen, but tread carefully. The ideal scenario is that you would want to be dealing with the trusted family solicitor regulated by the Law Society in your jurisdiction (for instance in England and Wales at www.lawsociety.org.uk) and you would want a solicitor accredited on their Wills and Inheritance Quality Scheme (WIQS). If you depart from this route the following questions may help your selection process:

- What are the specific legal and tax qualifications and regulating body of the individual that will be responsible for talking with you, understanding your position and then advising you? Check their name on that organisation's register. This could be one of the biggest transactions you make so obtain at least two quotations and seek recommendations from trusted family members or friends.

- Does the trust documentation provide certainty of what was intended; certainty of what was going into the trust; and certainty of the beneficiaries (who they were)? Ask what happens if the scheme does not work. How big is the firm advising you and how long have they been around? A quick search of their latest accounts filed at Companies House (search at .gov.uk) can be illuminating if they show a recently formed company, low assets on the balance sheet or late filed accounts. It would normally be disclosed to you in an initial letter of engagement sent to you before your proceed but if not do ask what professional indemnity insurance cover they have?

- Extras? Have the total costs of all aspects from start to finish been set out in advance in writing so that you have clarity before proceeding? If changes are needed, what is the fee/ hourly rate? This helps to avoid the issue of cost creep.

- What are the pros and cons? There will always be some risks to any scheme – how well are these set out and how prominent are they?

- What are the tax charges – what types of tax will the trust incur and when?

- What happens if the government rules change? Are the schemes amended and updated and at what hourly rate or other cost?

Notwithstanding the above the family trust remains a legitimate and useful tool in inheritance tax and family succession planning and when properly utilised can offer tax advantages, asset protection, retention or centralisation of control, and flexibility as to who in the family is benefitted, and how.

Top tip

There is no such thing as a magic wand that makes inheritance tax disappear on your main home if you continue to live in it or guarantees local authorities will not chase down assets deliberately given away to avoid claims for care home fees. Tread carefully if someone offers you a magic wand for a fee and satisfy yourself on the above questions.

Top tip

Proceeds from life insurance policies will form part of your estate unless you take steps to divert the proceeds, perhaps using a trust, directly to another party - perhaps children or grandchildren. This is not a complex area of tax planning and many life assurance companies can provide simple free trust forms for you to complete to shelter the funds from inheritance tax or consult a financial adviser or

solicitor if you remain unsure.

Tax treatment of trusts

It is a common error to believe that assets in trust are exempt from inheritance tax. There may be IHT to pay when assets – such as money, land or buildings – are transferred into or out of trusts (currently 20%) and when they reach a 10-year anniversary (currently 6%). Finally, IHT will need to be paid again when the trust is closed, or if assets are removed. Tax is based on the most recent 10-year anniversary valuation up to 6%, charged on a pro-rata basis. There are complex rules that determine whether a trust needs to pay IHT in such situations so ensure you have clarity on the tax consequences and if unsure get further clarity on this with professional advice (usually a financial adviser, solicitor or chartered accountant could help). Further information is available on the website: www.hmrc.gov.uk – 'inheritance tax and trusts'.

Main residence nil rate band and IHT

The 'main residence nil rate band' was introduced in April 2017 is a relatively new and a very significant tax break that may remove the inheritance tax worry to the vast majority of UK married couples and civil partners. Here is how it works. Remember the £325,000 threshold allows married couples or civil partners to transfer the unused element of their IHT-free allowance to their spouse or civil partner when they die, giving an effective threshold of £650,000 before any inheritance tax will become payable. Then remember that IHT will be levied at 40 per cent above the IHT threshold (£650,000 for a couple or £325,000 on the estate of anyone who is single or divorced when they die and the threshold is fixed to April 2028).

There is an extra relief available where the value of the estate is above the IHT threshold and contains a main residence that is being passed on to 'lineal descendants'. It will raise the IHT-free allowance to from £325,000 to £500,000 per person where married couples jointly own a family home (worth less than £2 million) and want to leave this to their children. The joint IHT exemption between the married couple will be £1 million. The key aspects are:

- The relief was introduced on 6 April 2017, for deaths on or after that date. It was phased in, starting at £100,000 in 2017/18, rising to £125,000 in 2018/19, £150,000 in 2019/20 and £175,000 in 2020/21 and currently remains at £175,000. For a couple, the £175,000 each plus the existing £325,000 each, makes up the £1 million maximum relief that is now achievable.

- The relief applies only on death, not on lifetime transfers.
- The amount available will be the lower of the net value of the property and the maximum amount of the main residence nil rate band. The net value of the property is after deducting liabilities such as a mortgage.
- The property will qualify if it has been the deceased's residence at some point.
- The property must be left to lineal descendants: children, grandchildren, great-grandchildren etc. or the spouses of the same. Children include stepchildren and adopted children.
- The relief is transferable, so the estate of the second spouse to die can benefit from the main residence nil rate band of their deceased spouse, regardless of when that spouse died.
- The relief will be tapered away for estates with a net value over £2 million, at the rate of £1 for every £2 over that limit, so will be reduced to zero on an estate of £2.35 million. The Autumn 2024 budget announced that the start of the taper at £2 million will continue until April 2030.

The Nil Rate Band (NRB) threshold is not *automatically* doubled for married couples and civil partners. If the deceased spouse left their entire estate to the surviving spouse, they did not use their own NRB and will instead have made use of their spousal exemption and there will be no IHT to pay on that basis. The surviving partner then 'inherits' their deceased spouse's unused NRB (or the portion of it which went unused), which combined with their own IHT NRB is a maximum of £650k. Married couples therefore need to ensure they maximise the transferable NRB by drafting wills accordingly and the advice of a solicitor is recommended (see Chapter 11, Sandwich Generation and 'Wills').

IHT and pensions

The Autumn 2024 budget announced significant changes to the treatment of pensions which may, in turn, cause significant changes to the way wealthier individuals plan to spend their wealth and /or gift it away where the wealth includes significant pension funds. Until the announcement the use of pensions was a key part of IHT planning as most pensions fell outside of IHT and pots could be passed on without a tax deduction. On the other hand, sometimes complex situations could result in taxes at rates of up to

55% for unauthorised payments from pensions. There were complex rules depending on age at death, type of pension and whether it is a lump sum or an annuity and so on. Having said all that the general view, pre Autumn 2024 budget, was that individuals or couples with an Estate (before taking account of any pension pots) worth more than the IHT exempt amounts should consider their pension pot strategy especially in the years up to age 75 and professional advice usually proved beneficial results in such circumstances.

The Autumn 2024 budget changes everything. It was announced that the value of most unused pensions savings and death benefits will be brought within the scope of an individual's estate for inheritance tax purposes from April 2027. This currently (December 2024) and as proposed is in addition to any income tax charges that may apply. The changes still have some way to go as I write as the Finance Bill 2024/25 was introduced to Parliament on 7 November 2024 and legislates for the measures introduced in the October 2024 budget and earlier. MPs are expected to consider the clauses by 4 February 2025 and the bill will move onto the report stage and its third reading before proceeding to the House of Lords. The bill will become law when it receives Royal Assent. This issue, if potentially relevant to your retirement plan, must be watched closely and if passed into law may cause you to take professional advice and consider altering your plans accordingly.

> **Top tip**
> **The Autumn 2024 budget potentially changes everything on pensions and IHT. It was announced that the value of most unused pensions savings and death benefits will be brought within the scope of an individual's estate for inheritance tax purposes from April 2027. If implemented and you are impacted then take professional advice and consider altering your plans accordingly.**

Business Property Relief (BPR) and Agricultural Property Relief (APR)

The Autumn 2024 budget also announced that Business Property Relief (BPR) and Agricultural Property Relief (APR) will be restricted from 6 April 2026. These reliefs are currently uncapped and can reduce the taxable value of certain assets by 50% or 100%. The changes proposed are significant as the scope of assets that can attract 100% relief will be reduced, and the amount of relief at 100% will be capped at £1million. As proposed relief at 50% will be available on qualifying assets in excess of the cap. The budget proposals still have some way to go before they become law at the time of writing (December 2024) as I outlined in the preceding section. If implemented they will impact many business owners, landowners and farmers. If potentially relevant to your retirement plan, the budget proposals must be watched closely and if passed into law may cause you to take professional advice and consider altering your plans accordingly.

Other IHT planning

The Autumn 2024 budget also announced that the current domicile-based IHT system is to be replaced with a new residence-based system from 6 April 2025. Those who are 'long term resident' at the time a chargeable event (including death) arises will be subject to IHT on worldwide assets. The status will normally apply where the individual has been resident for at least 10 of the preceding 20 tax years, but special rules apply to those who have already left the UK or who have spent fewer than 20 tax years in the UK by the time they leave.

The Autumn 2024 budget also announced that from April 2026 the IHT relief on AIM listed shares will be capped at 50 per cent resulting in a 20% effective tax rate. The Alternative Investment Market ('AIM') is a sub market of the London Stock Exchange that allows smaller, more risky companies to raise capital with less regulation. Up until then AIM listed shares get relief from IHT which may have formed part of the IHT planning of the wealthy.

Other IHT planning includes the charitable donations exemption, with a reduced rate of IHT payable on estates that give at least 10 per cent of the value of their estate above the nil rate band (£325,000) to charity. The remainder is taxed at 36 per cent against the usual 40 per cent IHT rate.

Gifts or money up to the value of £3,000 can be given annually free of tax. If you didn't use last year's allowance you can carry it forward and use it this year to give £6,000 away to your children, for example. The allowance is per donor, not per child.

It is possible to make small gifts to any number of individuals free of tax, provided the amount to each does not exceed £250. You cannot combine this with the £3,000 allowance.

Gifts to mark a wedding or civil partnership. The limits for these gifts are up to £5,000 given to a child, £2,500 given to a grandchild or great-grandchild or £1,000 given to anyone else.

Perhaps the most generous of these reliefs, though, is that gifts made out of surplus income and which have a degree of regularity and do not detract from the donor's standard of living or capital worth may be made free from IHT without any fixed monetary limit. The greater your income and lower your living costs, the more can be given away in this fashion. It could be worth rethinking your plan as the gift, if given to a younger dependent, may be put to greater effect and impact if that younger person receives it at a time they need it the most (wedding, childcare, house deposit, help with education etc).

Top tip
Planning and longevity go hand in hand, as most lifetime gifts to individuals do not trigger IHT if you survive for seven years. The timing of gifts is a recurring theme in this book and the key question is: could the gift also be put to better effect if the recipient receives it an earlier stage (which might also reduce IHT)?

There are also provisions to enable the tax and other advantages of ISAs to be passed onto the deceased's spouse (for instance in the case of ISAs that funds could remain in the ISA tax-effective wrapper). Could it be tax-efficient to ensure that your spouse inherits your ISA under your will rather than the investments passing to other family members? Remember that the government can change the tax rules without notice and exemptions can be withdrawn or reduced.

Wills

Finally, remember the importance of a will and how it ties into IHT. Without a will in place it will be the intestacy laws that decide how your estate is distributed, not you. Having a will allows you to state precisely who your beneficiaries are and what they receive and allows you to appoint administrators who will administer the estate after your death. So make a will either through an online or postal service or, if your affairs are more complicated, with a face-to-face professional adviser, and consider a power of attorney. Keep them up to date so that they are effective and efficient from both a legal and a tax perspective. For further information, see 'Wills' in **Chapter 12, Sandwich Generation**, within this book and also find more at www.gov.uk (search for 'probate and inheritance tax').

Help in dealing with a tax investigation

You might find yourself or your business the subject of a 'tax enquiry' if HMRC believe something does not look quite right about your tax affairs. 'Enquiry' sounds a very bland word but the reality is far from bland. It basically means an investigation to try and recover tax that HMRC believe could be due as a result of taxpayer error or a taxpayer failing to take reasonable care or, worst of all, some form of deliberate behaviour by the taxpayer to evade paying tax. HMRC is increasing its investigation capability, arming itself with more staff and more power.

HMRC usually has a year from the date you filed a tax return to open an enquiry. If it finds errors, however innocent, it can go back 4 years. It can go back 6 years for careless errors. HMRC can go back 12 years for offshore income errors and 20 years for deliberate errors and fraud. Add in interest on any late tax and further additional penalties of up to 200% of the tax shortfall and you could be facing an eye-watering tax assessment.

HMRC will listen carefully to facts that may mitigate any penalty due. If you are looking at serious amounts of tax due then early discussion with a professional adviser will assist you in dealing with the unwelcome situation you may find yourself in. You should also check whether any insurance or professional association memberships that you have could provide free tax investigation cover. This is a very useful piece of cover.

If HMRC discover an error during an investigation, they can re-open other closed years as well. Tax investigations can prove to be extremely stressful and very expensive so I would suggest the following.

1. ***Engage an accountant.*** HMRC can't go on fishing expreditions into your tax affairs but it does not stop them trying. Information requested by HMRC must be 'reasonably required'. If you are the subject of anything but the simplest of HMRC interventions, find an accountant who holds themselves out as a specialist in this area and take some advice, even if it's only some tips and help in dealing with the enquiry yourself, and ensuring that HMRC are playing by the rules.

2. ***Get tax investigation insurance cover.*** Many accountants will offer this type of insurance; specialist providers such as Markel do too, as well as trade membership bodies such as the Federation of Small Businesses. But if you get an enquiry and don't have a specific policy, it's worth checking things like your house insurance in case they provide some level of assistance.

3. ***Keep good records.*** When HMRC come knocking and you have contemporary written evidence supporting your position you will immediately be on the front foot and the onus will be on HMRC to undermine your stance. If you're relying on advice, get it in writing. And certainly don't think that a recollection of something an HMRC staff member told you on the phone will hold water if the inspector in front of you thinks differently.

4. ***Consider disclosing interpretations.*** If you're declaring your taxes based on an interpretation of a grey area or otherwise in circumstances which HMRC may not agree with, consider offering a full explanation in the tax return white space. The 'discovery' assessment provisions allow HMRC to look back beyond the usual 4 year period to 6 years (if you were careless) or 20 years (if they consider your actions were deliberate), but a full set of details on your return may limit their enquiry window to 12 months post filing, giving you tax certainty a lot earlier.

5. ***What about when HMRC messes up.*** Contact HMRC with your national insurance number and Unique Tax Payer reference (UTR) and explain your concern. If nothing happens move on to making a formal complaint and say how you would like your complaint resolved- head the letter 'formal complaint'. If you are still not happy you can request a second review by another officer at HMRC and mark it 'second complaint'. If that does not work you can ask the Adjudicator's Office to review your complaint. If you disagree with Adjudicator's Office you can ask your MP to refer your complaint to the

Parliamentary and Health Service Ombudsman.

Retiring abroad

A vital question for some readers is the taxation effects of living overseas. There are examples of people who retired abroad in the expectation of being able to afford a higher standard of living and who returned home a few years later, thoroughly disillusioned as they had not planned through the costs and implications – more in the 'Your Home and Property', Chapter 2 including notes of caution about the impact of Brexit on tax. Part of the plan has to be a consideration of tax.

Tax rates vary from one country to another. Additionally, many countries levy taxes that don't apply in the UK and complications can usually be expected from wealth taxes and estate duty on overseas property. Localised and national property taxes can also combine to trip up well-laid plans.

In addition to the tips and pointers in Chapter 2 you should also review the free and quality information available on most countries from our own Foreign and Commonwealth Office – access via www.gov.uk and search for 'living in [country]'. The World Factbook by the US Central Intelligence Agency is also a useful source of quality information on every country in the world. As things advance, independent and appropriately qualified legal advice is absolutely essential when moving and/or buying property overseas and then financial and tax advice from a regulated financial adviser familiar with the transition from the UK to the overseas location.

Many intending emigrants cheerfully imagine that, once they have settled themselves in a dream villa overseas, they are safely out of the clutches of the HMRC. This is not so and your first step is to work out your residence status. Whether you are a UK resident usually depends on how many days you spend in the UK in the tax year which runs from 6 April to 5 April the following year. According to HMRC: 'You're automatically resident in the UK if either you spent 183 or more days in the tax year or your only home was in the UK – you must have owned, rented or lived in it for at least 91 days in total – and you spent at least 30 days there in the tax year.' On the other hand, HMRC state that you're automatically non-resident 'if either you spent fewer than 16 days in the UK (or 46 days if you haven't been classed as UK resident for the three previous tax years) or you work abroad full-time (averaging at least 35 hours a week) and spent fewer than 91 days in the UK, of which no more than 30 were spent working.' In the year you move out of the UK (or back in) the year is usually split into two – a non-resident part and a resident part. More information is at www.gov.uk –

go to 'statutory residence test' – and you can also use HMRC's tax residence indicator toolkit and go to 'check your residence status'.

So **why is this 'residence' status so important for tax**? Well, residents pay UK tax on all their income, whether it's from the UK or abroad. Non-residents only pay tax on their UK income and they do not pay UK tax on their foreign income. In addition, non-residents only pay UK Capital Gains Tax either on UK residential property or if they return to the UK.

The usual scenarios that may require non-residents to complete a self-assessment tax return include:

- if you are in receipt of UK rental income;
- if you make capital gains from the sale or disposal of assets in the UK;
- if you are a director of a UK company or
- if you receive profits from a UK partnership;
- if you earn an income in the UK through self-employment;
- if you do not live in the UK, but you do some or all of your work in the UK.

In addition, HMRC's Non-Resident Landlord Scheme requires landlords with a usual place of abode outside the UK to have the tax on their UK rentals collected by their UK letting agent or tenant and the tax is due for payment within 30 days of each quarter ending 30 June, 30 September, 31 December and 31 March. Where property is owned jointly, the share of each joint owner is considered separately. If you want to pay tax on your rental income through self-assessment, fill in HMRC form NRL1 and send it to HMRC. You must tell HMRC if you're either leaving the UK to live abroad permanently or going to work abroad full-time for at least one full tax year. You do this by HMRC's Form P85 and send it to Self-Assessment, HM Revenue and Customs, BX9 1AS, United Kingdom.

Double tax agreement

The country where you live might also seek to tax you on your UK income. This is where a double taxation agreement between the country you live in and the UK may save you being taxed twice by claiming a tax relief in the UK for foreign tax paid. The conditions for tax relief vary from agreement to agreement; find more at www.gov.uk and go to 'double taxation treaties: non-UK resident with UK income'.

> **Top tip**
> Tax is one of the most complex twists of moving overseas. Don't guess or listen to pub talk. Get professional advice both in the UK and the overseas country.

Important wealth warning

Importantly, this chapter is only a guide and it is neither legal nor taxation advice. Any potential UK tax advantages may be subject to change (the 2024/25 budget remains subject to approval and there may be changes following another budget or after a general election) and will depend upon your individual circumstances, and individual professional advice should be obtained.

Further information

- HMRC general enquiries number: 0300 200 3310 and Income Tax correspondence is sent to Pay As You Earn and Self-Assessment, HM Revenue & Customs, BX9 1AS.
- Complaint about HMRC: www.adjudicatorsoffice.gov.uk.
- Tax Help for Older People (TOP): free tax advice service for vulnerable and unrepresented people on low incomes: www.taxvol.org.uk.
- Tax Aid is a charity that helps those with low incomes: www.taxaid.org.uk.
- Citizens Advice for what to do if you have a tax problem. They can also provide face-to-face and telephone support: www.citizensadvice.org
- The government funded service www.moneyhelper.org.uk and their "A Guide to Inheritance Tax" and "Tax and Pensions"

Useful reading

The Daily Telegraph Tax Guide by David Genders, published by Kogan Page.

> **Reminder: Take any action points or follow up points to Chapter 13, Your Plan For A Better Retirement.**

RETIRETMENT PLANNING EXPERT 2025   TAX ANNEX
MAIN PERSONAL TAX RATES

INCOME TAX

Rates and bands (other than savings and dividend income) after the
personal allowance

Band £	2025/26 Rate %	Band £	2024/25 Rate %
Under £12,570	0		0
Over £12,570* - £50,270	20	£12,570*-£50,270	20
£50,271 - £125,140	40	£50,271 - £125,140	40
Over £125,140	45	Over £125,140	45

*Assumes individuals are in receipt of the standard personal allowance.
The threshold at which basic rate tax starts being paid and the threshold
for paying higher rate tax will be frozen until April 2028.
Income tax rates in Scotland and Wales on income other than savings
and dividend income have been devolved. You pay Scottish Income Tax
if you move to Scotland and live there for a longer period than anywhere
else in the UK during a tax year (6 April to 5 April the following year).

DEVOLVED INCOME TAX

Scotland rates and bands

Band £	2025/26 Rate %	Band £	2024/25 Rate %
Under £12,570	0		0
£12,571 - £15,397	19	£12,570 - £14,876	19
£15,398 - £27,491	20	£14,877 - £26,561	20
£27,492 - £43,662	21	£26,562 - £43,662	21
£43,663 - £75,000	42	£43,663 - £75,000	42
£75,001- £125,140	45	£75,001- £125,140	45
Over £125,140	48	Over £125,140	48

SAVINGS AND INVESTMENT INCOME

Savings income	2025/26	2024/25
Savings allowance basic rate	£1,000	£1,000
Savings allowance higher rate	£500	£500

A starting rate of 0% may be available unless taxable non-savings income exceeds £5,000.

Dividend income	2025/26	2024/25
Dividend allowance	£500	£500
Dividend ordinary rate	8.75%	8.75%
Dividend upper rate	33.75%	33.75%
Dividend additional rate	39.35%	39.35%

INCOME TAX RELIEFS

	2025/26	2024/25
Personal allowance **	£12,570	£12,570
Personal allowance income limit	£100,000	£100,000
Marriage allowance	£1,260	£1,260
Married couple's allowance	£11,270	£11,080
minimum amount	£4,360	£4,280
income limit	£37,700	£37,000
Blind person's allowance	£3,130	£3,070
Property allowance and trading allowance (each)	£1,000	£1,000

**The Personal Allowance reduces where the income is above £100,000- by £1 for every £2 of income above the £100,000 limit.

PROPERTY TAXES

Stamp Duty Land Tax

Land and buildings in England and Northern Ireland

Residential Band	2025/26 Rate %	Non-residential Band	2025/26 Rate %
£0 - £125,000	0	£0- £150,000	0
£125,000- £250,000	2	£150,001- £250,000	2
£250,001 - £925,000	5	Over £250,000	5
£925,001 - £1,500,000	10		
Over £1,500,000	12		

The 0% band extended to £250,000 until 31 March 2025

Rates for **first time buyers**

(providing the property you are
buying costs £625,000 2024/25
reduced to £500,000 2025/26 or
less)

2024/25 £0 to £425,000	0%
2025/26 £0 to £300,000	0%
Over £425,000 2024/25 or £300,000 2025/26	The standard rates above apply

Not a UK resident
Different rates of Stamp Duty Land Tax will apply to purchasers of residential property in England and Northern Ireland who are not resident in the UK. The rates are 2% higher than those that apply to purchases made by UK residents.

Second homes
In England and Northern Ireland you will be charged an additional 3% stamp duty on each portion of the price and this was increased **to an additional 5% from 31 October 2024.** There are opportunities to reclaim this additional stamp duty where the original home is sold within 3 years. You may still be able to apply for a refund if you were unable to sell your previous home within 3 years in exceptional circumstances.

Non-natural persons such as companies
A higher rate of 17% (15% prior to 31 October 2024) may apply to all the consideration where certain 'non natural' persons such as a company purchase an interest in a single residential property for more than £500,000.

**Land and Buildings Transaction Tax
('LBTT') in Scotland**

Residential Band	2025/26 Rate %	Non-residential Band	Rate %
£0 - £145,000	0	£0- £150,000	0
£145,001 - £250,000	2	£150,001- £250,000	1
£250,001 - £325,000	5	Over £250,000	5
£325,001 - £750,000	10		
Over £750,000	12		

First-time buyers
A relief for **first-time buyers** in Scotland is available, which increases the residential nil rate band of LBTT to £175,000.

Second homes
In Scotland you will be charged an additional 6% stamp duty 'additional dwelling supplement', on each portion of the price. With effect from 5 December 2024 the rate was

increased to 8%. There are opportunities to reclaim this additional stamp duty where the original home is sold within 18 months. On 4 December 2024 it was announced that a review of LBTT legislation will start in Spring 2025.

Land Transaction Tax ('LTT') in Wales	2025/26 Rate %	Non-residential Band	2025/26 Rate %
Residential Band			
£0 - £225,000	0	£0- £225,000	0
£225,001 - £400,000	6	£225,001- £250,000	1
£400,001 - £750,000	7.5	£250,001- £1,000,000	5
£750,001- £1,500,000	10	Over £1,000,000	6
Over £1,500,000	12		

First-time buyers
There is no additional relief for **first-time buyers** in Wales.

Second homes- higher residential tax rates
In Wales you will be charged higher stamp duty (the "higher residential tax rates") on each portion of the price of a second home. There are opportunities to reclaim this additional stamp duty where the original home is sold within 3 years. Up until 10 December 2024 this was calculated at 4% above the LTT rate and from 11 December 2024 the following rates apply:

Higher residential tax rates: Second homes in Wales	2025/26 Rate %
Residential Band	
£0 - £180,000	5
£181,001 - £250,000	8.5
£250,001 - £400,000	10
£400,001- £750,000	12.5
£750,001 - £1,500,000	15
Over £1,500,000	17

PENSIONS

	2025/26	2024/25
Lump sum and death benefit allowance	£1,073,100	£1,073,100
Annual allowance limit	£60,000	£60,000
Money Purchase Annual Allowance	£10,000	£10,000

The annual allowance is reduced by £1 for every £2 of adjusted income(broadly net income plus any relievable pensions savings) over £260,000. The annual allowance may be increased with unused allowances from the previous three years.

INDIVIDUAL SAVINGS ACCOUNTS

	2025/26	2024/25
Overall investment limit	£20,000	£20,000
Junior account investment limit	£9,000	£9,000

CAPITAL GAINS TAX

	2025/26	2024/25
Individuals		
Exemption	£3,000	£3,000
Standard rate	18%	10%/18%*
Higher/additional rate	24%	20%/24%*
Disposal of second homes/certain residential property		
Standard rate	18%	10%/18%*
Higher/additional rate	24%	24%
Trusts -Exemption	£1,500	£1,500

*Higher rate applies for disposals made on or after 30 October 2024

Business asset disposal relief		
The first £1m of qualifying gains	14%	10%

INHERITANCE TAX

	2025/26	2024/25
Death rate		
£0 - £325,000	Nil	Nil
Over £325,000**	40%	40%
Reduced rate (for estates leaving 10% or more to charity)	36%	36%
Lifetime rate		
£0 - £325,000	Nil	Nil
Over £325,000	20%	20%

** The £325,000 threshold will be frozen until April 2028. A further nil rate band of £175,000 may be available in relation to current or former residences with a taper threshold applying at £2,000,000.

NATIONAL INSURANCE

	2025/26	2024/25
Class 1 (employed)		
Employee		
Earnings per week		
Up to £241	Nil	Nil
£242- £967 (upper earnings limit)	8%	8%
Over £967	2%	2%
Employer		
Earnings per week		
Up to £175	n/a	Nil
Over £175	n/a	13.8%
Up to £96	Nil	n/a
Over £175	15%	n/a
Class 1a	15%	13.8%
Employers - on employees taxable benefits		
Class 2 (self employed)		
Weekly rate	£3.50	£3.45
Small profits threshold	£6,845	£6,725
Class 3 (voluntary)		
Flat rate per week	£17.75	£17.45
Class 4 (self employed)		
Below £12,750	0%	0%
£12,570 to £50,270	6% on profits	6% on profits
Over £50,270	2% on profits	2% on profits

Social Security ('welfare benefits') including pensions and child benefit

The government will continue to protect pensioner incomes by maintaining the **'triple lock'** and increasing the State Pension, New State Pension and Pension Credit in line with the highest of the three measures (average earnings growth, CPI inflation, or 2.5%) by average earnings growth of 4.1% from April 2025.

The majority of social security payments are to rise by the September 2024 Consumer Price Index of 1.7% from April 2025. Some disability benefits are devolved in Scotland, so it is for the Scottish Government to decide uprating. Department for Work and Pensions (DWP) benefits are fully devolved in Northern Ireland, so it is for the Northern Ireland Executive to decide uprating in Northern Ireland. The high-income child benefit charge, if one person earns more than £60,000, will result in you paying back 1% of your child benefit received for every £100 earned above £60,000.

Chapter Six
Clear debt

"Fundamentally we're all the by-product of not what has happened to us, but how we choose to handle it."

STEPHEN BARTLETT

Ugly debt can be like a python and squeeze the life out of you. My years of work in Corporate Recovery and Insolvency provided me with three vital 'debt' lessons which I share in this chapter to help you get ready to start your glidepath into retirement.

Lesson 1: Understand and learn how to handle good, average and ugly debt.

Lesson 2. Understand your net wealth position as you glide towards the start of the retirement glidepath.

Lesson 3: Understand how and why any debt has been built into your net wealth and handle it (restructure it, cut costs, improve income and learn from previous debt mistakes) before starting your retirement glidepath. This might involve changing some key beliefs and habits of a lifetime. The liberating effect is powerful and you should achieve a better retirement.

I've quoted Stephen Bartlett at the start of this chapter- the millionaire businessman that many readers of this book will know- his blogs, books and Dragon's Den role gives him a great platform. He has a great knowledge base which he shares freely. I like his quote "Fundamentally we're all the by-product of not what has happened to us, but how we choose to handle it."

Understand and learn to handle good, average and ugly debt

I have seen decent business people destroyed by debt and I've learnt three lessons which should give some help to those trying to plan their glidepath into retirement where they have debt problems. It could be the individual saddled by a large mortgage where health issues may have reduced the family salary income and they feel they have to work on and on to clear the mortgage. Or the individual that has taken out an interest only mortgage and is now facing the problem of how to repay the capital as they hit retirement. Or the individual who has taken on two expensive car loan contracts, other bank loans an overdraft, credit card and several store cards.

Lesson 1: Understand and learn how to handle good, average and ugly debt.

Debt is necessary as it provides a bridge or pathway to build assets which will help you in the future. The easiest to grasp is the mortgage that all home owners probably remember sweating over that first time you signed on the dotted line to take on a debt that may have seemed unimaginable a few years earlier. Fingers crossed and you (and I) hoped that property values increased above inflation and wages growth. As you will have seen from **Chapter 2, Your Home and Property** it was probably a good move when viewed over the longer term and your 'net wealth' has soared. Debt that was taken on for a good financial reason and which produces an asset worth more than the liability (debt, interest and any costs) is **good debt**.

Then we have debt taken out to bridge a financial cashflow over the medium term. An example is a loan to help finance the kids through college or to pay for a dream 'holiday of a lifetime' at a time when the kids will love it. Maybe you couldn't really afford it at the time but thought 'screw it, let's do it'; did the numbers (the financial forecast over the medium term) and determined that it was 'safe' to take the loan. Even better, maybe you could access the loan at a decent rate (via a mortgage top up?) and realised you can cover it all in the medium term or that expected future salary increases should cover it. I call this **average debt**.

Then we move to the final category. Debt taken out for something that isn't really thought through or for stuff we don't really need or to fund an expensive lifestyle that we really can't afford. Or worst of all to plug a hole caused by some toxic spending habit – maybe there is an addiction issue or gambling. Or, on a less toxic cause, but sometimes just as consequential it may be impulse buying via the 'click bait' driven society that has emerged in recent years. Driven by social media and influencers this is pouring more petrol on the "spend now pay for it later" UK society in 2025. **This is 'ugly debt'** and then gets **a double ugly strike** as the debt may be subject to higher than usual debt rates of interest i.e. a rate of interest more than, say 4% above the current Bank of England base rate which stands at 4.75% (December 2024). Others may have fallen prey to ugly debt life's unfortunate twists- maybe the death of a partner or following a divorce. The financial restructuring after both can be significant at a time when you least need it.

Starting your glidepath to retirement by handling your debts more effectively should be a target- it will give you more control over your finances and is completely liberating.

Lesson 2: Understand your net wealth position

As part or your plan for a retirement glidepath you should know your net wealth and how it changes over time. I set this out in **Chapter 1** at the section '**know your net wealth**' and the pages thereafter. As I said there *"Net wealth takes me back to my earliest days in finance. It is a simple but important concept if you strip it back to the basics. On the one hand it is everything you own (assets) and on the other it is everything you owe (liabilities). The assets less liabilities calculation varies over your lifetime and probably peaks in your late 50s for homeowners".*

Refer back to Chapter 1 and take the work done there as your starting point for assessing your debt. Then determine whether your debts are good, average or ugly. Set out in a table showing the debt, the amount, the repayment terms and period, the interest rate, early repayment charges and the reason why the debt was taken on.

Lesson 3: Handle debt better- the 6 steps

Handling it. Now that you have established the base line the next steps are pure restructuring and put simply, 'handling ugly debt' and I use a six-step model. Again, I am going back to those basic (and actually very simple, when you know how) steps that are undertaken in corporate restructuring. They apply just as well to any personal position. I say again its actually very simple once you strip the emotions out of it.

My 6 recommended steps to handle debt better are:

1. Establish the base line of your current net wealth position and the good, average and ugly debts therein.
2. Focus firstly on the ugly debts and restructure them.
3. Determine how and why you took out ugly debt.
4. Share 1,2 and 3 with your partner and/or a trusted friend who understands finances. A problem shared is a problem halved
5. Assess other debt and how it could be cleared by cutting costs or increasing income.
6. Choose how you handle debt differently going forward.

Step 1, just to repeat, is establishing the base line i.e. your current net wealth position.

Quick wins are always good so **step 2** is to identify the ugly debts and restructure them. That means diverting income to clear the worst ugly debts as a priority picking off those with the highest interest first (after assessing any repayment charges)- usually credit card and store card arrears and overdrafts.

Top tip
Start with the ugly debts and make a plan to repay those with the highest interest first (after assessing any early repayment charges).

Step 3 is to then pause to determine how and why you took on ugly debt. It's a tough exercise and one that goes right to the heart of our behaviours and beliefs. As Stephen Bartlett advises at the head of this chapter the key bit is not so much the situation but learning how we got there and handling it.

Step 4 draws more on handling it and my memories of those business owners who were losing their businesses and potentially their homes with the old saying of a problem shared is a problem halved. This underpins step 4. Jumping back to my

Corporate Recovery and Insolvency work we were brought in to rationalise the finances of a troubled business. We were outsiders with no baggage but again were not industry experts (how could you be in a range of businesses that varied from Kitchen and Bathroom wholesalers; a Formula Ford team to Mirror manufacturers to name just a few). We brought the financial razor eye and the business owners helped with the knowledge to run the business until a sale was achieved after some restructuring or it was broken up. There were always savings to be made- I repeat 'always' and sometimes these were significant. The poor business owners were under so much debt stress they just couldn't see it. So, I'd say you must bring in your partner or significant other to review your net wealth and plan how to clear ugly debt. Even better if you don't feel comfortable with the numbers, issues and options is to discuss this with a trusted friend or family member who has a grasp of finance. I repeat "A problem shared is a problem halved". Plot out the numbers; be open and transparent and make a plan and stick to it. In addition to family and friends Citizens Advice can also help with debt clearance support and Step Change (the Debt Charity) has some of the best resources of all in the UK at www.stepchange.org. Step Change promises to treat you as an individual, to give comprehensive support is non-profit and their advice is free. If debt is out of control obsess about it until it is resolved and be prepared to make tough decisions- the restructuring you do will be like a great weight lifted off your shoulders.

Let's now go back to the start of this chapter and the individual saddled by a large mortgage where health issues may have reduced the family salary income and they feel they have to work on and on. They could be driving themselves into an early grave. There could be a whole chapter analysing the situation and pros and cons of different solutions. An early option on the list could be simply to downsize or relocate to a cheaper area after stripping out all the behaviours and beliefs that could be holding back the individual from releasing the shackles of debt. Or the individual who has taken on two expensive car loan contracts, other bank loans, an overdraft, credit card and several store cards. This introduces **the fifth step** of restructuring debt. It goes again to the heart of restructuring any financial issue involving debt that has been become a noose around the neck. It involves the two-pronged approach of cutting costs and/or increasing income to, in turn, allow you to clear the debt. I can illustrate this fairly easily by highlighting some of the opportunities set out elsewhere in this book- and remember these are just a few of the examples but you'll get the gist.

- If an individual owns a property it could involve, potentially, creating a tax-free lump sum to clear all ugly debt (and maybe all debt) by downsizing or relocating to a cheaper area. At the same time this step may reduce their ongoing property costs so potentially a double win. More on this at **Chapter 2, Your Home and Property.**

- Reviewing **Chapter 7 and the Cut Costs in 2025 chapter** in this book and save hundreds of pounds a month by cutting costs and waste to help repay all ugly debt.
- Developing a side hustle to bring in extra income **(Chapter 8, Starting Your Own Business).**
- Renting a spare room for extra income **(Chapter 2, Your Home and Property).**
- Getting a part-time job for extra income **(Chapter 9, Career Transition: Paid work)**
- Reviewing pensions and savings to see how this could improve income or create cashflow **(Chapters 3 and 4).**

You'll see now that the basic mantra is very simple- cut costs and increase income. That takes us onto the **sixth and final step** which also takes us back to Stephen Bartlett's opening quote. *"Fundamentally we're all the by-product of not what has happened to us, but how we choose to handle it."* This sixth step is to learn from the habits in the past that created the ugly debt and don't repeat and bad habits of the past.

The great mortgage puzzle- to repay or not to repay

One of the lowest forms of interest on any schedule of debts and repayment prioritisations is usually on mortgages. But that does not mean it is set to one side and left to just take its course until it is repaid. There are usually opportunities that involve a trade-off and it could be worth keeping your mortgage under review and trying to repay it before your retirement glidepath commences. The usual issues that warrant review include:

1. Giving yourself time to compare and contrast mortgage options on the point of taking out a mortgage and upon renewal. There are decent comparator sites but remember that not all deals are available on the open market and the UK leading brokers may have access to other products.

2. Understand that the earlier in the month you set your repayment date the

more you will save on interest – can you change the date without penalty?

3. Understand the early termination charges on your current mortgage so that if rates reduce and you want to change products you can do the cost / benefit analysis. Or even better if you receive a windfall you may be able to pay off the whole mortgage and be mortgage free.

4. Understand that overpayments are often allowed on mortgages. Assess whether you can overpay your mortgage each year to the maximum allowed which could shave years off your mortgage end date.

5. Understand if you can 'top up your mortgage' for no or minimal charges. This could be handy if you have ugly expensive debt and wish to restructure it into low interest debt.

6. You can usually 'port' a mortgage from one property to another so if you are moving house there may be an opportunity to retain a mortgage- especially if you are locked into a low rate of interest.

The 50:30:20 rule

Professor and later Senator (of Massachusetts) Elizabeth Warren promotes a basic and understandable budgeting rule that could help younger readers of this book avoid ugly debt and get their finances into shape well ahead of the start of any retirement glidepath. I like Elizabeth's rule which she set out in her book "All your Worth: The Ultimate Lifetime Money Plan" so I'm giving it space here. It is called the 50:30:20 rule and it involves dividing your money into three pots based on your after-tax income. 50% goes to needs; 30% to wants and 20% to savings and debt payments. The 50% needs are expenses that are necessary for survival and basic wellbeing such as housing, utilities food, transportation, healthcare and childcare. The 30% wants are non-essential expenses such as self-care and beauty, eating out, gym memberships, digital TV and streaming services, entertainment, non-basic clothes shopping. The 20% savings and debt repayment can include retirement pension contributions, building up savings as an emergency pot and paying off high interest debt. The precision will vary from person to person and there will, inevitably, be some blurring around the boundary edges. The concept seems sound and I like the simplicity. It could represent a model for some readers of this book to try and adopt and the earlier in your life journey the better. It may not work quite so well for those on very low incomes or who live in London or other high living cost areas. Overall, I believe it is a worthwhile addition to include it in my book and help your glidepath to retirement.

Further information

Step Change the Debt Charity at www.stepchage.org.

> **Reminder: Take any action points or follow up points to Chapter 13, Your Plan For A Better Retirement.**

Chapter Seven

Cut your 2025 costs. Complaints and Scams

"A fool and his money are soon parted."

This is the final chapter of the 'save more' parts of this book. Combine chapters 2 to 7 together (the six 'save more' chapters) and theywill make a significant difference to achieving a better retirement. Indeed, this chapter alone will save some readers an absolute fortune from the staying safe from scammer tips. The quotation at the head of this chapter shouts out that *"A fool and his money are soon parted"* and is one I re-review each year as it seems a bit harsh. But I leave it in as every year I encounter case study after case study of entirely sensible people being made to feel foolish by clever scammers. They are not fools but are made to feel very foolish with the benefit of hindsight. It's a harsh reminder and therefore remains at the head of this Chapter. If it is too good to be true, heed your instincts and walk away. Remember also that there is no law against a shop, business or trader overcharging and setting a price that is way too high if folk come along and pay that price. Overall, this chapter help you 'save more' and achieve a better retirement.

If it is too good to be true heed your instincts and walk away

This chapter at a glance

- *There is no law against over-charging*. Whilst 'click bait' (some enticing story or offer) and internet online scams present threats, the flip side should be recognised. There are massive opportunities to use the internet to turn information into power for yourself. So why do we accept the price, over-pay and we do we not research the offer that appears to be 'too good to be true'? But no longer – welcome to this chapter and tools and tips to empower you and also welcome a cold wet Winter's day that can save you, potentially, hundreds of pounds on services that you may have been overpaying. You will save £££s.
- *How to **cut the cost-of-living** and recession proof your finances.*
- *Inevitably in life things do sometimes go wrong*. If you do lose out and someone is clearly at fault you may wish to complain. The **complaint process** can be frustrating and some people and organisations may not have the time or ability to deal with your concerns. Worse still is encountering a brick-wall approach to your concerns or some Artificial Intelligence driven 'automated reply' to your complaint which oozes initial comfort but turns out to wholly lack any precision on your concerns and/or action/remedy that amounts to anything. You have the right to complain and should expect justice, fairness, equality and accountability. Tips are provided on how to be heard, how to spell out what you want and then what you can do to up the ante.
- *Five simple **golden rules for staying safe from scammers**. Follow them and you will be safer.*
- ***Scams** tend to follow a pattern and just get dressed up in different guises each year*. The more common scams are set out and you will learn the pattern and spot the next one that comes along.

It's time to review and start cutting costs – a 10 point checklist to get you started

1. Revisit Chapter 1, Your Plan and the **financial budget** you created. The starting point is to do an annual budget and then work out what you 'need' rather than just want. Revisit all those direct debits and standing orders and get rid of unnecessary subscriptions. Remember the budget needs the sanity check I mention at Chapter 1. It also must cover a full year as it's the 'one offs' that always spoil a budget and most people underestimate their spending if

they try to 'guess this'. If the budget does not balance then restructure it until it does.

2. **Clear, reduce or restructure your ugly debt in overdrafts, credit cards and store cards or loan debts** as per Chapter 6, Clear Debt. Talk with Step Change, the national debt charity, to get help with your options via www.stepchange.org and things will start to get better. Just take a quick glance at their 'your debt questions answered' on the home page of their website to see how they can help lift that big cloud that could be hanging over you. As I said in Chapter 6, ugly debt can really drag you down mentally. A thorough review with someone you trust can help as the answer may be right under your nose but you just don't see it.

3. There is no law against **over-charging** – go through the 'Are you being over-charged- think straight' section immediately following these 10 tips and see if you can slash down your costs by the review and some radical thinking.

4. Declutter, have a clear out and **sell off stuff you don't** need via ebay, facebook marketplace or local sales.

5. Check if you are eligible for any **benefits or grants** at www.turn2us.org.uk and **HMRC** have provided more advice about getting help with childcare, claiming tax relief on work-related expenses and help if you cannot pay your tax bill. Every little bit may help and you can check it out at: **gov.uk/guidance/check-what-financial-help-you-can-get-from-hmrc**

6. Having a spending behaviour reset- ignore discounts, special offers and all the tempting 'click bait' and influencer recommendations. I appreciate that this is tough, actually really tough, but you owe it to yourself to re-set buying behaviours if your finances don't quite stack up. Try **"do you actually need it and is the end price worth it."**? And try the most powerful of all- **set up a treat pot,** make a list of what you'd like (achievable, rather than desirable and I said in Chapter 1) and stick to it and the treats when bought will seem even better!

7. Try using other retail stores- habit can be a bad thing. Trolley.co.uk lets you compare supermarket prices.

8. **Know your consumer rights and get your money back when things go wrong.** If goods are faulty or not as described, the buyer should take it back for a refund. If you buy online you usually have 14 days under the Consumer Contracts Regulations to return the goods provided you have not broken the seal or it is perishable/personalised. Keep your receipts. You can find out more at www.which.co.uk and their consumer rights section. Later in this

chapter you will read about **Section 75 and chargeback protection** if you use a credit card or debit card to make a purchase. There is also some protection by using paypal. Try to stick to these payment routes for some added protection.

9.   Ohh I know this is going to be a tough call but folk tend to go into a spending frenzy at Christmas. But so many of us just can't keep up and it can be a tough time for some on a budget. Is it time to go **'secret Santa'** with the adults and just look after the kids i.e. there's a draw and each adult gets another adult in the family group to buy for. There's a spending cap and maybe even there is a prize for the most thoughtful pressie (or funniest or whatever)? This focuses everything back onto the thought rather than the spend. I'm sorry if this sound a bit bah humbug but I do worry about the impact on the spending frenzy on family members who may not have the same resources especially when times are tough.

10. Think creatively about how to have **free magical moments** and experiences with children, family and friends. The UK is one of the best places on earth for experiences, activities and fun. Websites like Martin Lewis's Money Saving Expert prides itself on not just saving you money (and that's another tip pointer of course) but also in pointing you to ways to create free or very cheap magical summers, Halloween and Christmas moments.

Are you being over-charged- think straight?

Those ten points are a good starter but there is then another way to slash your spending in these tough times. There is little protection against over-charging, and the buck usually stops with you on what you choose to pay for things so I wanted to drill down further into tip number 3 about over-charging. Quite often, suppliers rely on lethargy, as there just never seems to be enough time to sit back, think straight and review some regular financial transactions. You might just be amazed at how much you can save. Choose any cold, wet winter day and dedicate it to checking all your current deals and contracts and seeing what you can save. It may help you balance your budget, or pay for a few nights out but if you get good at this it will pay for another holiday.

Insurance

Log your insurance renewal dates: home buildings, home contents, car, pet and any others. Contact them and ask what discounts can be applied to a renewal and then check out their biggest competitor with equivalent policies. Remember some insurers (for instance Direct Line) don't take part in some comparison websites. Be careful, however, about life and health insurance policies and pet insurance so you don't lose any existing cover for pre-existing conditions.

Utilities

Check with your supplier if you are on their best tariff and compare this to other options via Ofgem-approved comparison sites such as uswitch.com. I do get frustrated at the jargon thrown in by the energy companies and various contract offerings- focus on the standing charge, unit cost and term of the deal and that may help you cut through the smoke and waffle.

TV and broadband bundles

So, who is paying more than £100 a month on TV packages and streaming services? This is a hugely competitive market, with Sky, Virgin Media and BT all bidding for your money and Amazon, Apple TV and Netflix providing great entertainment platforms. Compare the deals and start to make the switch. There will be dramatic price drops when you tell them you are leaving and are passed through to the 'business retention team' or whatever they call it these days. But also… gulp… is it finally time to ditch them and just learn how to use internet TV or link a laptop to older TV and try that if it helps you manage the budget. I'm truly astonished at how much some folk pay for their TV bundles when money is tight. Could this be one of your 'stop doing' actions at Chapter 13?

Mobile phones

The costs can mount up if you are paying for the mobiles of yourself, children and/or parents and providers rely on lethargy. So it is a case of holding back from the early upgrade offer and then just using someone like www.uswitch.com to compare the current offers on handset, calls and that vital data package and then you call the shots. A simple 5 minute call explaining you have found a better deal will usually see you passed through to some form of 'business retention department' and you may receive a matched or bettered deal. You should also check for mobile providers who offer data sharing facilities across several mobile phones if you find that children keep going over their data limits - some providers offer this facility which can save you money. A really quick win here is to get a decent reconditioned phone and then combine that with a SIM only deal- it can more than half the cost if times are tight.

Cash back and air mile credit cards

A quick look at www.moneysavingexpert.com could find you cutting your existing card in half and shifting to someone who will reward you properly. Some even come with neat little complimentary extras. Folk continually tell me about quidco.com and topcashback.co.uk and the money they save so these may be worth a look. A reminder at this point. Unlike some other publications I take no sponsorship, advertising or kickbacks – never have and never will as I depend on being completely impartial.

Pensions, savings and investments

Revisit Chapters 3 and 4 and the pointers on pension, savings and investments and renegotiate fees and account charges. Consider these in line with the quality of the related advice you receive and the returns you receive of dividend, interest, capital growth or other income. Again, I'm fairly staggered at the fees that can be charged due to lethargy and a long connection/ relationship but often these just keep going on year after year and amount to thousands and thousands of £££.

Lost premium bonds or other National Savings and Investment

These can be traced via mylostaccount.org.uk.

Switch or overpay your mortgage

Mortgages usually cost more than savings interest can earn and after the rapid rise in mortgage rates in 2023 they seem to be falling again. After checking out any early redemption fees consider switching mortgages. Weigh up the fees, rates, early redemption penalties and make the choice. Ask mortgage advisers about fee rebates (ie where they rebate to you a percentage of their fee/commission)- this can work well with smaller more 'flexible' brokers. Assess whether you can start over-paying on your monthly mortgage payments or make one-off repayments without penalty and save money. Another trick is to move your monthly payment earlier in the month and the effect can mount up to more money saved.

Estate agent fees

If selling your home compare and contrast the costs and benefits between a low cost and/ or online only estate agent and a traditional high street estate agent as the cost differences can be significant. If you are selling in a sought-after or premium location a local agent's knowledge and contacts is usually worth the extra premium.

If you can't save ££ try a change and vote with your feet

Business is all about making money and if you are dissatisfied with customer service vote with your feet. Stop paying them the money and just go elsewhere.

Top Tip

The 'oops, I forgot about that direct debit' moment. This is a must do. Get your bank statements and credit cards statements together, sit down with your partner and check you recognise and can account for all those direct debits and standing orders. Most online banks/phone banking apps can generate a list at the press of a button. If you don't use that club or gym membership, stop paying for it. Do this review with any elderly relative once a year, especially if they are now living on their own.

The Section 75 magic wand to being ripped off. Use it or lose it!

Section 75 of the Consumer Credit Act 1974 gives us the shorthand of a 'Section 75 claim'. It means that you may never need to follow the complaints process when something goes wrong with a purchase and hence the 'magic wand' term that I use. It protects you on purchases you make on a **credit card** between the value of £100 and £30,000 (note credit card only i.e. not debit cards and that's really important to remember). **Section 75** makes the credit card provider jointly liable if something goes wrong with your purchase. The simple claims are when the seller goes bust or the item never turns up but it can also work if the item is not as described or is faulty.

It's powerful as it is the law. Then there is another form of protection available for bank purchases such as debit cards. It's called 'chargeback' but isn't as powerful as it is a voluntary arrangement (rather than the law) so always try and use a credit card for purchases between £100 and £30,000.

'Chargeback' works by you contacting the bank and stating: 'I want to chargeback the (describe transaction, amount and date) of the original debit card payment'. Importantly the request must be made with 120 days of the original transaction (this may not work for holiday accommodation or tickets booked more than 120 days in advance and you find out it was all a scam too late). Chargeback is usually used where goods do not show up, are damaged or differ from the description (i.e. breach of contract-type claims). If the bank rejects your claim you can appeal to the Financial Ombudsman (details below) to have your case reviewed.

Top Tip
The protection given by a credit card is awesome - reread the Section 75 magic wand above and add an action to your 'start doing' list of changes at Chapter 13.

Complaints- fobbed off and brick-wall culture

Things in life inevitably go wrong and sometimes you lose out when it was not your fault. It is always satisfying when you explain your complaint and an organization says:

'We are really sorry for the inconvenience we have caused you. Thank you for taking the time to set out your concerns. We have now fixed the issue and it will not happen again and we would like you to accept a bunch of flowers as our way of saying sorry.'

This sort of response is rare and it's irritating the way more and more companies hide behind websites and make it almost impossible to find someone to speak to directly. You may get fobbed off or, worse, you encounter a **'brick-wall culture'** involving the **dreaded four D's of dismissing** you, **delaying** responding in then hope you may go away, **denying** you the right to complain and present your side of the story and your evidence and finally **deflection** as they try to move away from your concern onto a different issue to throw you off your trail. This is a culture in an organisation where there may well be procedures and policies that are written up and look impressive and you get reasonably quick answers BUT they just avoid dealing with the actual evidence, issue and any offer of a remedy and just side-step any inconvenient point. This usually signposts an organisation with a poor governance culture. It's a particular shame if you find there is no independent escalation route that can provide some oversight into the resolution of your concerns. Communications may ends with an email along the lines of *"we will place any further communications from you on file but will not respond any further"* or *"a take it or (effectively) take us to court"* approach. By then they hope you have no appetite or energy to carry on. In other cases (and one that I am seeing more and more of) it seems like a computer is auto-generating replies. And I'm afraid to say it is probably Artificial Intelligence writing most of the reply which can often seem quite long and detailed and oozes comforting words but the reality is (usually) little focus on the evidence you have presented and deflecting down side alleys and avenues that leave you difficulty in following up.

Perhaps some businesses will see the benefit of reverting to two-way communications and proper customer care. I believe you should expect **'justice, fairness, equality and accountability'** – the mantra of the radical lawyer Michael Mansfield, QC. This chapter will help you achieve this with four easy steps.

Step 1: You have the right to complain and expect justice, fairness, equality and accountability- three paragraph complaint

When something goes wrong, contact the firm or organisation responsible straight away and give them a chance to sort out the problem. Clearly state your complaint. Spend time thinking about this beforehand so that you can be clear and concise about what has happened and, more importantly, what you expect. If you are vague and unclear when you complain, then you can expect a vague and unclear reply. If you want an apology, say this and say why. If you want compensation, state how much and why. If you want more time to formulate your complaint after getting some information from them say this.

So set aside things that are just annoying from where they are flawed/ wrong or at fault. Construct a three-paragraph complaint that is written in tight sentences.

Paragraph one is the issue. Paragraph two is what you expect (spell it out). Paragraph 3 is the channels you've already tried. It really is as simple as that but do spend time getting it factually correct and attach supporting evidence. Time and time again I find that it is the quality of the evidence that makes or breaks a complaint i.e. most organisations would wish to take an evidence-based approach to complaint handling as the evidence tells the story and is difficult to counter by dismissing, delaying, denying and deflecting. If it goes beyond one page it sounds like you could be rambling. Don't worry – we all do this when we feel aggrieved. But it probably means you need to set it aside and come back to it with a clearer head, re-read it and relegate some information to an attachment. The evidence should also be attached. Get a friend or relative to read it and help keep things 'tight'. Send it by email and ask for confirmation of receipt by return, or send by recorded delivery and keep a copy, together with the post office tracking receipt.

The Consumer Rights Act 2015 might also help you. It came into effect on 1 October 2015 and covers what should happen when goods are faulty, services don't match up to what was agreed, or the service was not handled with reasonable care and skill. It also covers unfair terms in a contract, and extensions to existing laws brought in coverage of digital content (such as online films and games). For more details, including summaries of your rights, use www.citizensadvice.org.uk and the section on 'The Consumer Rights Act 2015'.

Step 2 up the ante - 'formal complaint'

If the issue is not resolved or you encounter the tactics employed above, take steps to make it a formal complaint. Ask the organisation for the name, address, telephone number and email of the person or department that deals with complaints. Write a letter or email and head it up 'FORMAL COMPLAINT' quoting any reference you have.

Try something like:

Dear [name]

FORMAL COMPLAINT: Your ref [reference]

X weeks have now passed and I am dissatisfied with the way you have handled my complaint. You appear to be [dismissing/ delaying/denying/deflecting] from my complaint dated x/x/x a further copy of which is attached. Please now deal with my complaint <u>and</u> let me have a copy of your complaints' policy. If you have not got a complaints' policy please let me know how I may escalate my complaint within your organisation. Please also let me know of any ombudsman scheme, arbitration service or suchlike that I may go to outside your organisation if I continue to remain dissatisfied about my complaint.

Yours

[your name]

Some organisations will try to get rid of you by sending you a 'go away' letter saying that they have 'fully considered' your complaint and have now exhausted all opportunities to reach a conclusion. The punchline is that they will no longer respond to any further letters or communications from you and they will close their file. At this stage it is up to you to decide whether to give up (that is what they want) or take if further.

Step 3 up the ante again - 'obtain your complaint file'

There is a very useful route that few people know about and most organisations/companies have to sign up to. This should help you both exert pressure and probe a little further before considering the next step. And it really is simple. Just ask for a copy of all data relating your complaint including, but not limited to, all internal notes, telephone transcripts or phone recordings, manager review notes and any other document bearing your name or referring to you. State the request is made under the General Data Protection Regulations (basically a new improved Data Protection Act 1988) and is a 'subject access request'. State that your request should be passed immediately to their Data Protection Officer. The information has to be supplied to you within a month and provided for free. When you have your complaint data file review how they have considered your complaint; have they gone back to get the other side of the story to ensure 'fairness' and is it correct; have the other side said anything that is unfair or untrue or made derogatory statements about you.

Sometimes firms may blank out (or 'redact') parts of their files and there are strict rules about what can and cannot be redacted. If you believe information has been unfairly redacted you have a right of appeal to the organisation that oversees fair play. The Information Commissioners Office (ICO) have lots of helpful information and template letters that can help you access your personal information at www.ico.org.uk – go to 'for the public'. One word of caution – it can take many months for the ICO to investigate your request for help and currently, December 2024, they appear to be taking about 14 weeks.

Step 4 up the ante again- 'pull in some free help with clout'

It is then time to consider some final routes if you feel you are not receiving justice, fairness, equality and accountability and feel that it is worth the effort. Some organisations have independent assessors, and their service is completely free (for instance, Companies House and other quasi-government agencies). Some have a free ombudsman service (banks, financial advisers and estate agents as we have signposted below). Others have regulating bodies (solicitors, surveyors and chartered accountants) that may be able to intervene on your behalf. Others have oversight organizations such as Ofcom (mobile phones) or Ofgem (utilities). The route to accessing the relevant organisation should be in the firm's complaint policy. If not try googling complaints about [name of firm] to see if that can provide a pointer.

Other help

Another useful route is to consider if mediation, arbitration or conciliation services are possible. These routes are referred to as 'alternative dispute resolution'. For instance, the National Conciliation Service handles issues about vehicles (including service and repairs) and can be found at www.nationalconciliationservice.co.uk (there is also www.themotorombudsman.org for resolving motor disputes). Then there is the ABTA arbitration scheme which deals with alleged breaches of contract and/or negligence between consumers and members of ABTA, the travel organisation, and has been in operation for over 40 years.

These schemes are provided so that consumers can have disputes resolved without having to go to court and without having to go to the expense of instructing solicitors. It is important to understand that some are a legal process, which means that if you do go through the process but are not happy with the outcome you cannot then go to court. Alternative dispute resolution is extending its reach following the Consumer Rights Act 2015 and if you are in dispute with a business they will now need to make you aware of the relevant certified alternative dispute resolution provider. Citizens Advice may know if there is an alternative dispute resolution process available for your complaint and it also has very useful template letters and advice for complainants at www.citizensadvice.org.uk or give them a call.

If there is no external organisation, you could choose to use a complaints management service. These charge a fee so make sure you understand the costs you will have to pay. You could also consider legal proceedings so remember the costs you will pay include the other side's costs if the court decides you are wrong. There is a 'do it yourself' service via the County Court online (www.gov.uk and go to 'make a court claim for money').

Finally - vote with your feet

The final tip is to consider whether or not your complaint is really worth the effort of pursuing or do you just vote with your feet and go elsewhere – and tell your friends about it?

Stay safe from the scammers

Scammers are basically clever crooks who deploy sleight of hand, fast talk and clever technology and a few back-up techniques such as vanity and knowing that people never want to admit to being stupid. You may never spot what they have done, in the same way as a good magician really will leave you believing that they made someone 'float' on stage. The equivalent of smoke, mirrors and sleight of hand can make anything look plausible. This chapter underlines the tricks and tips to help you ignore the smoke and mirrors deployed by the scammers and stay safer and you won't feel you've been made to look a fool. The tips below will help you stay safe from the scammers.

The five golden rules for staying safe from scammers

1. Trust your instincts

It's a simple common-sense approach: ignore the smoke and mirrors and sleight of hand that crooks and scammers are so capable of pulling off that are used to distract you from the real issue. Does it look, feel, and 'smell' like something is not quite right? Does it get your hackles up? If so, trust your instincts and walk away, put the letter in the bin or put down the phone, shut the door or make an excuse and walk away/leave. Instincts have been honed in the human species over thousands of years – if they have served you well in the past, learn to trust them.

2. Actions speak louder than words

Scammers, generally, are all talk (unsurprisingly, they are very good at it) and no action. It should also come as no surprise that they are also charming and 'nice and friendly'. So, here's the nub of the issue as, quite simply, any reasonable person should be able to deliver against what they promise or apologise and explain before you have to ask, *'what's going on*?' If the actions don't happen just walk away and don't give them a second chance to take advantage of you. If some reasonable questions (it's good to ask and ask) provoke a hint of aggression or anything to put you down then that should tell you all you need to know. Remember the motto - its actions that count not words.

3. Too good to be true?

Scammers know that greed often gets the better of many people (remember the quote at the heading of this chapter) and employ it to their advantage. If it sounds too good to be true, it is probably a scam. Again, just put down the phone, shut the door or make an excuse and walk away/leave.

4. Thank you, but I'll just check with...

We have great financial institutions in the United Kingdom and this goes to the very heart of the UK economy. Our regulatory system is sound. You should therefore check precisely who you are dealing with, and if it involves big money or risk ensure you are dealing with a professional adviser. For anything to do with savings, investments and pensions you must check that the firm is regulated by the Financial Conduct Authority at www.fca.org.uk.

Sometimes individuals hide behind the cloak of a firm or a company. If the company is not a high-street name you can do some free and easy research at Companies House. Go to 'Companies House' then 'find company information' then 'start' and enter the company name or unique number in the 'search the register' box and then look at the filing history documents (which has lots of juicy detail). Check how long it has been in existence and whether it has filed its accounts on time. Both can flag up warning signs and accessing the service is completely free and easy to do.

Also linked to the 'I'll just check with...' tip is the simple fact that crooks have one other objective in addition to taking your hard-earned cash – and that is not getting caught out. This is where nosy neighbours are brilliant – a stroll over, a smile, a look in the eye and a few questions (after talking about the weather for 10 seconds!) can be of great assistance armed with tip number one, 'trust your instincts'.

5. If in doubt, stay out

Over the last two decades the online world has gained a deeper reach into our lives, our information, and our wealth. Regulation has not been able to keep up to date to protect us as, literally, anyone, anywhere in the world can reach us and interact with us online and they probably know quite a bit about you already. Remember all those quirky facebook prompts to list your porn star name i.e. your pets name and your mother's maiden name. Errr guess what passwords are derived from! We really must accept that, to a large extent, it's up to us how much we use the online world acknowledging that everyone (including the government) is encouraging us to use it. For safety follow the golden rule - if in doubt stay out. That means if your browser does not display the 'secure' padlock on the site you are looking at you have no protection. It means you keep people out by knowing and checking your profile settings on social media.

Share the 'golden rule' with any elderly relative

If you only do one thing as a result of this chapter, do this: require any parent or elderly friend or relative to learn one simple golden rule. The rule is … if anyone contacts about anything to do with money they should only take down 1. The name of the person who spoke to them 2. A brief context (they called about a roof repair etc) 3. Full name of any company they represent and contact information. It is simple, effective and it works. Armed with points 1-3 you or someone else follows it up. If need be place the rule by the phone or on the front door by the latch. Giving your elderly relative or friend or neighbour the knowledge and confidence of your complete support is one of best things you could give (is this another action point at Chapter 13?).

Some common scams

Amazing concert tickets, beautiful holiday cottage – and it's all make believe

We probably know the reputable ticket resale sites and bona fide sites where you can get holiday accommodation. So why ohh why do folk think they have found a bargain and then just send some crook in a suit money by a bank transfer. Hey presto and, just like a magician, the scammer, concert ticket and holiday accommodation has disappeared. Stick to the reputable sites and if you do think you have a found a bargain, and it really is too good to be true, the acid test is in the payment route.

The warning bells have a range of sounds. They range from a non-bank transfer overseas (the alarm bells are sounding so loudly we can't sleep) to a bank transfer (still not good and a very uncomfortable night's sleep- it's the … *"I can't take credit card payments at the moment so would you mind just doing a bank transfer"* maybe adding that dose of pressure like *"I've had a lot of interest in this …"*). You can only really settle down when they take a credit card payment and it is over the value of £100 (great, a good night's sleep). This is because the credit provider is equally liable if something goes wrong and more is set out in the Section 75 'magic wand' paragraphs above within this Chapter.

Solicitor and invoice scams

Your bank, solicitor or other trusted professional will email you to finalise payment of a transaction you currently have in progress. You diligently follow their instructions but end up being scammed and losing it all – perhaps a six-figure sum if it was a house deposit. So how did that happen? It's the world of the internet and hackers and someone, somewhere in the world identified your transaction was in progress and the parties involved. They simply created bogus emails drawing on the bank, solicitor or other professionals publicly accessible information. Then with a bit of clever graphic design and amending their real email so that it somehow displays in your email account as having come from the bank, solicitor or other professional you're ready to be hooked. In some cases the individual's account has been hacked so it comes from their genuine account. You duly make the payment. Unfortunately, the scammer has set up bank accounts in the UK with false ID and the payment is cleared out and 'gone' before anyone has worked out what has really happened.

A variant is a scammer impersonating a regular supplier (to you individually or to your business) stating that they had changed their bank details and requesting the recipient amend their records.

To counter these attacks ensure your anti-virus software is up to date, use extra secure passwords (see below for more on this) and, on emailed bank details, call the firm and secure confirmation from a known person and then send a test £1 transfer to confirm it gets through.

Click bait and other 'hooks'

The ingenuity and creativity of email and phone scammers is reaching new heights. Someone somewhere has gathered thousands of email addresses and mobile phone numbers, including yours, and mass-mails them with a piece of information – designed with only one purpose in mind. That purpose is to gain your attention and engagement and a 'click' on their planted dodgy button/link etc. All have one purpose and one purpose only and that is to get you to 'click on a link' hence the term **'click bait'**. The same applies to pop ups and adverts you may see on your phone. Here the scammers know your browsing habits and lure you with a fake advert whilst you are browsing a site or an app. The site you are taken to may be fake even though it has been designed very professionally and looks like it is representing your cherished brand or interest. You are lured with an offer, click, enter your bank details and the rest, as they say, is history. Unfortunately, the reality is that the message you received, or saw has been built by scammers and they want to steal your money.

Top tip

Never, never, never click on any links from strange email accounts, or offers you see whilst you are browsing on your phone unless you are sure it is the real thing. If in doubt check it out with the organisation directly – hover over the displayed email address to show the actual email account the scammer. 'If in doubt, stay out'. On websites check the padlock sign by the website address (secure site) and you will be safer and only pay by credit card for Section 75 'magic wand' protection.

If it is a UK business they must clearly show the company or business operating the website (usually in the 'contact us' or 'about us' section), which you can then check out. If it is a company and it is not a high-street name check out the company at Companies House as suggested in the 'thank you I will just check with' section above – the service is free. Again, the watchwords here are *'If in doubt, stay out'* and back to the headline quotation *'A fool and his money are soon parted'*.

The surprise prize-ballot win

This one has faded away in recent years but like all good scams will return so it's worth a paragraph. There is usually a premium-rate telephone number to call in order to claim the prize or a fairly small-value payment to make but at the end of the day, and after much excitement, the ultimate actual prize is probably worthless or trivial. File anything like this under 'B' for bin. This is how it works: there will be a few flashy big prizes (always something eye-catching to get you excited) and then other prizes for which there may be 5,000 or more 'winners' and will probably take you more than £10 in phone or other 'processing' charges to 'win'. Your chances of winning are remote and cunningly the scammers do not state the odds of actually winning. Watch out for words such as 'your assigned numbers could match', which means you may not have won anything at all and what you have is just a chance to enter some sort of ballot. The scammers rely on you getting distracted by the official-looking website/ social media post or paperwork and the mention of prizes - the equivalent of the magician's smoke and mirror distractions mentioned earlier. As a final deterrent, if you are foolish enough to reply to something you didn't enter in the first place you are likely to be put on a 'suckers list' (the term the scammers use) and will be bombarded by even more junk ballots and scams.

Credit and bank card cloning or snatching

Again, this one is reducing as the banks have improved their technology at cash dispensers to stop cloning devices being attached. But how about the scammer who calls you and pretends to be from the police, explaining they have just arrested someone who 'apparently' was caught with a clone of your card? They arrange for a courier to call and collect your actual card as part of their investigations. Unfortunately, it is all just another scam and the supposed police officer is just another scammer. These guys really do have guts but the bottom line is never, ever, be worried about feeling made to look silly.

Top tip
Don't be worried about being made to look silly and just act confused; ask them to write down exactly what they want so you can show it to your daughter/neighbour etc. If they won't and they tell you it's a secret then they are a scammer and are lying.

Advance fee fraud

This is one of the scammers' favourites and has been dressed up in a hundred different guises. The scam is remarkably simple. A payment is made by you with the promise of a bigger payout in return. Perhaps it is cloaked in terms of funds left to you by a mystery relative or a prize you are entitled to and where you pay a processing fee of £50. The routine follows a route where next you are asked to pay another release fee of £150 and on it goes with a promise of £10,000 sucking you in (which, of course, you will never actually receive). Walk away.

Doorstep scams

National Trading Standards tell us that 85 per cent of victims of doorstep scams are aged 65 or over. These scams follow a regular routine. A knock on the door and a stranger. There is a request. Can I use the phone as it is an emergency? I noticed a broken window/broken roof tile/there is a gas leak or water leak etc. Once inside the crook will distract you whilst their sidekick steals something, or else they provide some emergency service and then overcharge you. Remember you don't have to answer the door and always use a door chain and fit a spy hole on solid doors. Trust your instincts, ask for ID and if unsure ask them to return at a later time when someone will be with you. Again, this is where 'nosy neighbours' are brilliant so look out for each other.

Romance, dating fraud and sextortion- tinder swindlers

The new lover, or someone showing you interest, gives you attention you crave just when you may need it (maybe you are at a low point – remember, these scammers are clever crooks in suits- they even have a name in these current times 'the tinder swindlers'). After a while the sob stories start – maybe money for a sick mother or child. Scammers know how to manipulate you to get the response they want. They usually want you to keep things 'secret' as they know that any friend you confide in will tell you to run a mile. Sadly, emotional involvement and shame prevent some people from acting rationally – and the scammers know this. Charming chat, sleight of hand and, just like a magician, your money is gone before you know it. A more extreme version is sextortion where blackmailers (organised crime, sometimes using entrapment) believe they have information on you which they threaten to disclose to compromise you. They want cash or a favour in return.

> **Top tip**
> **Romance scams – trust your instincts when you smell a rat. Be brave and confide in someone you really trust and call in the Police. The Police have specialist teams to deal with organised crime-based blackmail.**

Call in the police

If you spot a scam or have been scammed, report it and get help. Contact the Police Action Fraud contact centre on 0300 123 2040 or online at www.actionfraud.police.uk, or contact the police in your area. If a crime is in progress or about to happen, the suspect is known or can be easily identified, or the crime involves a vulnerable victim, then dial 999 if it is an emergency or 101 if it isn't.

For more information, take a look at the Police guidance the *Little Book of Big Scams*: visit www.met.police.uk and go to 'The Little Book of Big Scams' – I think it is an absolutely top piece of work.

BBC's Rip Off Britain 'Top Tips'

The team at BBC's Rip Off Britain do a great job on championing consumer rights. Their website is at bbc.co.uk and then search Rip Off Britain and I'd recommend reviewing the 'top tips' section of their website. The tips currently (December 2024) include:

How to avoid fraud on social media

Avoid the pitfalls when buying from overseas

How to spot fake reviews

Real email or fake email

How to handle a run in with your builder

Simon Calder's staycation scam watch

> **Top tip**
> I'd recommend reviewing the Met Police's 'The little book of Big Scams' and adding a review of the BBC Rip Off Britain 'top tips' on their website as a follow up action point at Chapter 13?

Keeping safe from telephone cold calls and online fraud

Cold callers on the telephone can be irritating at best and sometimes downright scary. They may not take 'no' for an answer. The way these calls are intruding into our life is becoming a real problem. The Telephone Preference Service (TPS) is a free service. It is the official central opt-out register on which you can record your preference not to receive unsolicited sales or marketing calls. It is a legal requirement that all organisations (including charities, voluntary organisations and political parties) do not make such calls to numbers registered on the TPS unless they have your consent to do so. More at tpsonline.org.uk.

Premium rate phone call scams

A recorded phone message, text message, email or even a missed parcel note or debt collector note through the door (clever eh!) asks you to call a phone number (and then insert some words that lure you... take your pick - a threat (debt collector), a prize, free holiday, free meal, free shopping voucher, missed parcel etc.). Use who-called.co.uk to check out their number as this is used to log suspicious activity and can give you some decent intelligence. Remember the scammers are clever and they sometimes leave partial messages on your phone to lure you into being intrigued and you then call their premium rate number.

Anti-virus software

Keep your anti-virus software up to date. There are free options such as AVG free (www.avg.com). For free online security advice, visit www.getsafeonline.org.

Have a backup

What happens if your laptop/other device is stolen or you get hacked and your data is stolen and then wiped. Take a secure back up on devices such as Apple's iCloud or external hard drives or a USB flash drive.

Review and change you social media profile settings

We expose a massive amount of personal information on social media without locking out the bad boys and girls. Ensure your privacy settings are as you would want - usually friends only. Don't overlook this in Chapter 13, Your Plan, especially if you are about to post photos online showing you are thousands of miles from your home on holiday.

Pay securely

Pay securely using a credit card for the section 75 magic wand protection I outlined earlier in this chapter. When you pay, look for the closed padlock in the web address bar which means your connection is secure.

The worst passwords

This almost beggars belief, but PCmag.com reports the worst passwords in 2024, and the worst and most-used nightmare passwords include; 123456, 123456789, qwerty1 and, yes, you've guessed it 'password'. Your password should be, where allowed, at least 12 digits long, contain a mix of upper- and lower-case letters, numbers and a character. The National Cyber Security Centre recommends that you use three random words passwords on the especially important email account security.

Top tip
The easiest way to spot that you've been scammed is to know your finances inside out. Watching what goes in and out of your bank and credit cards will show up a problem quickly.

Top tip
Trust your instincts. If something doesn't feel right it's probably because it isn't. Walk away.

Useful reading

Martin Lewis's website, www.moneysavingexpert.com

There are many useful template letters and advice for complainants at www.citizensadvice.org.uk or give them a call on 03454 040506.

The Little Book of Big Scams, published by the Metropolitan Police Service at www.met.police.uk – go to 'The Little Book of Big Scams'.

BBC's *Rip Off Britain* – go to www.bbc.co.uk, search for 'Rip Off Britain'

For free online security advice visit www.getsafeonline.org.

Citizens Advice: www.citizensadvice.org.uk and their 'scams' section.

Reminder: Take any action points or follow up points to Chapter 13, Your Plan For A Better Retirement

Chapter Eight

Starting your own business

"Screw it – let's do it!"

Sir Richard Branson

Running a business can carry additional risk and if things go badly wrong you could, at worst, lose your home as I saw when working in Corporate Recovery and Insolvency in the deep brutal recession of 1989 to 1993. But, on the other hand, it can be immensely rewarding. Maybe it's just the opportunity to earn £1,000 per annum tax free to supplement your pension income or to push on with a business or consultancy type idea (using all your experience) to bring in much more significant money. I've seen all sorts of businesses start up and thrive through my day to day work in my Chartered Accountancy and Tax practice. I'd add that starting a business can also keep you active, mentally fit plus earning and occupied for years to come and beyond your intended retirement date. You've nailed it if you do something you love and enjoy. This chapter marks the start of the 'earn more' sections of Retirement Planning Expert 2025.

You've nailed it if you do something you love and enjoy

More and more people are setting up their own business and becoming their own boss for reasons of personal freedom, supplementing their pension or leveraging a hobby they have always enjoyed and which can make some money. It's been a rising trend in recent years which has been propelled by the **'re-set'** many of us have encountered since the lock-downs of the Covid-19 pandemic years. The two more frequent reasons I've encountered in my accountancy practice are folk just want to do more of what they enjoy and try and make a bit of income from it <u>or</u> they have a burning ambition to take their business skills (honed over many decades) forward in their own way and maybe also escape the corporate jungle with its shackles of set employment days and limited holiday leave. Remember the core of this book is based around the four essential steps to achieving a better retirement: plan more, save more, earn more and live better. We're now into **'earn more'**.

If you have dived straight into this chapter looking to find your first piece of inspiration the biggest message of reassurance is, simply, you are not alone. According to the Department for Business and Trade there were 5.5 million private-sector businesses at the start of 2024. You are not alone as 4.1 million of businesses did not employ anyone aside from the owner(s). 3.1 million trade as sole proprietorships (sometimes called the self-employed), 1.1 million trade as companies and 0.4 per cent are partnerships. These terms are explained in more detail in this chapter to help you decide which could be right for you. But for now the main message is that one or two person businesses are the absolute back-bone of the UK economy. Even better there is plenty of help out there and this chapter will signpost you to free help and support (it is just a matter of knowing where to look to find the quality material!). This chapter goes to the heart of this book as prosperity is not just about material wealth it's also about what we get out of everyday life through the social and emotional benefits. It may also be a route to escaping corporate structures when there is still time to learn a new trick or two and, therefore, could be another option to help you save more / earn better in this section of the book.

Importantly, this chapter is only a guide and it is neither legal nor financial advice; it is no substitute for taking professional advice from a financial adviser or other professional adviser. Any potential UK tax advantages may be subject to change (and the 2025/26 budget remains subject to Parliamentary review and then Royal Assent in 2025). There may also be changes following another budget and your own choices will depend upon your individual circumstances and individual professional advice should be obtained. The information outlined in this chapter may, however, assist you in understanding some of the issues you may face and the terminology which will help you in planning for and achieving a better retirement.

This chapter at a glance

This chapter will give you the confidence to get started and provide plenty of straightforward advice. The key issues covered are:

- A one page quick-start guide (you can get going today if you want!).
- Understanding the differences between starting a small business and employment, especially if both options are still open to you.
- Help with the question: 'Do I really need to bother with a business plan?'
- Administration, finance and tax – keeping on top of the paperwork.
- Filling the diary with work, and tips for marketing that will make a difference.
- The trading format and understanding personal risk – should you set up your own limited liability company, work as a sole trader or maybe go into partnership?
- Other ways of getting started and some operational issues.
- Where you can go for further help – remember you are not alone!
- A summary checklist to help you get started in business.

How to start a small business today in 1 page

This one page will get you on the way to starting a small business:

- Find something you enjoy doing that you know you can sell.
- Grab all the free help you can from your local enterprise partnership or equivalent (signposts are in this book).
- If you have a trading income of more than £1,000 register as self-employed with Her Majesty's Revenue & Customs (HMRC) via www.gov.uk (then go to 'working for yourself'). Complete HMRC's self-assessment form each year and declare your business taxable income.
- Acquire some files or set up an electronic equivalent (with a back-up) and keep a list of your income and costs and all receipts. This helps 'prove' your business transactions and no ifs, no buts you must keep it for six years.

- The big lesson: HMRC don't like people evading tax (it is illegal!). If you can't prove your transactions then you will be charged the tax that HMRC believe they were due, plus a penalty of up to an extra 200 per cent plus interest.

- Think really carefully about risk – as a self-employed person your personal wealth is backing your business and anything that goes wrong. If you are worried about risk then investigate and take out appropriate insurance and don't start trading until this is in place. If risk is potentially significant don't trade as self-employed but do look into the benefits of having a limited company (more in this chapter and the clue is in the name 'limited').

- Take a deep breath and start living your new business. Involve yourself with other people who run their own businesses and listen and learn from them. Join the best business club or organisation that you can find; a Federation of Small Business membership should be on your short list but listen to other recommendations from other business owners who you know and respect.

- Make sure that you can sell your product or service for more than it costs – do the numbers and remember to think about marketing, packaging and transport costs/postage and then 'administration/office costs'. To help your business grow further just jump to the marketing section in this chapter. The tips should take you to the next level and, in time, you may benefit from delving into even more of this chapter and its hints and tips.

The secret ingredients

Over the last 30 years I've seen one great big secret ingredient for starting your own business and potentially bringing in a vital extra income. It's actually quite simple: it is the 'belief/can do' and positive attitude of the business owner. They have the ability to press on with their ambition and actually deliver on the goal they have set themselves. Forget the all-talk no-action folk here – they tend to flounder.

The more successful individuals are those that involve others and are good at identifying and listening to those who can help. Unsurprisingly, the folk who can help most (in my view) are usually those who have experience of running their own successful businesses. After that you have the professional advisers the business person surrounds themselves with (their accountant, commercial solicitor, business orientated financial adviser and any 'free' adviser help via their local authority- free is usually good!).

The successful business start-ups quickly recognise, at the end of the day, that it's 100% down to them and get on with it using some form of a plan. As one client once said to me in the initial weeks of starting up- "I get it, the buck stops with me!" and I answered 'yes- you've got it'. The businesses that falter seem to do the opposite of all the positives I've mentioned above and never quite reach their potential. There are then three other secret ingredients, as follows:

Understanding and accepting the differences between starting a small business and employment

In some cases where there is an opportunity to start a small business there could be a similar opportunity to take a full- or part-time employed position. Make sure you are content with the route you are going down and that it's the right route for you?

Here are some of the main reasons for starting a small business:

- focusing on what you are best at or enjoy;
- being your own boss and therefore benefiting from very rapid decision making;
- flexibility (around other interests/responsibilities);
- freedom to organise things your way;
- no commuting;
- less involvement in internal politics and no more attending meetings that you have started to believe were becoming a bit pointless;
- being able to work on your own;
- developing a unique idea or delivering a better solution/product;
- providing a legacy for your children to pass on to them to run or sell tax efficiently creating a 'windfall';
- the more you put in, the more you get out.

On the other hand, here are some of the reasons for seeking a part- or full-time employed position:

- having a local employer with known travel requirements;

- security of income and extra 'free' money (via pensions or employee share schemes);
- benefits of holiday pay, pension, paid sick leave, and perhaps private health and life cover;
- flexible working policies such as part-time work, hours based around child-care or the provision of career breaks:
- bonuses;
- having a team and the friendship of colleagues;
- no personal liability if things go badly wrong;
- staff discounts or other perks.

Having a decent written business plan

There are thousands of success stories about those who took the plunge to build a business that provided involvement, enjoyment and a new or extra income. However, for every three success stories there is a business that does not work out and your money could disappear fast if you set up in the wrong way or overstretch yourself. Worst of all, you could lose your home if things go badly wrong. So, yes, you need some form of a plan and the information below and tips throughout this chapter should help you plan and also help you understand and deal with the risks.

Learning from history on why businesses fail

Businesses can fail for many reasons. Learn from the mistakes of others. From my experience working in Corporate Recovery and Insolvency in the 1989 to 1993 recession I see many factors that remain the same today. We were battered for two years and the government funded vast parts of the economy through the Covid-19 pandemic either directly into the health service or via business help and support. The massive national debt now needs to be repaid at the same time and the economy growth we need appears to be stumbling. We also need to be really watchful of the impact of borrowing in an era of higher interest rates.

The other lessons have remained much as they have done over the last thirty years. The first one is simply that *the market dries up or moves on and you are left behind.* Just look at fashion and related retail industry where many of the big traditional stores finally toppled (Laura Ashley, Debenhams) as they just could not complete with the more agile new entrants. The basic of reacting to difficult business times remains the same as in 1989 to 1993 - take time out to think and keep abreast of what your customers really want (have you tried asking them?). Then where are your competitors and what are they doing to keep on top of or ahead of the market and, overall, how is the market moving?

A second reason, and one that will continue to increase, is the *failure to deal with tax affairs properly*. The implications of penalties and interest levied by HMRC are often ignored and only hit home when it is too late. Keep your books properly and retain all records for six years after the year end – in brief, if you can't prove it, you may lose the tax benefit and pay additional tax, penalties and interest. If there is a problem, HMRC can go back and inspect previous years' accounts (for up to six years or even longer). If, ultimately, you fail to pay your tax fully when it is due, HMRC will pursue you vigorously and you are giving them a reason to have a closer look at you and your business. On the other hand, if you have genuine cash flow difficulties and cannot pay your tax on the due date, talk to HMRC and you may find their attitude refreshing (especially if it is your first time of asking).

Other reasons include a failure to plan and also bad debts – if a customer goes bust and cannot pay your invoices, this will come off your bottom-line profit and can really hurt. There are a few simple steps that you can take to reduce the potential of taking such a hit. What are your credit terms and have you encouraged all customers to pay electronically and promptly? Do you contact them as soon as your invoices become overdue? Require cash on delivery or prepayment if there are some worrying signs emerging and do trust your instincts here. PayPal and mobile credit card machines are transforming payment services. In some cases it is worth remembering that a bad customer is sometimes worse than no customer at all.

In today's environment and if struggling financially it is also about doing *a top down cost review* based on your expenditure pattern- do you absolutely need to spend the money? Is there a better or cheaper option and talk things with your accountant and any advisers. Let's return to the question: 'Do I really need to bother with a business plan?' The answer is usually 'yes', even if it is just one or two pages, as you are improving your chances of succeeding and may even do rather better than you first thought.

What goes into a business plan?

'*I have always found that plans are useless but planning is indispensable.*' This is a quote from General Eisenhower and is about planning for battle. Pause and take in the wise words 'planning is indispensable', as too many people run a mile when the subject of a business plan comes up. Or, armed with confidence gained from a book on setting up a business, you may start a plan but never get it finished. The reason for this 'block' is usually fear of the planning process or feeling intimidated by daunting business plan templates and spreadsheets seen in some books or banking literature.

So try this. If you want to travel somewhere you use a map. In business it's just the same except you get yourself a *plan*. Do write it down and don't expect to get it right first time (no one does!). A few pages are fine to start with based on objectives, your market research and a budget for the year (accountants call this a profit-and-loss forecast). Review it with your accountant and/or a trusted friend who runs a business, then build it up.

Top tip
Have some sort of thought-out plan when you start and keep refreshing it. With experience you can tweak it and make it that bit slicker but you must put it down in writing.

Stage 1 of the plan: Objectives

What, financially, do you need to set as objectives to bring you in that £2,000 or £20,000 or £60,000 you need to help reach and attain the lifestyle you desire? This takes a bit of thinking through but you should be able to come up with two or three simple objectives based on income, gross profit (if you sell stock) and overheads.

As an example for someone who sells advice-based services and who does not sell stock it's easy and you only need two objectives.

Objective 1: I aim to invoice £30,000 in my first year of trading based on working at least 100 days at an average billing rate of £300 per day. I will review my billing rates quarterly and my performance monthly.

Objective 2: I aim to keep my overheads (after expenses recharged to clients) in my first year to £5,000.

Then, for the more complicated businesses, for example one that trades in buying and selling stock, you will need a further objective based around the difference between sales price and purchase price.

Objective 3 will be something like: I aim to achieve the following gross profit percentages:

- product line A: 30 per cent;
- product line B: 40 per cent;
- product line C: 50 per cent;
- gross profit percentages are calculated using (sales price less cost of materials/product sold ÷ sales price) × 100.

The key point with objectives is that less gives more: you don't want a long list of objectives and try and ensure each objective is Specific, Measurable, Achievable, Realistic and Timed (or S.M.A.R.T) and you will improve your chances of success.

Stage 2 of the plan: Your market research

The next page of your plan should be all about your marketing effort: this is a topic that is often misunderstood and mistaken for advertising. Think about approaching this section under the following three headings: products, customers and competitors.

Products/ Services

Start with your main product or service and think about the features and benefits of what you are selling. Understanding these and discussing them with your trusted advisers will allow you to start thinking about other related services or goods that you could offer.

Top tip

What is your unique selling point ('USP') that sets you or your products aside from others. If you are not sure ask others as it will help you underline the point in all that follows.

Customers

For each main product area ask lots of questions to tease out your research. Who are my customers? Where are they based? When do they tend to buy? How and where do they tend to buy and at what price? How should I contact them? Keep asking those important questions of who, what, why, where, when and how – they tease out all sorts of quality research information that you can action.

Competitors

Again, ask yourself who, what, why, where, when and how? This should lead to a series of activities that you can do to help secure new quality work and customers (note that the marketing section later on in this chapter has further tips). If you end up with a jumble of unfocused ideas try ranking each idea on the basis of priority, impact and cost (free is good!).

Stage 3 of the plan: Your income and expenditure forecast

This third stage is the tricky one but hang in there as it is worth pushing your plan to include this: your income and expenditure forecast for the year. It is your financial map and will allow you to check your actual performance against the plan. You can then do something about it when you are off target. You should be able to do this yourself, but if it becomes a struggle ask your accountant or a friend who has their own business to help.

Is there more?

Once you have completed your first plan keep it alive and keep reviewing how you are doing against it and you should find that the planning process itself teases out things that will make things that little bit better – guaranteed! Initially I would recommend at least a quarterly review.

Practical and emotional tips

Your partner's attitude is crucial. Even if not directly involved, he or she may have to accept (at least initially) the loss of some space in the house to give you an office. Do you have space available to work from home initially? Or as an alternative would you need/prefer to rent accommodation? The rental market has transformed in the last decade with many 'serviced' office providers opening up and renting out space by the hour, day or month on flexible and economic rents. These offices can be great places to meet and network with like-minded small business owners. If you are selling products or crafts google for craft and market events and try negotiating on a first attendance rate so you can try it out as attendances, site pitch and quality can vary.

If you work from home will you need to spend a bit of time managing the expectations of neighbours and/or friends about your new life and 'work hours'?

There will be the added distractions of out-of-hours phone calls and, perhaps, suddenly cancelled social engagements, depending on your business. Can your family/partner cope or help?

Can you cope without the resources/back-up provided by an employer (IT/HR/training/marketing/legal and/or administrative support)? You will have to do it yourself or buy it in at a cost (a potential overhead cost for your business plan).

Running a small business means developing new networks and the network that provides vital practical and emotional support is other like-minded individuals that run their own business, so join the best trade or professional association you can find (there are some listed further on in this chapter).

Keep on top of the paperwork/accounts

Generally, this one topic causes the most groans! But simple bookkeeping, if done properly, is just a by-product of your business and flows naturally from raising sales invoices or receipts to tracking income and tracking what you pay for, when and how. As a bonus, you will never miss an unpaid sales invoice if you are on top of your bookkeeping.

An even more compelling reason for doing your own bookkeeping is the HMRC 'prove it or lose it' viewpoint when enquiring into an aspect of your tax return. Under the system of self-assessment, HMRC relies on you completing your tax returns. In the case of an enquiry, HMRC tells you precisely what part of your tax return is under investigation and you are expected to be able to validate sample payments or receipts. If you are unable to prove the expenditure, you lose it as far as HMRC is concerned, resulting in, for example, fewer purchases being accepted as a deduction from your profits and more tax to pay. There will be penalties and interest to pay and the scope of HMRC's enquiries will be widened, which means more time, distraction from your business and, probably, stress.

Basic bookkeeping

All incoming and outgoing payments need to be recorded throughout the year. Records of outgoings need to be categorised according to type, and examples of some categories you might need to consider are stock, subscriptions/meeting fees, office equipment, office supplies, post and courier costs, travel fares, parking and subsistence, telephone and internet, sundry, accountancy and professional fees, and insurance.

Many small business owners opt to do their own bookkeeping, with or without the help of computer software. If you opt for software choose one that your accountant understands as their fees should be lower. For many small businesses your accountant should be able to provide some Excel spreadsheets that will do the job, together with a bookkeeping guide to help get you started.

If you are really averse to bookkeeping yourself, consider hiring a bookkeeper. Bookkeepers currently charge between about £17 and £28 per hour, depending on geographical location and experience, and can be found by recommendation from your accountant or business network contacts.

Finding a good accountant

Depending on qualifications and experience, accountants can charge from £35 to £120+ per hour (plus vat) to assist you in setting up in business and to prepare your accounts and tax. But as anyone can call themselves an accountant it can be a bit hit and miss, with very variable quality when things go wrong. Unreturned calls and not dealing factually with enquiries and questions, vague verbal assurances, and not dealing with formal complaints are all part of the 'deal' when you choose wrongly. If there are mistakes in your accounts and tax you will also find that you are very much on your own when it comes to dealing with HMRC enquiries.

> **Top tip**
>
> **Don't end up with the wrong accountant. What should you look for? The letters ACA or FCA, ACCA, CIMA after the accountant's name mean that you can be assured that you are dealing with a highly qualified accountant used to commerce but the key is that qualifications, professional indemnity held, any regulating body and complaints procedures should all be set out in writing for you at the start and before you sign up. If not, start shopping around.**

Some accountancy firms offer a combination of bookkeeping, accountancy and tax services and, if so, you can expect to pay a premium on the bookkeeping hourly rates quoted above.

So how can I find a good accountant? Ask your trusted family members or friends if they can recommend one. Then ensure you get clarity on four things:

1) confirmation of the accountant's qualifications (the type of qualifications);

2) the professional body you would complain to if there is ever a problem;

3) confirmation that they hold professional indemnity insurance; and

4) confirmation that they know and understand your business area.

It is advisable to meet at least two accountants and, importantly, see how you feel about rapport and the availability of proactive hints and tips. Make sure you believe you can get on with the accountant you select as it is likely to be a long and mutually beneficial relationship. Ask if the person you meet will be the person who does your accounts and tax and whether they will provide proactive advice. Get written confirmation of hourly rates plus an estimate of fees for the year and get clarity on what happens if you decide to change accountants halfway through the year if fees are paid up front or monthly. Most accountants should be used to providing clients with a 'retainer', clarifying the above and what you and the accountant will do and by when. Best of all is a good accountant who knows your industry area as they will be able to help with general guidance and offer input to your plan on marketing and pricing, drawing on experience beyond accounting and tax.

Finally, there is sometimes some confusion over the term 'audit of accounts'. Many years ago, smallish companies in the UK had to have an audit of their accounts. The turnover threshold (one of three thresholds) for being required to have an audit has been increased and currently stands at £10.2 million, so the vast majority of start-ups need not concern themselves with audited accounts.

Taxes and National Insurance

There are quite significant differences in the taxes you will pay if you run a small business so consider this before getting started.

Sole traders

Self-employed individuals running their own businesses are usually called 'sole traders'. Nearly all new small businesses that trade as sole traders need to register as self-employed via www.gov.uk (then go to 'working for yourself').

First the good news if you just want to earn an extra £1,000 by doing odd-jobs or gardens in the warmer months to help pay for a holiday. From 1 April 2017 HMRC introduced a 'trading allowance' for individuals with trading income and you can keep the money and don't have to tell HMRC providing the total income (before costs) is £1,000 or less.

If your trading income is above £1,000 you must register for self-assessment with HMRC and complete a self-assessment tax form and submit this to HMRC each year (www.gov.uk and search 'register for self-assessment'). However, if turnover is above £1,000 then you can claim partial relief. You can choose to either deduct the actual trading expenses from income the usual way or elect to use the £1,000 allowance as a deduction from income. If you claim partial relief you cannot deduct any other expenses, just the £1,000 allowance.

While tax can be daunting, some sole traders with relatively straightforward billing and overheads do their own self-assessment and pay Income Tax on their profits. With Income Tax, you first have a Personal Allowance, which gives you a tax-free amount, and then any excess income (including your profits) is taxed at 20 per cent, then over a certain limit at 40 per cent and then 45 per cent. In very broad terms you currently (December 2024) have a tax-free allowance of £12,570 which is remaining fixed up to April 2028 (this may change following any new budget).

You are then taxed on the *next* £37,500 at 20 per cent so an individual will be able to earn £50,270 before having to pay tax at 40 per cent (i.e. £12,570 Personal Allowance at 0 per cent tax and then £37,500 at 20 per cent). Then 40 per cent tax applies to further taxable income up to £125,140. Anything above £125,140 gets taxed at 45 per cent. The rates are different in Scotland (see the **Chapter 5, Tax**).

Many sole traders choose to run their bookkeeping for the year to 5 April to coincide with the tax year end (or 31 March, which HMRC effectively accepts as equivalent to 5 April).

If you are past the state retirement age there will be no National Insurance Contributions (NICs) to pay. Sole traders are liable for Class 2 NICs of £3.45 per week 2024/25 rising to £3.50 2025/26. You are also liable for the much more significant Class 4 NICs that are assessed and collected by HMRC at the same time as assessing your Income Tax on profits at 6% between £12,570 and £50,270 reducing to just 2 per cent on profits over £50,270.

The payment of sole-trader Income Tax is reasonably straightforward but there is a twist in your first year of trading. Assuming that you have a year end of 5 April 2025, the first payment will be due by 31 January 2026 so you have a long period of (effectively) interest-free credit, as some of the profits on which the tax is due may have been earned as long ago as May 2024. With the first payment, however, you get a 'double whammy' as you also have to pay on 31 January 2026 a payment on account of your second year's trading. Then on 31 July 2026 you have to make a second on-account payment of the second year's trading. Both on-account payments are set by default on the basis of your year 1 profits. Under-estimate this cash flow impact at your peril as it can hit hard if you don't 'get it'. You can 'claim' a reduction if year 2 is proving to have lower profits than year 1; your accountant will help you with this if it is appropriate.

After the initial tax famine, followed by (effectively) a double payment of tax, you will thereafter pay tax twice a year. Payments need to be made by 31 January (during the tax year) and then by 31 July after the end of that tax year, with any overpayment or underpayment sorted out by the following 31 January.

Top tip

Many sole-trader businesses set up a reserve bank account in addition to their current account, and place a percentage of their income aside, which is earning interest each month. This tactic should help you resist the temptation to raid money that is not for spending – and

ensure you can pay your tax on time.

Additionally, as a self-employed person you are allowed certain other reliefs. Ask your accountant or check the HMRC website and 'expenses I can claim', but the following expenses and allowances are usually tax deductible:

- *Business expenses*: These must be incurred 'wholly and exclusively' for the purposes of the trade. Office supplies that you buy will probably qualify; however, any business entertaining will not.

- *Partially allowable expenses*: These mainly apply if you are working from home. They include such items as the part of your rent (or mortgage interest), heating, lighting and telephone usage that you devote to business purposes, and also possibly some of the running expenses on your car, if you use your car for your business.

- *Spouse/partner's wages*: If you employ your spouse/partner in the business, his or her pay (provided this is reasonable) will usually qualify as a legitimate expense, in the same way as any other employee's, but must be accounted for through a PAYE system.

- *Pension contributions*: Tax relief is generally available for pension contributions at the higher of £3,600 (gross) or 100 per cent of relevant earnings up to a maximum of £60,000 (this is subject to a tapered reduction for taxpayers with 'adjusted income' in excess of £260,000). You can go above the £60,000 'maximum' if you have not used the £60,000 maximum in the previous two years and a reduced £40,000 in the third year back. You should take professional advice if there is the potential to make very significant pension contributions and obtain the associated tax reliefs as there are both opportunities and risks with pensions and much more is set out in **Chapter 3, Pensions.**

- *Capital allowances*: This is a tax break for expenditure on equipment.

Making Tax Digital is a major change for the £3.1 million self-employed tax payers and a relatively new term for some self-employed. It is the term HMRC use for bringing in onerous new record keeping and digital reporting standards for landlords and the self-employed. So far it has been applied to vat reporting. The implementation has been delayed as follows:

6 April 2026 if you have an annual business <u>or</u> property income of more than £50,000

6 April 2027 if you have an annual business or property income of more than £30,000

No decision has been made yet on businesses with an income below £30,000. Some businesses and agents are already keeping digital records and providing updates as part of a pilot. For more information go to .gov and 'making tax digital for income tax'. Making tax digital involves keeping digital records of accounts and sending summaries to HMRC every quarter in addition to filing your annual self-assessment return. The idea is that the information you supply will be used by HMRC to give you an estimate of tax due. In reality I this is an attempt by HMRC to gain more data from businesses so that they can assess if there is a tax gap (HMRC speak for potentially undeclared income and hence lost tax).

Partnerships

Partnership tax is broadly similar to the process described above for a sole traders, with the exception of there being some more paperwork due to submitting each partner's individual personal self-assessment tax return and a composite partnership tax return.

Limited company

Companies pay **corporation tax** on their profits (currently as of December 2024) at rates between 19% to 25% but most small one person companies will continue to pay tax at 19%. This is because a small profits rate (SPR) applies for companies with profits of £50,000 or less so that they will continue to pay Corporation Tax at 19%. Companies with profits between £50,000 and £250,000 will pay tax at the main rate reduced by a marginal relief providing a gradual increase in the effective Corporation Tax rate. If profits are above £250,000 the tax rate is 25%.

The key point with a company is that the money coming in is not your money – it is the company's money – so how do you extract your money? The first option is salary and this means running a **Pay As You Earn (PAYE)** system: another form of tax with a rigorous calculation regime and payments that have to be made to HMRC. PAYE carries the **Income Tax** rates as featured for the sole trader, but NICs (**National Insurance contributions**) are much higher as these are a composite of both employee *and* employer NICs (as the company is an employer). In 2024/25 these are 8% **employee**

NICs on a salary from £12,570 and £50,270 reducing to 2% for amounts above £50,270. Then there is an additional 13.8% in 2024/25 rising to 15% in 2025/26 **employer NICs** on all salary above £9,100 in 2024/25 and £5,000 in 2025/26. The 15% above £5,000 was announced in the October 2024 budget and created shockwaves across the UK business population. There is help for many small businesses through a tax relief called the employment allowance but this relief does not apply to a one-person company. This seems unfair but, currently that's the way it is and it seems to drive many to look to a different route to profit extraction involving less salary and more dividends. Salary and employer's NICs are deductible when calculating corporation tax but dividends are not which complicates the scenario and doing the numbers.

The second option for extracting funds is **dividends** but, repeating for emphasis, these are <u>not</u> deductible when calculating your corporation tax. The tax is as follows:

- An annual dividend allowance which means £500 of dividends are tax-free.

- Then tax on dividends are 8.75% if the dividend falls in the basic rate tax band, 33.75% if it falls in the higher rate tax band (£50,270 to £125,140) and 39.35% if it falls in the additional rate tax band (£125,140 plus).

For some contracting or consultancy-type businesses that trade as companies there is a 'tax trap' for the unwary known as **HMRC regulation number 35 (IR35)**. HMRC is particularly interested in ex-employees setting up service companies that work exclusively for their former employer or for just a few clients (sometimes called 'personal service companies' to use an HMRC term). This is an extremely wide-ranging and difficult subject but, in very simplified terms, IR35 is to be avoided if at all possible; it only applies to companies (not sole traders). Most contractors/freelancers working on assignments with the public sector (or public-sector quasi-agencies) are likely to be caught by IR35.

There are many hints and tips and some urban myths about IR35, all of which are outside the scope of this guide. It is a big issue and one that you have first got to recognise and then, if potentially applicable, do something about. One of the key players in helping freelancers guide themselves through the minefield of IR35 is the **Association of Independent Professionals and the Self-Employed (IPSE) at www.ipse.co.uk.** This organisation, working in conjunction with a chartered accountant who understands IR35, is probably your next step if you are concerned. Briefly, if you fall foul of IR35, the tax inspector will seek to set aside the dividends you have paid and treat the dividend payment as if it were subject to PAYE and NICs (including employer NICs) and the tax advantage you thought you may have had could disappear.

Registering for VAT

Value Added Tax (VAT) was introduced in 1973 and it seems that many people have lost sight of the name of this tax and especially the word 'added'. You are adding a tax to your supplies, collecting it on behalf of HMRC and paying it over to HMRC. In effect you are an unpaid tax collector.

If your taxable turnover is likely to be more than £90,000 in a 12-month period you must register for VAT unless your supplies/services are outside the scope of VAT. Any expenses that you recharge to clients need to be included in the calculation of taxable turnover.

UK business clients are invariably registered for VAT so are not concerned about having VAT added to your invoice as they can reclaim it. For that reason, some businesses register for VAT before reaching the compulsory registration limit so that they can claim VAT on their purchases - it's like buying equipment, supplies and services for 20% off. If your turnover is less than the threshold, before voluntarily applying consider whether registration will really be of benefit to you; whether reclaiming the VAT paid on items needed for your business (such as office equipment) is worth the trouble of sending in VAT returns and keeping separate VAT records.

You can claim back VAT on pre-start/pre-registration expenditure incurred in setting up the business so keep those VAT receipts. If you elect for 'cash accounting' status, this means that VAT only becomes payable or reclaimable when invoices are actually paid. It avoids having to pay the VAT on your own sales invoices before slow-paying clients pay you, which creates cash-flow problems. One final positive note, if you do register for VAT it seems to give you added credibility with clients.

Making Tax Digital has been implemented by HMRC if you have a VAT registered business. This is a HMRC requirement to keep digital records and file your vat returns using compatible software and provides HMRC with more data about your business to assist you with record keeping and improve their oversight on your business. You can apply to be exempt from this requirement if you are digitally excluded and some other criteria. More at .gov and 'making tax digital for vat'.

VAT flat-rate scheme

HMRC introduced the flat-rate scheme in 2004, with the aim of simplifying record keeping for small businesses. This allows you to charge VAT to your clients at the standard rate of 20 per cent and to pay VAT as a percentage of your VAT-inclusive turnover (instead of having to work out the VAT payable on your sales less purchases).

You can apply to join the scheme if your taxable turnover (excluding VAT) will not be more than £150,000 in the next 12 months.

HMRC publishes a list of business categories from which you need to decide which best describes your business. A further bonus is that you can deduct 1 per cent from the flat rate that you use for your first year of VAT registration. As a tip, do not do anything without checking it out with your accountant as there are a few twists and turns that could make the VAT flat-rate scheme unsuitable, especially since the introduction of a new 'limited cost trader' category which many small businesses with low purchasing levels are forced to use.

Marketing

It is a sad fact that many new business owners believe that marketing simply means placing an advert in some well-known directory. This will achieve only a fraction of the sales of any comparable business with a decent grasp of marketing. So how can you generate sales for a new business? The following tips will get you started:

1. *Your own website and/or social media.* Business and the public rely heavily on the internet and a presence is usually vital either through a website and/or harnessing social media. Is there a vital domain name that you need to secure and register? If this one question alone fills you with fear the solutions are nearer than you think – just try asking friends and don't ignore help that is right in front of your nose: young friends or relatives who may know more than you. It is also worth checking out websites run by trade or professional associations that may allow you to register and set up a profile. You can set up profiles on various social media networking websites such as LinkedIn. Depending on your business, Linked-In, Facebook, Twitter, YouTube and Instagram can provide the benefits of building your online contacts and allow you to showcase your expertise in a certain area. Social media (very like networking, below) is about building relationships and trust with an ever-increasing contact list.

2. *Personal contacts and networking.* Once you decide to set up your own business, your personal contacts, ex-colleagues or other small business owners are a potential source of work. Too many small businesses forget that behind every contact there is another layer of potential contacts who are just one introduction away, so ignore this multiplier effect at your peril. In your first year you should be re-educating your contacts to think of you not as 'Jane

who used to work at IBM' but 'Jane who now runs her own business advising small businesses on their IT needs'. Do not be afraid to pick up the phone or send business cards explaining your new business and what you can offer. Joining the best trade or professional association you can find will be a great way of developing your business contact network, with the added bonus of research facilities, information and other fringe benefits.

3. *Discounts and offers*. These can be used to great effect during seasonal dips, introducing a new service or clearing old stock. Whether it is 20 per cent off, a buy-one-get-one-free offer or the numerous variations of this basic approach, there are three golden rules:

    —   always state the original or usual price (to show the value in the offer);

    —   always specify an expiry date;

    —   always explain that the offer is subject to availability.

4. *Flyers and business cards*. A response rate of 1 per cent to a flyer is considered fairly good, but with some clever thinking you can improve this. Have you targeted the flyer? A good example would be a wedding gown designer who neatly persuades a sought-after wedding location hotel to keep a flyer dispenser in their foyer. Are you able to include your professional or trade association logo on your flyer and business cards? Have you asked if this is possible? There are two sides to a flyer and business card – have you thought about putting information on the blank reverse side? Could this contain some useful tips or, perhaps, a special offer or discount? Anything that ensures the card or flyer is kept rather than dumped will help your business to edge ahead.

5. *Testimonials*. People buy on trust, and testimonials show prospective customers that you have done a good job and can be relied upon. Positive testimonials can be powerful and should never be underestimated.

6. *Agencies*. Agencies will be especially important for prospective consultants or contractors, as many recruitment agencies also place full- and part-time contracts (as opposed to employed positions). The contract market is growing and offers dynamic and fast-moving industries the opportunity to hire (and fire) swiftly. When marketing yourself through an agency the same rules apply as when marketing yourself to a potential employer. Good personal and written presentation will help the agency to sell you on to its clients – and it

is in their interest to find you work, given the fee they receive for placing you.

7.   *Advertising*. There are many options for advertising yourself and your business, such as website banners, and free and paid-for directory listings. Another approach could be 'free' advertising through a press release that you forward to local or trade press with an interesting story. A clever variant is advertising yourself and your skills by writing articles in professional or trade journals – what do you have that is new or novel or leading edge?

8.   *Sponsorship*. Another subset of advertising is sponsorship. The driving instructor who sponsored the playing shirts of the local under-17s football team is a great example of cost-effective and rather clever sponsorship.

9.   *Awards*. Business awards can offer new businesses an opportunity to make a splash in the local area, introduce you to other vibrant businesses, and there may even be a category for mature business owners newly starting up. These are often sponsored by local press and the Federation of Small Businesses (www.fsb.org.uk) where more information can be found.

Learn when to say 'no'

This is one of the hardest lessons to learn and comes with experience. The fear of losing a sale to a competitor, or the uncertainty of where the next piece of work or sale will come from if you reject this one, may induce you to overstretch or undercut yourself. If you continually face this dilemma the resulting stress means you may not survive in business for long. So learning how to say 'no' in a way that does not burn bridges is important.

Business alliances

Business alliances can work well and when you first start up in business all sorts of folk and businesses may approach you. You will quickly learn that some are all talk and no action or seem more interested in accessing your contact network than building a mutually beneficial longer-term business relationship. Lord Alan Sugar's words on what makes an entrepreneur, in his book *The Way I See It: Rants, revelations and rules for life* (Pan Macmillan 2011, website: www.panmacmillan.com) gives a clear and simple lesson on this: 'If you have partners, they have to bring something to the party.'

Trading formats

You need to choose a type of business format and each carries a different level of personal risk and a different level of bureaucracy. The following will help you decide which one is right for you.

Self-employed (also sole trader/sole proprietor)

A self-employed person is someone who works for him/herself, instead of an employer, and draws an income from their personally run business. If the profits from the work are accounted for on one person's tax return, that person is known as a sole trader. If the profits are shared between two or more people, it is a partnership (see below).

There is no clear definition of self-employment. Defining an employee, on the other hand, is slightly easier as it can be assumed that if Income Tax and NICs are deducted from an individual's salary before they are paid, then that individual is an employee.

Importantly, the business has no separate existence from the owner and, therefore, all debts of the business are debts of the owner, who is personally liable for all amounts owed by the business. This strikes fear into the hearts of many business owners. You only need to think of the number of business owners who go bust every time a recession comes around and lose their house. Should this be a worry?

First and foremost, you must consider the risk to you in any work that you do. Could it go wrong and could you be sued? Is that a realistic prospect or so remote that it does not even warrant thinking about? Or is it somewhere in the middle? Can insurance help? (More on insurance later.) Remember that such insurance is only as good as the disclosures you make and the levels of cover provided. At the end of the day you know your business, your customers and the work that you do, so the risk assessment can only be done by you.

How to start up as a sole trader

- You can start trading immediately.
- You can trade under virtually any name, subject to some restrictions that are mostly common sense, such as not suggesting something you are not (connection to government, royalty or international pre-eminence). A B Jones trading as Super Lawns, for example, is fine.

- The full name and address of the owner and any trading name must be disclosed on letters, orders and invoices.

- Register as self-employed by going to www.gov.uk and searching for 'working for yourself'.

Partnership

Two or more self-employed people who work together on a business and share the profits are trading in partnership. The profits from the work are accounted for on a partnership tax return and extracts from that partnership tax return are then copied into the partners' individual tax returns.

The business has no separate existence from the partners and, therefore, all debts of the business are debts of the partners, so they are personally liable for all amounts owed by the business. In addition, partners are jointly and severally liable for the debts of the business or, put more simply, the last person standing pays the lot. There is a saying that you need to trust your business partner better than your husband/wife/civil partner.

As with sole traders, the first consideration is the potential for business risk, since your personal wealth is backing the debts of the business. First and foremost, you must consider the risk to you in any work that you do and, given the 'joint and several liability' point explained above, the trust and faith you have in your business partner. Again, as with sole traders, can insurance help reduce the risk?

How to set up as a partnership

- You can start trading immediately.

- You can trade under virtually any name, subject to some restrictions that are mostly common sense, such as not suggesting something you are not (connection to government, royalty or international pre-eminence). As before, A B Jones and A B Smith trading as J & S Super Lawns is fine.

- You will need to consult a solicitor to assist with the preparation and signing of a partnership deed. The partnership deed is for your protection and is essential because it sets out the rules of the partnership including, for example, the profit or loss split between partners, what happens if one partner wishes to leave or you wish to admit a new partner.

- The full name and address of the partners and any trading name must be disclosed on letters, orders and invoices.

- Register the partnership with HMRC with form SA400 via www.gov.uk (then go to 'register a partnership for Self-Assessment').

Limited company

A limited liability company (often the shorthand of 'limited company' is used to describe this trading format) is a company whose liability is limited by shares and is the most common form of trading format. The benefit of the limited liability status should not be underestimated as it could, potentially, protect your personal wealth if the company goes bust. The company is owned by its shareholders and is run by directors who are appointed by the shareholders. This can be the one same person and indeed many companies in the UK are one person companies.

The shareholders are liable to contribute the amount remaining unpaid on the shares – usually zero, as most shares are issued fully paid up. The shareholders therefore achieve limited liability.

How to start up a limited company

- A company needs to be registered with Companies House and cannot trade until it is granted a Certificate of Incorporation. The registration process is quick and inexpensive using the Companies House web incorporation service (it currently costs £50 and is completed within 24 hours). Some people use a company formation agent (Google this term to find such an agent – there are plenty of them) and the process should cost less than £100.

- The company name needs to be approved by Companies House. No two companies can have the same name and approval is usually completed in a day. Names that suggest, for instance, an international aspect will require evidence to support the claim and certain names are prohibited unless there is a dispensation (for example 'Royal').

- You must appoint a director and this 'officer' of the company carries responsibilities that can incur penalties and/or a fine. The appointment of directors should therefore not be done lightly. The full range of responsibilities is set out in the Companies Act; further guidance is available from the Companies House section of www.gov.uk (go to 'running a limited company'). Some examples of responsibilities include the duty to maintain the financial records of the company, to prepare accounts, to retain the paperwork and to avoid conflicts of interest. Small businesses no longer need to have a separate company secretary but it can be useful to have another office-holder signatory and the risks associated with this position are relatively light. In addition, you will need to appoint a registered office, which is a designated address at which official notices and communications can be received. The company's main place of business is usually used as the registered office but you could also use the address of your accountant or solicitor (there may be a charge for this).

Top tip
A limited liability company costs just £50 to set up. It provides enormous protection in managing the risk to your personal wealth due to limited liability.

Alternative ways of getting started

Umbrella company

This isn't really running your own business but it is a quick and easy way to get work and earn without all the red tape and time involved in running your own business. The downside is there are less tax planning opportunities. It is worth some description here as it may be an option for you or come up in conversation. Essentially, it is a company that offers you a shelter (umbrella) from administration. You are employed through the umbrella company and the end firm that actually uses your services keeps you at arm's length. You don't accrue the usual employment rights that will be available to employed staff in that end firm. The umbrella company is very limited in its function - almost 'just' processing your payroll, deducting PAYE and national insurance and paying it over to HMRC and paying you the net salary. It can offer a win: win for both you and the end firm that uses your services. For example, for someone who wants flexibility and earnings – perhaps working ad hoc or a few days a week. It also offers firms that need staff a flexible labour pool that is easy to hire and fire as their only obligation is to pay the umbrella company a fee to cover your wages. The tricky bit is the administration charges levied by the umbrella company for running the payroll and who pays the employer's national insurance (which increases to 15% over £5,000 in

2025/26) and you'll want to check out how that works - possibly in deductions and charges from what hits your pocket. This NIC increase will be problematic for freelancers who use umbrella companies and the employers NIC is taken out of the freelancer's daily rate.

Overall the umbrella company used to be a useful route to earning some cash in a flexible way but if you have ambitions for earning over the longer term and over about £250 per day the other options for setting up your own business in this chapter could be more rewarding and tax efficient (subject to IR35 which I have explained earlier in this chapter).

Buying a business

Buying an established business can be an attractive route to becoming your own boss, as it eliminates many of the problems of start-ups. The enterprise is likely to come equipped with stock, suppliers, an order book, premises and possibly employees. It is also likely to have debtors and creditors. Take professional advice before buying any business, even one from friends. You must establish why the business is being sold. It may be for perfectly respectable reasons – for instance, a change of circumstances such as retirement. Equally, it may be that the market is saturated, that the rent is about to go sky-high or that major competition has opened or is about to open up nearby.

Before parting with your money, verify that the assets are owned by the business and get the stock properly assessed for age, quality and sell-ability or get it professionally valued. You should also ensure that the debts are collectable and that the same credit terms will apply from existing suppliers. Get an accountant to look at the figures for the last three years and have a chartered surveyor check the premises. A solicitor should be engaged to vet any legal documents, including staff and other ongoing contracts.

The value of the company's assets will be reflected in its purchase price, as will the 'goodwill' (or reputation) that it has established. For more information, agents specialising in small business sales have useful guides (for instance, see www.christie.com).

Franchising

Franchising continues to be a popular form of business entry route with attractions for both franchisor and franchisee. The franchisor gains, as their 'brand' is able to expand quickly. The advantage to the franchisee is that there are normally fewer risks than with starting a business from scratch.

A franchisee buys into an established business and builds up his or her own enterprise under its wing. In return for the investment, plus regular royalty payments, he or she acquires the right to sell the franchisor's products or services within a specified geographic area and enjoys the benefits of its reputation, buying power and marketing expertise. As a franchisee you are effectively your own boss. You finance the business, employ the staff and retain the profits after the franchisor has had its cut. You are usually expected to maintain certain standards and conform to the broad corporate approach of the organisation. In return, the franchisor should train you in the business, provide management and IT support and give you access to a wide range of backup services.

The amount of capital needed to buy a franchise varies enormously according to the type of business, and can be anywhere between a few hundred pounds and £500,000 or more. The franchisee is normally liable to pay an initial fee, covering both the entry cost and the initial support services provided by the franchisor, such as advice about location and market research.

The length of the agreement will depend on both the type of business involved and the front-end fee. Agreements can run from three to 20 years and many franchisors include an option to renew the agreement, which should be treated as a valuable asset.

Many franchises have built up a good track record and raising money to invest in good franchises may not be too difficult. Most of the leading high-street banks operate specialist franchise loan sections. The franchisors may also be able to help in raising the money and can sometimes arrange more advantageous terms through their connections with financial institutions.

The British Franchise Association (BFA) represents 'the responsible face' of franchising, and its members have to conform to a code of practice. When considering opportunities, a good franchisor will provide a great deal of invaluable help. However, some franchisors may be less helpful and this will usually tell its own story. Make careful enquiries before committing any money; as basic information, you should ask for a bank reference, review several years accounts and appointments and resignations of directors (all available for free from Companies House), visit their head office and cost out and prepare a business plan and profit and loss forecast for at least the next year (see above on how to do this) and review this with the potential franchisor. Also check with the British Franchise Association whether the franchisor in question is a member and visit some of the other franchisees to find out what their experience has been. Before signing, seek advice from an accountant or solicitor. For more information, see the British Franchise Association website: www.thebfa.org.

Operational and other issues

Banking

If you operate through a limited company you have to set up a separate business bank account into which all income is paid and out of which you pay all costs. Most self-employed and partnerships will operate a separate bank account for their business as it can make the accounts easier and it can also help stop you muddling personal and business funds. Shop around for the best deal that suits your business (often a trade-off between the conveniences of a local 'bricks and mortar' branch accompanied by internet banking versus free or reduced charges for internet-only accounts) but often the convenience of maintaining business and personal bank accounts at one bank wins the day.

Inventions and intellectual property

If you have a clever idea that you would like to market you should ensure that your intellectual property is protected if you believe there is a special value in the name (trademark) or something special or unique about the product (patent). For information about patenting an invention, trademarks, copyright and much more, look at the UK Intellectual Property Office website at www.gov.uk (go to 'Intellectual Property Office').

Licences and permissions

Certain types of business require a licence or permit to trade; these include pubs, off-licences, nursing agencies, pet shops, kennels, minicabs or buses, driving instructors, betting shops, auction sale rooms, cinemas, street traders and, in some cases, travel agents and tour operators. You will also require a licence to import certain goods.

Depending on the nature of your business, other permissions may need to be obtained, including from the environmental health department, licensing authorities and the fire prevention officer. In particular, there are special requirements concerning the sale of food, and safety measures for hotels and guest houses.

Your local authority office will be able to advise you whether you require a licence, and in many cases your council will be the licensing authority. More information is available at www.gov.uk (go to 'licence finder').

Employing staff

Should you consider employing staff, you will immediately increase the complexity of your business. As well as paying salaries, you will have to account for PAYE, keep National Insurance records and conform to the multiple requirements of employment legislation. If you are worried or don't want the bother of doing the paperwork yourself, your accountant is likely to be able to introduce you to a payroll service, which will cost you money but will take some of the burden off your shoulders. Keeping personnel records will bring you into the scope of data protection: see ico.org.uk.

Employment legislation

As an employer, you have certain legal obligations with respect to your staff. The most important of these cover such issues as health and safety at work, terms and conditions of employment, and the provision of employee rights including, for example, parental leave, trade union activity and protection against unfair dismissal. Very small firms are exempt from some of the more onerous requirements, and the government is taking steps to reduce more of the red tape. However, it is important that you understand in general terms what legislation could affect you. You will usually find free support on this subject via membership of a trade association or organisation such as the Federation of Small Businesses (www.fsb.org.uk). The Health and Safety Executive also has a useful website: www.hse.gov.uk.

   An employer, however small the business, may not discriminate against someone on the grounds of sex, race, disability, religion, marital status, sexual orientation or age. This applies to all aspects of employment, including training, promotion, recruitment, company benefits and facilities. More information can be found at: www.equalityhumanrights.com.

Disputes

If you find yourself with a potential dispute on your hands, it is sensible to approach the Advisory, Conciliation and Arbitration Service (ACAS), which operates an effective information and advisory service for employers and employees on a variety of workplace problems, including employment legislation and employment relations. It also has a wide range of useful publications, giving practical guidance on employment matters. See website: www.acas.org.uk.

Insurance

Insurance is more than just a wise precaution. It is essential if you employ staff, have business premises or use your car regularly for commercial purposes. Many insurance companies now offer 'package insurance' for small businesses, which covers most of the main contingencies in a single policy. This usually works out cheaper than buying a collection of individual policies. An insurance broker should be able to guide you through the risks and the insurance products available:

- *Employers' liability*: This is compulsory if you employ staff. It provides indemnity against liability for death or bodily injury to employees and subcontractors arising in connection with the business.

- *Product and public liability*: This insures the business and its products against claims by customers or the public.

- *Professional indemnity*: This is essential if a client could suffer a mishap, loss or other damage in consequence of advice or services received.

- *House insurance*: If you operate your business from home, check that you have notified your house insurer of this fact.

- *Motor risks*: Check that you have notified your insurer if you use your motor vehicle for your business.

- *Life assurance*: This ensures that funds are available to pay off any debts or to enable the business to continue in the event of your death.

- *Permanent health insurance*: Otherwise known as 'income protection', it provides insurance against long-term loss of income as a result of severe illness or disability by paying a regular income.

- *Critical illness insurance*: This provides insurance against long-term loss of income as a result of severe illness or disability by paying a lump sum.

- *Key person insurance*: This applies to the loss of a key person through prolonged illness as well as death. In small companies where the success or failure of the business is dependent upon the skills of one or two key executives, key person insurance may be demanded by lenders.

You should discuss these points with your insurance company or a broker. To find an insurance broker, see the British Insurance Brokers' Association website: www.biba.org.uk; or the Association of British Insurers website: www.abi.org.uk.

> **Top tip**
> If you work from home or use your car for work remember to notify your insurer.

Pensions

Starting a business opens up opportunities to manage your remuneration and pensions. Review existing pension provision against pension aspirations with a suitably qualified financial adviser. But remember there are also pension predators out there. More information on pensions is at **Chapter 3, Pensions.**

> **Top tip**
> **Pensions planning can be dramatically effective and very tax-efficient but there are traps for the unwary. Review Chapter 3, Pensions in detail and then follow up with your IFA and your accountant should help you achieve a better retirement.**

Useful reading

The government website (www.gov.uk) contains the government's online resource 'Set up a business' with tools and guidance for business.

Regional or country-specific support is also available at:

- Northern Ireland: www.nibusinessinfo.co.uk and www.go-succeed.com;
- Scotland: www.findbusinesssupport.gov.scot;
- Wales: www.businesswales.gov.wales.

Other useful organisations

- *Solicitors*: Many solicitors offer a free initial consultation. To find solicitors in your local area use the 'find a solicitor' in your regional law society.

- *The Federation of Small Businesses* (www.fsb.org.uk): The networking opportunities and benefits make it a 'must have' for small businesses.

- *Association of Independent Professionals and the Self Employed* www.ipse.co.uk and is good for freelancers and IR35 issues.

- *Business start-up websites and exhibitions*: A useful example is www.greatbritishbusinessshow.co.uk. The exhibitions are usually free, well attended, with free workshops and inspiring guest speakers.

Reminder: Take any action points or follow-up points to Chapter 13, Your Plan For A Better Retirement

Starting a business – checklist

When starting or running a business you will encounter a vast range of information and this can lead to you feeling swamped. This checklist has been developed to help you on the journey. Try annotating each item – N: not applicable; W: work on now; A: review with accountant; C: complete.

- If you want to travel somewhere you use a map. In business it's just the same except you get yourself a *plan*. Commit it to writing and don't expect to get it right first time (no one does!).

- **Choose your *trading format***, i.e. company (usually signified by 'limited'), sole trader or partnership or limited liability partnership. This is an important step and one to talk through with your accountant. You can set up a company for £50 at Companies House. Understand the personal liability risks of sole trader/partnership and, indeed, joint and several liability if trading in partnership ('last person standing pays the lot'!). If things go badly wrong your personal wealth could be at risk.

- **Choose your *accountant*.** Accountants are usually prepared to see you for an initial 'no obligation' meeting. Be clear about who your regular contact will be, their qualifications and knowledge of your industry, their hourly rates and whether they have professional indemnity insurance.

- Make sure you have a source of *legal help*. Could your local solicitor help? Alternatively, your trade association may offer a free legal helpline that may suffice initially.

- There is *free government help* that you can find at www.gov.uk search under 'Set up a business' for tools and guidance for business.

- **Regional or country-specific support** is also available at:
- Northern Ireland: www.nibusinessinfo.co.uk and www.go-succeed.com;
- Scotland: www.findbusinesssupport.gov.scot;
- Wales: www.businesswales.gov.wales.

- **Join the best *trade or professional association*** that you can identify – compare the benefits (networking, helplines, tax investigation cover etc).

- Choose and, if appropriate, protect your *business name*. There is some useful free help available on intellectual property (patents, brands, etc.) at at www.gov.uk/government/organisations/intellectual-property-office.

- Choose a **business bank account**. New internet-only accounts may be free.

- Combine business plans with your wealth and pension needs with a **financial adviser** regulated by the Financial Conduct Authority (FCA).

- **Sort out your *tax and record keeping*** (documents need to be kept for six years and you need to become a receipt/invoice hoarder with a logical 'system for filing'); as the taxman will say, 'Prove it or lose it.' Check first with your accountant before buying any bookkeeping system.

- Understand the implications of failing to deal with your ***tax*** affairs properly. Penalties can range from 30 per cent to 200 per cent plus interest. Some trade associations include 'free' tax investigation cover.

- Understand your key ***tax obligations* and deadlines**. Companies file annual accounts at Companies House nine months after their year-end and the *confirmation statement* on each anniversary of setting up the company.

- Understand your obligations on ***VAT***. The registration threshold for compulsory registration is £90,000.

- Set up your ***premises*** so that you can work effectively. If you work from home, manage the expectations of your family and neighbours – suddenly the phrase 'time is money' takes on a new meaning.

- Set up your ***suppliers*** (set up contracts and bills in the company or business name) and, if appropriate, set up stock control and delivery systems.

- Consider ***insurance*** policies for identified business risks (professional indemnity, public liability, product liability, etc.). An insurance broker can advise on this and you should also consider policies available via trade associations as these can provide increased cover at less cost (don't forget to notify your home and car insurers if you use these for business).

- Consider **protecting the income** you take from your business (especially if you have dependents) in the event of long-term *illness* or *death* and if in doubt take advice from a financial adviser regulated by the FCA.

- If you are not from a selling/marketing background, talk to trusted friends who run their own business and your accountant/adviser or mentor about your **market research and marketing plan**. Plan the *pricing* strategies for your product or service. A different package means a different price. How have you benchmarked your price and how have you differentiated your offering (features and benefits) to allow you to charge that little bit more? Conversely, what features and benefits have you stripped out to allow you to offer a price beneath the competition?

- Get paid promptly for your sales. What are your **payment terms** (terms and conditions)? Follow up on outstanding debts. If you sell stock, have you included a reservation of title clause if your client goes bust?

- Set up your **IT system** and support and have a system to back up your data securely. Check whether you need to notify the Information Commissioner under the *data protection* laws (ico.org.uk).

- Consider **other** **red tape**, especially if your area is a specialised sector (food, health and safety, etc.). Investigate and apply for the licences and permits that your business may need.

Top tip
Review and update your business plan in the light of experience and keep it a living, written document throughout your business journey. It's not a one off that's done and forgotten. A good business plan grows with your business can be the difference between a good business and an average business.

Chapter Nine

Career transition: Paid work and volunteering.

"We need to do a better job of putting ourselves higher on our own 'to do' list".
MICHELLE OBAMA

Is it time to put yourself first? The first reaction of many people approaching retirement is often 'great, no more work' and they may be puzzled at the space I give to career transition and other paid work. In 2025 there are so many possible opportunities to rethink your retirement glidepath by adjusting the balance of your working life. This could be via improved flexible working policies which I see being offered by more and more employers. But, and it's a BIG but, remember you can also 'retire' more than once. Re-set and restart. Or maybe even start that retirement glidepath five years early as I set out in Chapter 1 and then take a new approach to any future work after a late 'gap year' and a personal re-set.

You can retire more than once. Re-set and restart

After the last five years 'career transition' may be a bit higher in your mind as many of us go through a **'re-set'** moment after the Covid-19 years and then the inflation busting cost of living crisis. High responsibility, high stress jobs with perhaps lots of travel within the UK or internationally really can be rebalanced especially in a relatively full UK employment economy. It's also easier where you have a progressive employer who is keen to retain their experienced staff. If not maybe it is a gap year and a new job?

A full-on career may keep you busy and provide the finances you need. But there is another way that perhaps starts about 10 years from retirement and which provides more of a **'glidepath'** into retirement rather than a **'cliff-edge'** halt. Put another way, can you **'re-set'**, put yourself first and 'right-size' your employment? Is putting yourself first something for your start doing list at Chapter 13? You can pull the levers of a new job, part-time working or 'compressed hours' and maybe even glide into and even past some retirement age you had previously fixed in your mind.

Even if you enjoy your work and find it satisfying it may be restrictive in ways you don't see. You stick to the rules – specific tasks, regular timekeeping, keep going through thick and thin and limited personal freedom to do as you wanted. Have you heard folk explain that 'their life isn't their own' due to the demands of the job? So can the pressure be turned down or even off? Career transition describes the process of reassessing what you can offer, what you really want and exploring opportunities to achieve a better last decade of employment. If you get it right could any new employment (or rebalancing your existing employment) maybe even last beyond state retirement age if it helps you achieve a better retirement?

Alternatively, your needs may be financial as, quite simply, having reviewed your retirement plans at Chapter 1 you now need to supplement your present anticipated or actual retirement income and earn, earn, earn. This, therefore, sits as the second chapter within the **'earn more'** essential step of retirement planning in my book. As a brief recap, the core of this book is based around the four essential steps to achieving a better retirement: plan more, save more, earn more and live better. The other key readership for this chapter are those looking to retrain or just do some part time work to provide some interest and a bit of finance to pay for an extra holiday ('earn more'). Maybe after a bit of break (I sometimes call it a late gap year) a new job may also provide the mental and physical activity that seems to be so important to maintaining a good health (see next **Chapter, 10, Well Being**). Finally, I explore the wonderful opportunities in volunteering where 'giving back' could be just the right thing for you and society and can also assist with physical and mental activity- a win:win.

This chapter at a glance

- Is it time to put yourself first?
- Employment 'right-sizing' and using career transition to help you change career to provide a smoother glidepath into retirement.
- How to assess yourself and find the right positions for you.
- Tips to help you get that role.
- Tips on redundancy situations.
- Help on getting full or part time employment in retirement.
- There is also information and advice on training opportunities and other employment ideas, including finding public appointments.
- How to find volunteering opportunities.
- Some examples of volunteering types of work.
- A detailed look at one organisation that depends on volunteers who all make a difference, Citizens Advice.

Career transition and rightsizing your employment

This comes down to blue sky thinking on a blank sheet of paper. You've worked for decades and probably have seen all sorts of positive and negative work experiences and your knowledge of work experiences of those close to you can be illuminating. This career review has five broad components: what type of job I'd like and where and when; what I bring; how I can make the best impression; what opportunities are out there and finally is the package sufficient?

What type of job I'd like and where and when?

It begins with a review of what you value in life - list it in importance. This is the big stuff in your life- your wants and desires. Is it remaining close to family and perhaps caring responsibilities, a location or community or more freedom to pursue your passion in life (sailing, riding, refurbishing a cottage etc.)? Conversely what do you want to avoid? Is the role to be full time or part time? What travel limits would you like to see? Remember it's a tough ask to have a job that you love all the time and as with many things in life it is probably a case of compromising on some issues. But at the end of the day if it's fairly local, useful, purposeful and stimulating you are ticking some good boxes off.

Then assess how you respond best in a work situation and with what sort of management style above you. What causes you to thrive and what causes you stress? What really motivates you and conversely what demotivates you and learn from past experiences - both the best and worst? Is it team working that you enjoy and dealing with people or do you prefer to get on with things on your own?

Then think about the types of work you could do and whether they are in a declining, stable or increasing market. How does this influence the breadth of choice you should be looking at? Everyone is different and there is no right or wrong answer here. It's about reassessing what's best for you at this stage in life and as you move on from here.

The sort of jobs that I have seen clients build into their retirement glidepath following a '**re-set**' (and perhaps a career break to enjoy a holiday of a life-time) are:

- A similar role with their existing employer but part-time/ flexible hours.
- Doing what you have always done just less of it with another employer.
- Turning a hobby into a small business.
- Consulting or freelance work through an agency.
- Gardening.
- Pet sitting or walking.
- Becoming a driver.
- Substitute teaching.
- Tutor.
- Book-keeping for small business owners.
- Working at events.
- Starting their own business (see Chapter 7).

Finally think about the timing and 'when'. Do you owe yourself a bit of a break and a late gap year or a gap of 3 or 4 months? I have seen this plenty of times from folk wanting a Summer off to follow a sports passion (football or rugby world cup, Cricket tour of South Africa, Olympics etc). Maybe it's a 100 day world cruise or a desire to fly all the way around the world seeing all those places when they still have the energy, stamina and ability to move though. For instance beautiful India and Sri Lanka and onto Cambodia and Thailand and onto Bali (for a beach chill) and then Australia and New Zealand before stopping off at San Francisco and Vancouver on the way back (more on life experiences and how to make a wish list at **Chapter 11, Experiences, leisure and holidays**).

Do you owe yourself a bit of a break and a late gap year ?

What do I bring?

Then it's a case of identifying the skills you bring and especially how they are transferable to other roles and don't forget those learnt on hobbies or voluntary work. Discussions with people who know you and the potential jobs you could do can yield great intelligence here and some of those 'I'd never have thought of that moments.' Ignore the importance of these at your peril and try and set aside at least an hour for each and have a structure (maybe the points in this section) so you deal with specifics rather that vague notions. The more experienced your confidants the better the output.

A trusted and structured form of career analysis is the **'Birkman method'** which measures through a long questionnaire four main areas: your usual behaviour in the context of tasks and relationships; what you require in the environment and people around you to be at your best; the behaviours in stress situations when your needs are not met and, finally, your interests (that is the tasks and activities that offer you the greatest attraction and satisfaction). Your present employer may arrange for you to take this as part of a career review or you can access this via a number of HR type consultancies throughout the UK (just try googling 'Birkman method' and your location).

How I can make the best impression?

This is all about translating what you know about yourself into a credible statement that underlines your experience, skills and knowledge and how you can add value to the company or organisation in meeting the challenges they have.

Take care with application forms: In addition to your **CV** some firms may also ask you to complete an application form relating to the job in question. Read the questions they ask carefully and in your responses try to play to your own strengths and experience. Remember that in a competitive job market firms will use the application form to short-list those candidates they want to take a further look at through interview. Those short-listing decisions will be made solely on the quality of the application.

CV writing: This is so important, and presentation is key. If it's a few years since you've updated your CV, make sure it's current and contains the following sections: personal and contact information; education and qualifications; work history and/or experience and relevant skills to the job in question. Identify the key requirements and key characteristics required from the advertised role and assess how your CV mirrors this back to say "I'm the one you are looking for". Personal interests, achievements and hobbies can be covered briefly if relevant to the job. Use assertive, positive language, emphasising the skills you have gained from past work. CVs, in most cases, shouldn't run to more than two pages of A4 paper, attaching anything else as an annex to the CV.

Doing an interview: You may be called to do an interview. Take time to prepare for this and do research on the firm and the job vacancy itself. Study the attributes required for the role, you will find these on the job profile, and decide on examples you can show you meet these. You may be asked to do a presentation and, if so, expect guidance on the subject, slide length and time allocation for the presentation and then the time for questions (if not ask about this). Prepare a mental checklist of your own strengths and experience which might enable you to do the job in question – the interviewee/ panel will almost certainly want to explore this with you during the actual interview. Your decades of experience and loyalty will set you apart from youngsters so emphasise this with examples of achievements and extra work you did on the job and how you can add value and fit in the team. Prepare, prepare and prepare to do yourself justice and then, in the interview (which may be remote via 'teams'/ zoom or skype) just try to relax and be yourself.

Referees: These will not be required until you are at the point of receiving an offer. Have them ready: one should be a previous employer and the other someone who can vouch for you personally.

What opportunities are out there?

Get organised: Your career transition/job-hunting campaign needs planning. Don't leave something so important to chance.

Make use of your contacts: Within the network of people you know there are bound to be some who may not be able to actually get you a job, but can give some help with advice, information and possibly potential job leads.

Former colleagues and finder fees - a win-win: Introductions to prospective employers from a former colleague or a friend you know that already works for the target organisation can work well. It gives you a 'warm in' and may give the former colleague or friend a finder fee which can be significant. It cuts out the recruitment agencies and the fee they would otherwise get and can be a great win-win for all concerned.

Tactically you may want to explore these routes before signing up with recruitment agencies.

Recruitment agencies: Identify the recruitment agencies who operate in your targeted career areas. These can vary in size and quality so ask around for recommendations on the good and the bad.

Is the package sufficient?

The numbers are important and will be dealt with in a moment but now that we are more experienced there are other vital factors:

- The new boss and prospective colleagues. Did you like and respect them?
- What is their spirit and ethos? From an ethics point of view did you feel they fit with you?
- You will be listening and looking during any interview and perhaps you'll get a tour of the office. What do your instincts tell you? Trust them as they are usually well honed and tailored, of course, to you.
- What are the travel and overtime expectations - are these clear and understood?
- Do they offer a gym and other wellness activities?

Then onto the numbers. Are you clear on **the package** and what that means in terms of salary; any bonus expectations; health care, life cover; holiday entitlement, ability to buy extra days holiday (increasingly important as you glide into retirement); other flexible working options; pensions (what you contribute and they contribute and the latter can be significant) and share purchase or option plans and other benefits.

Employment rightsizing and compressed hours

The traditional view is that folk press onward and upward in employment and in the old days of final salary pension schemes (**see Chapter 3, Pensions**). This had a logic when pensions may have been calculated based on earnings when you finally retired as happened until the mid 1990s. Today the model is turned on its head and the final decade or years of employment, for most people, is more about a glidepath. So, can you re-engineer with your current employer less stress, less travel and less responsibility for the same or similar headline pay by agreement? Ask about the process for going part-time and talk with others who have done this as precedents are valuable in employment situations. What about compressed hours to give you a day off a week as you glide into retirement (and maybe on through it). This is where you work for only 4 days but a bit longer each day and still get paid for 5 days (or at 90% pay and benefits if, for example, you work 32.4 hours over 4 days rather than 36 hours over 5 days). If you can't find a glidepath solution with your current employer is it time to 'blue-sky' think and find that other role that meets your values and skills that provides a smoother glidepath into retirement? This is employment 'right-sizing'.

Top tip

As you glide towards retirement ask your employer about processes for securing flexi-working or compressed hours. More enlightened and progressive employers recognise the value in retaining their talented and experienced employees which is especially true in 2025's relatively full employment economy.

Redundancy

Managers feel that one of the worst jobs they will have to deal with is making someone redundant. Hopefully it will be handled with care and compassion with outplacement support ('outplacement' is the term the industry uses for the process to help move employees on when there is restructuring). The outplacement support can vary in length and quality but broadly may include a one-to-one relationship with a career counsellor who will assist you in the transition from one career into another or into early retirement. The process may include workbooks, seminars and workshops, webinars and the process should cover career research, the job application process, CV preparation and interview techniques. Other options such as early retirement or starting your own business may also be available.

Generally, employers will want to handle this well as cost cutting and redundancies can involve several rounds as a business restructures. If the first round goes badly motivation and productivity can decrease and the business continues to decline. If redundancy is likely or if it strikes the following pointers may assist.

- If your employer's pension scheme allows it can you take your pension early in lieu of part or all of the severance package?

- Up to £30,000 of redundancy can be tax free and anything above that is taxed at your highest rate of tax so could it help if it fell in the next tax year if this was an option.
- Review with your Human Resources manager whether you can ask for part of any termination payment beyond the £30,000 tax free sum to be paid into your pension. This can be tax efficient and professional advice should also be sought.
- If you have share options these may lapse on the date you leave (your employment contract and options offer will clarify this point). If you feel the options are likely to increase substantially see if you can extend the period so that they are spread over two tax years or more.
- Check out your rights if you are feeling pressurised to 'exit' by processes that appear to be challenging your competence in your role. Follow this through with any legal expenses insurance that you have which can help you understand your rights. You may find that, instead, you are offered a 'compromise agreement' to move away from your role and the company rather than a formal redundancy. These are not exceptional and legal assistance should be sought to help negotiate any such 'package'. Remember legal expenses insurance often comes as an extra to home insurance or professional association membership so check your policies. If the business is insolvent and an insolvency practitioner is appointed in control of the business the rules are different and there is less protection (but a government safety net still exists for unpaid salary and redundancy payments).
- Don't agree to anything verbally and ask for all proposals to be put in writing and review via any legal expenses insurance you may have or consider taking legal advice.
- Check what happens to your benefits during any notice period that you are not required to work. What is the value of these and how will you be compensated?
- Check specifically if life cover and health cover can continue during any notice period that you are not required to work whilst you find a new job especially if you have a challenging medical history as these can be costly to implement for a short period and can take time to arrange in such circumstances.
- Ask about retaining office equipment you were been supplied with as it is usually more bother for the employer to gather these in. Ask about retaining mobile phone or laptop (restored back to original state to remove company information).

Training opportunities

Knowing what you want to do is one thing, but before starting a new job you may want to brush up existing skills or possibly acquire new ones. Most professional bodies have a full programme of training events, ranging from one-day seminars to courses lasting a week or longer. Additionally, adult education institutes run a vast range of courses or, if you are still in your present job, a more practical solution might be to investigate open and flexible learning, which you can do from home. There are a number of vocational education and training opportunities offering such training for individuals of all ages. You are more likely to be successful if you learn at a time, place and pace best suited to your own particular circumstances. You should try to find out what is available locally via your local college of further education and check it out a year ahead of any potential need to start to get inspired. In addition the following organisations offer advice and a wide range of courses:

- Learn Direct: www.learndirect.co.uk

- online courses from universities and brands: www.futurelearn.com;
- Adult Education Finder: www.adulteducationfinder.co.uk;
- Home Learning College: www.homelearningcollege.com;
- Learn Direct: www.learndirect.co.uk;
- University of the third age www.u3a.org.uk;
- National Extension College: www.nec.ac.uk;
- Open and Distance Learning Quality Council: www.odlqc.org.uk;
- Open University: www.open.ac.uk.

Other paid employment ideas

Consultancy and contracting

If the idea of hiring yourself out as a consultant or contractor appeals, you may be able to build up a steady stream of assignments and be recommended to other companies who could use your skills. There is more on this in Chapter 8, Starting Your Own Business or you may get placements through an agency; there is a vast choice through mainstream and niche agencies. If you're not sure about who's who in the world of agencies ask around (former HR colleagues and other contractors/consultants are the usual starting places). More research and information can be obtained from:

- Association of Independent Professionals and the Self-Employed: www.ipse.co.uk
- Consultancy UK: www.consultancy.uk

Interim management

Interim management is the temporary provision of senior or director-level management resources and skills. It is a short-term assignment of a proven heavyweight interim executive manager to manage a period of transition, crisis or change within an organisation. Assignments could be full-time or involve just one or two days' commitment per week. More research and information can be obtained from the Institute of Interim Management: www.iim.org.uk.

Non-executive directorships

A non-executive director, or external director, is a paid member of the board of directors of a company or organisation who does not form part of the executive management team. They are not an employee and they do not participate in the day-to-day management of the organisation. Instead, they are expected to monitor and challenge the performance of the executive directors and the management and give advice on broad strategic issues. Such appointments carry heavy responsibilities and people who are qualified to take on such a role are usually chosen for their breadth of experience and personal qualities. More at www.nedonboard.com.

Public appointments

There are a large number of advisory and other public bodies or quangos (quasi-autonomous non-government organisations) that have responsibility for a raft of public services at national, regional and local level. Those services cover a vast spectrum, including health, education, the environment, agriculture and food, defence, policing, legal/judicial, culture, media, sport, science and technology, and transport. The list is by no means exhaustive and further details can be found on the Cabinet Office website (publicappointments.cabinetoffice.gov.uk), which outlines opportunities throughout the whole of the UK.

Most of the bodies have a large staffing complement and a managing board or executive of senior administrative and professional staff. However, as public bodies, most are also required to have non-executive directors or board members drawn from the general public. The role of these external appointments is to bring outside experience and expertise to the table and also to bring a degree of external challenge to the work and decisions of the executive body or board. There are also purely advisory bodies designed to give external advice in a wide range of areas.

It is not necessary to have been in the public sector in order to be able to make a contribution. Indeed, in many instances the body will be looking for the sort of practical experience that people gain in business or commerce outside of the public sector. The skill set will vary from body to body and, in addition to a lay person's interest in the subject matter, experience in areas such as finance, human resources and change management, along, perhaps, with specialist knowledge, will often be seen as valuable.

The time commitment can vary, but on average it is probably one or two days per month. Likewise, the remuneration varies from body to body – from a very modest attendance allowance to several thousand pounds per year. But for some people the idea of being involved in an area of particular interest may be as attractive as any financial reward. For the post of chairperson, the time commitment is likely to be much greater, but so too will be the remuneration.

There is a rigorous and open appointments procedure for all posts, usually looking at the extent to which any candidate measures up to the specific competence-based criteria that the appointment requires. Full details of the appointment, the criteria relating to it and general advice on applying will be available to those who apply. It is important that this information is looked at in detail as the shortlist for final interview will be based on an objective assessment of the extent to which the information provided in the application form meets the specific criteria relating to the post.

Virtually all posts are now publicly advertised in the national, regional or local press – so anyone interested should keep an eye on this. Further information, including vacancies, is also available on the Cabinet Office website mentioned earlier or at a regional level from www.gov.scot/public-bodies for Scotland, and www.nidirect.gov.uk/public-appointments for Northern Ireland.

Paid work for charities

There are some opportunities to work for money rather than as a volunteer in the charity sector, although it might be helpful to work as a volunteer before seeking a paid appointment. Anyone thinking of applying for a job with a charity must of course be sympathetic to its aims and style and it is likely that you may have already been involved with the charity before seeking paid employment with it. You can also keep an eye on job adverts in that sector.

Jobs with tourism and travel

The travel and tourism sector comprises many different industries such as tour operators, tourist boards, passenger transport (coach, aviation, waterways and rail) and visitor attractions, such as museums, theme parks, zoos and heritage sites. This industry is not just for the young – mature and experienced people are also sought after. If you have stamina, enjoy meeting the general public and like travelling, working in the tourism sector could be interesting. Some people with specialist knowledge sign on as a lecturer with one of the travel companies offering special interest holidays; others specialise in tourist attractions nearer to home. Air courier jobs are also good for people who like travelling abroad.

Teaching and tutoring

If you have experience of teaching, there are a number of possibilities open to you, both in the United Kingdom and abroad. With examinations becoming more competitive many parents require private tutors to help their children prepare for public examinations. There is always a demand for people to teach English to foreign students at the many language schools, and most UK universities offer language courses during the summer.

House-sitting

There are opportunities throughout the United Kingdom and abroad to look after a house and maybe a pet whilst the owners are abroad. Companies who specialise in this kind of work include:

House Sitters UK: www.housesittersuk.co.uk

Trusted House Sitters: www.trustedhousesitters.com

Volunteering

Lots of volunteering is inspired by friends and relatives who have taken the plunge or been touched by a cause. That's a good starting point so ask around and you could be introduced sooner than you think. It's a two-way process so expect some form of interview or chat and find out the benefits of working with the organisation, time expectations and flexibility. If it's not right don't waste each other's time and seek a different opportunity. Maybe you've been inspired by tipping your toe in the water? Do some more research thinking about the issues that really are important to you. Think about the skills that you bring and start your search.

Volunteering – finding opportunities

Finding opportunities are not as difficult as you may think. Community noticeboards, websites and the local library or Doctor's surgery notice board were the old-fashioned ways but are still worthwhile. Then, as you would expect, there is the online noticeboard and www.do-it.org is a great starting point- try it now with your postcode and you'll be amazed at what's nearby. Regional focused websites include:

Northern Ireland: www.volunteernow.co.uk
Scotland: www.volunteerscotland.net
Wales: www.volunteering-wales.net
England: www.ncvo.org.uk

Why people become volunteers
The most frequently cited reasons why people volunteer include:

- It's their interest or passion:

- maintaining friendships, teamwork, status and a sense of belonging;

- wanting to 'make a difference' to other people's lives;

- enjoying using their skills in new and valuable ways;

- feeling better both physically and mentally;

- supporting local activities and neighbourhood organisations;

- being a committed member of social and charitable projects;

- actively participating in democratic institutions such as parish/community councils, boards of school governors, or neighbourhood watch;

- finding opportunities to help in education, sport, culture, leisure, conservation and the environment.

The type of volunteer work

There are so many types of work available to volunteers, depending on what you enjoy doing and what skills you have – you should be able to find something to suit. It is entirely dependent on you what you choose – the range is enormous, from the large international or national charities to much smaller organisations. Always play to your strengths; you should be able to find many opportunities in your local community to volunteer. Types of work could include:

- *Administrative*: Any active group is likely to need administrative and financial help, from stuffing and labelling envelopes to organising committees to keeping the finances in order. This may involve a day or so a week or occasional assistance at peak times. Many smaller charities are desperate for help from individuals with IT expertise and accountancy experience.
- *Committee work*: This can cover anything from very occasional help to a virtually full-time commitment as chair, treasurer or secretary. People with business skills or financial or legal backgrounds are likely to be especially valuable, and those whose skills include minute-taking are always in demand.
- *Direct work*: Hands on building and maintenance work, driving, delivering 'meals on wheels', counselling, visiting the housebound, working in a charity shop, gardening in a community garden, running arts classes or sports clubs, helping with a playgroup, respite care for carers; the list is endless. There are many interesting and useful jobs for those without special training.
- *Fundraising and marketing*: Every voluntary organisation needs money, and when donations are static or falling, more creativity and ingenuity are required to help bring in funds. Events are many and varied, but anyone with energy and experience of organising fundraising events would be welcomed with open arms as a volunteer.
- *Overseas*: Many more people in later life are now combining volunteering with travel. There are many in their 50s and 60s who are seizing this opportunity as they may have missed their 'gap year' when they were young. Each organisation has a minimum period of service. One of the better-known organisations involved in this area is Voluntary Service Overseas (www.vsointernational.org).

A case study: Citizens Advice

There are, literally, thousands of opportunities in volunteering but picking one allows us to penetrate in and explore the 'what they do, why and how a volunteer can help'. The case study is **Citizens Advice** but it could, quite literally, be any organisation.

Have you ever had a problem or crisis in your life when you needed advice? Citizens Advice provides people with advice for all kinds of problems without judging them and the organization is powered by an army of volunteers who make a difference and benefit from all that volunteering brings. There is probably a role for you at your local Citizens Advice outlet. But first some context. Citizens Advice provide a reliable and consistent service by sticking to a few key aims and principles:

- providing advice people need for the problems they face;
- trying to improve the policies and practices that affect people's lives by showing the people who make the decisions what people's experiences are.

Citizens Advice are independent and provide free, confidential and impartial advice to everyone regardless of race, sex, disability, sexuality or nationality. They are the largest advice-giving network in the United Kingdom, with over 3,000 outlets (there should be one near you) and 20,000 volunteers. They help people deal with nearly 6 million problems every year by phone, email and outreach sessions. The volunteers come from all walks of life and are committed to providing an independent advice service. The advice is based on four principles. It is:

- *Independent*: They will always act in the interests of their clients, without influence from outside bodies.
- *Impartial*: They won't charge their clients or make assumptions about them. The service is open to everyone and they treat everyone equally.
- *Confidential*: They will not pass on anything a client tells them, or even the fact that they visited, without their permission.
- *Free*: No one has to pay for any part of the service they provide.

Putting these principles into action enables them to provide a vital service to millions of people each year. They, and therefore you, can help make a real practical difference to people with problems in your local community.

What do Citizens Advice volunteers do?

There are lots of different roles and a few are summarised below – there really is something for everyone.

- *Caseworkers/advisers*: An adviser will assist clients at drop-in sessions, appointments in the outlet, over the phone or at outreach sessions explaining the choices and consequences clients face. They need to be good at listening, work as a team, be open-minded and non-judgemental and enjoy helping people.

- *Administrators*: Help ensure everything runs smoothly with different roles to match your skills and time availability including developing administrative systems, helping to arrange events and receptionist activities.

- *IT support coordinators*: Support training and troubleshoot hardware and software problems, develop networks, design spreadsheets and databases.

- *Campaigners*: Conduct research on local issues and manage media campaigning.

Each area is run autonomously as a separate charity. You should be able to make contact with the organisation serving your area through the Citizens Advice website.

What training is available from Citizens Advice?

You will initially receive a briefing lasting about two hours, which will explain more about your local Citizens Advice and the potential opportunities that are available. It is a very comfortable session without any obligation. Following this session, if you do wish to volunteer, you then undergo the initial stage of training which lasts about eight weeks and takes about half a day per week. After that it's up to you what you want to give and how your new volunteering will progress. To find out more just check out www.citizensadvice.org.uk; in the volunteering section of the website you can search for opportunities by entering your postcode.

Top tip

Winston Churchill said "We make a living by what we get, but we make a life by what we give." You probably don't appreciate the talents you have and how wonderful they could be to one of our thousands of voluntary organisations or folk who just need a hand. Have a go and the real chances are that the art of giving will help you live better and achieve a better retirement.

Useful reading

Learn Direct: www.learndirect.co.uk

University of the Third Age www.u3a.org.uk

Northern Ireland: www.volunteernow.co.uk

Scotland: www.volunteerscotland.net

Wales: www.volunteering-wales.net

England: www.ncvo.org.uk

Reminder: Take any action points or follow up points to Chapter 13, Your Plan For A Better Retirement.

Chapter Ten
Well-being and personal relationships

"You don't develop courage by being happy in your relationships everyday. You develop it by surviving difficult times and challenging adversity."

EPICURUS

Well-being is the state of feeling healthy and happy. Personal relationships go hand in hand with this 'state' and, therefore, feature as must-read parts of this 'live better' essential step. It's time to give more time to your well-being, personal relationships and a healthier lifestyle. And it's time to spend a bit more money on assessing and maintaining your health. How much do you spend servicing and maintaining your car? That sort of puts things in perspective. Or think about the time you spend on social media against how much time is given to your well-being, health and personal relationships.

Positive personal relations will help achieve a better sense of well-being. Logic says that if you get your personal relationships right so much positivity will flow from them which should improve your overall health. Whilst relationships can make life much easier and more enjoyable the opposite happens if they become fractured.

Well-being is the state of feeling healthy and happy.

You can do so much to achieve a better retirement by following through on the preceding nine chapters in this book which have set out the first three essential steps of achieving a better retirement: **plan more (Chapter 1); save more (Chapters 2 to 7)** and **earn more (Chapters 8 and 9).** But all of your reading and all of your actions that have been developed are pretty pointless without the 4th essential step of 'living better'.

Whether you are part of a couple or single having good personal relationships also provides you with a group around you for emotional support, advice, different viewpoints that challenge you, shoulders to cry on and folk with whom to share daft jokes, social occasions and transport. A problem shared is also a problem halved. Don't forget the importance of having people around you who will take you down a peg or two if you sometimes tend to get beyond yourself.

More fundamentally it will be a rare person that is happy every day as there will always be difficult times and challenging situations so it is just as much about how you survive them as Epicurus said 2,300 years ago. His basic philosophy was about living a self-sufficient life surrounded by friends. Without getting too heavy about it he had a good point when he said *"You don't develop courage by being happy in your relationships everyday. You develop it by surviving difficult times and challenging adversity."* This seems perfect and is therefore chosen as the headline quote for this chapter.

This chapter at a glance

This is one of the shortest chapters but one of the most important in this book. If your personal relationships and health are maintained and improved you will have a better retirement.

- Retirement brings big changes to the **dynamics of your personal relationships**. If your life was your work and your friends were at work, the changes will be bigger than you could have realised. Those folk who allowed their work to become their life and who didn't glide into and retune for retirement may have to work harder on this.

- **Adjusting** to the new life balance with any partner will need care so that you do not get under each other's feet and learn how to say 'no' (nicely!).

- Reminders about those other **people who matter most to you** – children, grandchildren, parents if you have them and other close relatives and good friends.

- Pointers to the **new friends** that will emerge from your new social groups in retirement and that good friends tend to stick around during the highs and lows of life. You may have to let go of other friends who maybe had no real interest in you.

- Some pointers on the **key health focus points** and help to recognise the risk factors around physical and mental activity and some opportunities to improve things.

- **Exercise** is one of the greatest benefits to good health. This chapter shows you some options and choices, but then it's over to you and that willpower thing.

- You are what you eat. Suggestions on how to **eat more healthily**. It's worth repeating here that action could add years to your life.

- Perhaps most important of all (it's that question about the time to spend on the really important stuff!) have you had a **recent health screening check**? If not get something underway well before retirement as this may well give you actions and pointers around the key retirement red health flags.

Personal relationships

According to Relate, 91 per cent of people aged over 50 in the UK said that a close personal relationship is as important as good health and financial security. This emphasises the fact that as we grow older we find that strong and healthy personal relationships count for even more. This covers the spectrum from former work colleagues to your partner, your children, your parents and other friendship groups. It may come as a big surprise but your retirement brings a change in these dynamics and this means that some may change, some may be lost and some new ones will be found. With some preparation there shouldn't be too many bumps along the way but adjusting will take a little time.

Work

The chances are that most people will have spent a great deal of their time in a working environment where they will have established a whole series of relationships. Those will include work colleagues, fellow professionals, customers and suppliers; some of those colleagues may well have become close friends. Once retired some of those contacts will become much less significant in your life.

While individual circumstances can vary, the general advice on retirement is that you should not seek to return to your old working environment. You may initially be tempted to drop in to see how things are going and to have a quick chat with old friends, but generally it is not a great idea. Things can change very quickly, as can personnel, and life moves on. Whatever your previous role may have been and however important it was you will now be seen as an outsider. People in work will want to get on with the job in hand and will have little time for chit chat – just think how you may have reacted when you were actually working. So unless you have agreed some very specific role with your old organisation **it is probably best to stay away right from the very start**. That is not to say that you should not stay in contact with people with whom you were particularly friendly. But do so on the basis of an old boys' or old girls' or close friends' network outside the actual working environment.

Partner

If you are a couple you will now spend much more time together, and indeed this is something which you both may have been looking forward to. But you may need a little time to adjust to this new life balance and you need to be **careful not to get under each other's feet**. You may just need to give each other a bit of personal space and find or re-find hobbies and activities that could keep you challenged and occupied. There are literally thousands and **Chapter 11, Experiences, leisure and holidays** will give you inspiration. If only one partner has retired you may need to sit down and work out how responsibility for undertaking all those everyday but necessary tasks might have to be readjusted.

These very personal relationships will be a key factor in how happy your retirement years are likely to be. So, grab some time out and a cup of tea or glass of wine and sit down as a couple, talk through how best to work through what will be a new relationship, and be prepared to accept that it may take a little time to adjust to your new situation. Generally, you should find that things eventually do fall fairly neatly into place. Should the need arise, the following organisations can offer help and advice:

- Marriage Care: www.marriagecare.org.uk;
- The Spark (Scotland): www.thespark.org.uk;
- Relate: www.relate.org.uk and in Northern Ireland www.relateni.org

Learning to say no (nicely)

Learning to say no (nicely) needs to be on the list of techniques as you glide into retirement. Just about everyone around you will have plans for all that time you are going to free up – partner, parents, children and friends. The 'love sandwich' can help.

The meat of the love sandwich is what you are saying no to. It is in the middle but surrounded by a layer of good stuff (love) either side. It all about talking early on about what retirement means to you and gently managing people's expectations. It starts at the first layer and acknowledging the request or pointer that you are being given and why it is being made to you (i.e. there may be a garden that needs some help, or a child that needs childcare, or an organisation that needs help) so get clear on what is being asked of you. As part of this layer explain that you can see the need but at the same time re-explain the priorities of **your** retirement plans. Then deal with the meat of the question and say you can't help with x,y z. It will be hard the first time you try this approach but you really do need to avoid confusion and misunderstandings and explain clearly that you can't do x,y or z. Then take more time on finishing with the other layer which is some pointers or solutions to help that the person can explore. You may like it or hate it but it does works and what I can say with confidence is that so many people wish they were just that little bit better at saying no at this point in their life and managing the expectations of others.

> **Top tip**
> Learning to say 'no' nicely is a vital part of attaining the retirement you deserve. Is it something to 'start doing' at your plan in Chapter 13?

Children

You may also find that you have more time to devote to those wider family relationships. Your children may have moved on to start developing their own families, but it is likely they will continue to value whatever support you can give them. This may involve the occasional – or in some cases regular – babysitting duties. This can be a great bonus to both parties: you establish a closer bond with your grandchildren and your own children get a bit more freedom at an important stage of their own life. Also, if they are finding it difficult to get a foot on the property market, and you now find yourself with some available capital, you may want to discuss the possibility of giving or loaning them a helping hand to get started. But a word of warning: you should not impose yourself, your ideas of how things should be done or how to spend a gift –**'give and let go'** could be a useful phrase here. As in all things, a sensible balance is needed and don't forget that you need to retain your own freedom to do as you wish within reason. After all, you have worked hard for what you have now got and are entitled to enjoy it.

Parents

At the other end of the age spectrum your own or your partner's parents may now be getting to the stage where they may need some support or even just a little more of your time. Again, you need to tread carefully to avoid imposing your solutions on their problems and to ensure that they don't become overly dependent on you.

Sandwich generation

Those in their fifties and sixties are the 'sandwich generation' where dual pressures may influence the relationships. This could be caused by 'boomerang' kids who return home after University / College whereas, in previous generations, they tended to find their own independence at an earlier age. The same may apply if you have vulnerable or elderly parents that have needs and potentially care. More is set out in **Chapter 12, Sandwich Generation.**

Friends

You will probably already have a wide circle of social friendships and that is unlikely to change on retirement. Indeed, it is important to retain and even develop those links now that you have more time to do so. You should also take every opportunity to develop new friendships as you start to get involved with all of those activities you never had time to pursue during your working life. With more time there will be more opportunities to join new groups and if there is not a group around then take the lead and form one with the hints and tips provided in **Chapter 11, Leisure and Holidays**.

So, the general message is every person and relationship is individual and will differ slightly from another. Usually, things boil down to compromise and learning to work things out. An active social life, combined with building on those personal and family relationships is a sure-fire way of enhancing your retirement years and **'live better'**. Fractured relationships, on the other hand, usually have the opposite effect and it's maybe time to reflect a bit on those 'friends' that actually appear to have no real interest in your presence. You are not doing yourself a favour by offering those folk your time and energy and the glidepath may be a time to move on (and away from them).

Some people may stay as friends and some may come and go but the **true friends tend to stick around through the highs and lows of life**; sharing these events and getting through them is all part and parcel of your personal relationship 'network' and as a species we can be a resilient bunch!

Swedish death cleaning

I guess that may have got your attention. This came up quite a bit in the Retirement Planning courses I ran in 2024 and I admit the term was a new one for me at first, albeit I was aware of the thrust of the main objectives. It's now good to have a label for it! So, I've researched it a bit further and it makes so much well-being sense. It is a well-known concept in Scandinavian culture where decluttering and getting back a sense of control and order of your possessions comes first. It is all about having what you need, clearing out the waste and bringing some sense of order to your life. Some people start to buy less – do you really need yet another jacket or another pair of heels this Winter. It's not about being stingy it's about order. Maybe it sits best as you approach the passive stage of retirement that I outlined in Chapter 1 and where you may also be reducing the size of your home and scaling things down.

There are secondary benefits as the hordes of paperwork are razored down to what your loved ones may need to sort out your affairs at some point in the future. Decluttering involves three categories: there will be the 'skip' if you have lots to clear out (or boxes to fill and take to the tip). Some skip-hire companies offer a full recycling service. Next is sorting out the items to be sold to generate a bit of an extra income (either via vinted, ebay, facebook marketplace or equivalents or, if there is a lot, call in your local auctioneers); and then donating items that seem to be in decent condition and reusable (to charity or using the sort of local 'free in the local area' facebook groups that are popular).

Remember the attic, basement, deep cupboards and try to keep emotions out of it but do consult with your family or close friends for two reasons. Firstly, so they know what you are up to and that your affairs are in order and, secondly, just in case there are cherished memories in your possessions that are about to be 'Swedish death cleaned' and that they may want.

Health

The big picture- are you ready for ageing

It's a little old now as it was published back in 2010 but the House of Lords 'Ready for aging report' predicted the increases in demand for health and social care from 2010 to 2030 for people aged 65 and over in England and Wales and highlighted the key risks and trends:

- people with diabetes: up by over 45%

- people with arthritis, coronary heart disease, stroke: each up by over 50%

- people with dementia (moderate or severe cognitive impairment): up by over 80% to 1.96 million

The big picture- obesity

The NHS is clear in its advice: being obese puts you at raised risk of health problems such as heart disease, stroke and type 2 diabetes. Losing weight will bring significant health improvements. Achieving you targets can be tough and folk can, perhaps, be seen to give up too easily 'Ohh Peter is on another diet / health kick'. But face facts - it's simple and just requires a strength of mind to actually make and commit to a change of lifestyle.

Know exactly where you are on the Body Mass Index – visit www.nhs.uk and go to 'body mass index'. The body mass index is a measure that GPs like because it provides a relationship between your height and weight and then translates this into one of four categories: underweight, normal, overweight and obese. The worry points are the extremes of underweight and obese. If you are obese, start exercising more and eating better. The BMI calculator takes precisely one minute to complete by entering your age, height, weight and approximate activity level. There are also lots of advice, hints and tips on keeping healthy on the NHS website.

And did you know about the **'string test'**? It's brilliantly simple, costs nothing and takes 1 minute and is fanfared by, Professor Steve Bloom, the Head of Division for Diabetes, Endocrinology and Metabolism at Imperial College London who said

"If you manage to lose weight your cancer risk goes down to a half, your diabetes disappears, you live longer, alzheimer's disease is less and, of course, the long term effects in the human race of not having this tsunami of obesity is amazing. People

will live longer, they will be healthier, they will be more effective."

Here is how his string test works. Get a piece of string and measure your height with it and cut it off at your precise height level. Fold the string in half and now measure it round the widest part of your stomach. The two ends should touch and if you are left with a gap between the ends of the folded string you need to work on reducing the gap and work towards a healthier life.

Physical exercise

Well this sounds simple and – you've guessed it – it is something easy that most of us can do. Staying physically active improves our health and quality of life, and can help us live longer. Among the advantages of keeping active are a reduced risk of developing a life-threatening disease, a better chance of avoiding obesity, maintaining or reaching a healthy weight, improved sleep and increased daytime energy, feeling happier, and keeping your brain sharp. The more physically active you are, the longer you are likely to remain independent. Exercise makes you stronger, boosts confidence and increases your sense of well-being. Start slowly and build up gradually. Experts recommend 30 minutes of moderate exercise a day about five times a week and it can be something as simple as a brisk walk. You can then then start to work on your strength and mobility and a chat with a personal trainer ('PT') at your local leisure centre can help with the development of a programme that helps work on 'your core' – the area that helps build strength and stability. Maybe a programme of 10 sessions with a PT can then start make a real difference. These come at a cost but returning to the opening paragraph I'd ask how much you spend on servicing a car.

Radical changes in habits don't happen easily and I've two suggestions to help make the change in lifestyle and then embed it. The first is just writing down what you want to achieve. **Try the 'I'm going to start' box at Chapter 13**. Secondly, it then needs to become part of way your day runs- initially **obsess about** it for 10 weeks and create the time in your day to make this happen. After 10 weeks you'll be there and the chances always improve if you track and measure what you're trying to achieve. That tracking just takes a pen and a piece of paper. But do **obsess about these changes one at a time** (i.e best not to take on two big things to change in your life at the same time). Once you've sorted the first one after 10 weeks move on to the next 'I'm going to start' action. If you have a partner share what you are doing and you'll find they'll help you make the change.

> **Top tip**
> If you really want to make a lifestyle change take things one step at a time. <u>Obsess</u> about what you want to achieve and commit it to the 'I'm going to start...' as Chapter 13. If it's getting your activity and steps up pick a stretching target beyond your current average steps a day and aim to eventually get over that target and the impact could be amazing. If you have health issues just ensure you check your plan out with your Doctor/ health professional.

Organised activities

There are lots of ways of staying fit and in most local areas there are loads of classes to help you do it; some may even be free, or cut-price, at your sports or community centre or local park. Find out what's available in your area. There are all sorts of activities, including boxercise, pilates, table tennis, circuit training, swimming, running, cycling, walking groups and bowling. Getting fit as part of a group gives a social aspect to it and is probably more motivating but if you want to get started on your own. Try Fitness Blender, which offers more than 400 free workout videos, ranging from high-intensity interval training to yoga: www.fitnessblender.com.

Mental exercise

As retirement progresses and old work structures and boundaries change we may also face a risk of isolation and reduced mental activity. Learning opportunities were highlighted in **Chapter 9** – 'training opportunities' and can I give an extra mention again here to University of the Third Age ('U3A') which is profiled at **Chapter 11**. Their organised events tick the boxes of socialising and events/ hobbies and should be explored as part of your plan. **Chapter 11** also helps highlights hobbies and consider these for the same socialisation and mental activity opportunities. The health risks flagged in the House of Lords 'reading for ageing report' that I highlighted at the start of this chapter represent real risks to your retirement journey. You should not underestimate the power of physical and mental activity in helping to combat these risks in combination with a better diet which I look at next.

Healthy eating

There are a many special diets and the media are forever commenting on what we should and should not eat. Treat some of that with caution and focus on a balanced diet and try to avoid overeating/ grazing. Start with recognising that old boundaries are changing (from when you worked 5 days a week) and your diet could slip into bad habits without those old boundaries. For starters try to eat more fresh fruit and vegetables; cut back on bread; drink plenty of water and reduce or cut out high sugar e.g. fizzy drinks; eat more fish; drink less alcohol and limit your salt intake.

Top tip

- **Buy smaller plates – size is everything here- it promotes smaller portions.**
- **Colour is good - if your plate is colourful that means lots of vegetables and fruit.**
- **Willpower – 'I'm going to start …' or 'I'm going to stop…'. It's not about a diet fad. It's all about a new lifestyle for a lasting impact. Does that prompt a thing to 'start' at Chapter 13 or conversely is there something that you're now just going to 'stop'. Remember change can be difficult. Obsess about it for at least 10 weeks and you'll notice the change.**

Drink (alcohol)

There is so much reported about over-indulgence with alcohol that this topic may seem too obvious to mention. The more you drink, the greater the risk to your health. The **NHS suggested limit is 14 units a week** and a pint of lager or a 175 ml glass of wine count as two units. For people who suspect they may have a drinking problem, the first point of contact should be their GP. There are organisations to help those in need of support, such as:

- Al-Anon Family Groups UK & Eire: www.al-anonuk.org.uk;
- Alcohol Concern: www.alcoholconcern.org.uk;
- Alcoholics Anonymous: www.alcoholics-anonymous.org.uk.

Smoking

The only advice to give is that you should not smoke cigarettes or vapes – and if you still do you should stop and improve your health and save more. The start point is the NHS stop smoking service and can it massively boost your chances of quitting for good. www.nhs.uk and search 'stop smoking services'.

Top tip
Is it time to commit this to your 'stop doing' at Chapter 13 and become obsessed about making a real change?

Health insurance

Health insurance or private medical insurance (PMI) pays out for private treatment if you fall ill; it also allows you to avoid long queues for treatment, receive fast-track consultations, and be treated privately in an NHS or private hospital. PMI is not essential and the cost of it can increase significantly as you get older. You do, therefore, need to look very carefully at the balance between cost and benefit depending on your own situation. If you have an accident or serious illness such as a heart attack or cancer then the NHS steps in and can be world class. But problems can arise from other conditions that may be debilitating but not life-threatening; the challenge may be in getting a timely intervention so that you are more comfortable and can get on with enjoying your retirement years. If you have disposable income and your finances are in order you may be able to buy in the help you need for extra peace of mind. Not every eventuality is covered by PMI, so it is important to check your policy details and review the cost and affordability from time to time. Take care before moving from one provider to another and find out if pre-existing conditions are covered – get this wrong and you could be in for a very nasty surprise. The main providers are well known but there are other options such as wwwbendenden.co.uk which is a membership organisation where you can access reduced fee consultations on a pay as you go basis.

Private patients – without insurance cover

The NHS is crumbling in the Winter of 2024 and you may be waiting too long for a non-urgent procedure. If you or an elderly relative or child do not have private medical insurance but want to go into hospital in the UK as a private patient, there is nothing to stop you, provided your doctor is willing and you are able to pay the bills from your savings. Start the process by asking your doctor, **'Can I get this done privately?'** and they will guide you from there.

Medical tourism

The term 'medical tourism' refers to travellers who have chosen to have medical/dental/surgical treatment abroad. Cosmetic surgery, dental procedures and cardiac surgery are the most common procedures that medical tourists undergo. Since the standards of medical treatments and available treatments vary widely across the world, anyone considering undertaking medical treatment abroad should carry out their own independent research. Further information and advice can be found at www.nhs.uk/NHSEngland/Healthcareabroad.

Hospital care cash plans

A hospital healthcare cash plan is an insurance policy that helps you pay for routine healthcare treatment, such as eye tests, dental treatment and physiotherapy. They are totally different to private medical insurance and can be a cheap way of paying for everyday health costs. You pay a monthly premium, depending on how much cover you want. When you receive the treatment you pay upfront, send the receipt to the insurer and it reimburses you, depending on the terms of your policy. More information is available from the British Health Care Association: www.bhca.org.uk.

Income protection policies

Income protection insurance used to be known as permanent health - insurance. It is a replacement-of-earnings policy for people who are still in work (employed or self-employed). Critical illness benefit policies pay a lump sum on diagnosis of a critical illness (and some life policies may pay out on diagnosis of a terminal illness rather than awaiting death to make the payment – read the small print if you are unsure). Take advice on the appropriateness of these policies from a financial adviser and check that they are regulated by the Financial Conduct Authority (FCA). The FCA maintains a register of approved financial advisers. Find out more at www.fca.org and go to 'check the register'. In addition, help may be available through policies arranged by your work in the form of sick leave policies or stand-alone cover. If you are nearing retirement or have significant borrowings you may wish to revisit the adequacy of your cover from these sorts of products and check when they expire.

Health screening

Book a health MOT with your GP asking for a general health check and then listen to any advice offered. Beyond that and given that it is now time to focus more time (and perhaps money?) on health is it finally time to get a private personalised health assessment to give you an overview of your current general health and aim to identify any future health risks. Private health screening, outside the NHS, will give you an in-depth heath check and focus on preventative health. It should inform you of potential health risks specific to you and will underline good health habits and behaviours to support your health and it will usually provide a series of specific written tips and objectives. It may spot some red flags for follow up that might just be lifesaving. Many employers arrange these for staff and their partners at preferential rates. Ask HR or occupational health at your place of work if these are available. Otherwise, some of the UK organisations that offer a number of health assessment options depending on your personal needs and at various costs and locations throughout the UK include:

- www.bmihealthcare.co.uk;
- www.bupa.co.uk;
- www.nuffieldhealth.com
- www.privatehealth.co.uk.

> **Top tip**
> Get a GP health check or for a more in depth review a private personal health assessment. It's time to spend more time on your health. An action point for Chapter 13?

National Health Service

Choosing a GP

If you need to choose a new GP for whatever reason, is there a way of checking on how good they are? If you live in England or Wales you can do this quite easily via the Care Quality Commission (www.cqc.org.uk); at the top of their website toggle the drop-down box to doctors/GPs and then search by postcode.

Assessment ratings of outstanding, good, requires improvement and inadequate are provided for each of the following:

- treating people with respect and involving them in their care;
- providing care, treatment and support that meets people's needs;
- caring for people safely and protecting them from harm;
- staffing;
- quality and suitability of management.

Otherwise the usual best way to find a good GP is to ask for recommendations from trusted friends or, if you are new to an area, from your new neighbours – it's also a good ice-breaker.

Changing your GP

Since January 2015 all GP practices in England have been free to register new patients who live outside their boundary area. These arrangements are voluntary; if the practice has no capacity at the time or feels that it is not clinically appropriate for you to be registered, it can refuse registration and explain its reasons for so doing. If you know of a doctor whose list you would like to be on, you can simply turn up at his or her surgery and ask to be registered. You do not need to give a reason for wanting to change, and you do not need to ask anyone's permission. A request will then be made to your current GP for your medical records to be transferred to the new GP surgery.

NHS 111 service

111 is the NHS non-emergency number. It's fast, easy and free. When you call 111, you will speak to an adviser, supported by healthcare professionals, who will ask a number of questions to assess symptoms and direct you to the best medical care available. NHS 111 is available 24 hours a day, 365 days a year, and calls are free from landlines and mobile phones. For further information, see www.nhs.uk.

Prescriptions

The current prescription charge is £9.90 (2025/25) and reviewed annually from 1 April each year) but both men and women aged 60 and over are entitled to free NHS prescriptions. Certain other groups are also entitled to free prescriptions, including those on low incomes, and they are free in, for instance, Northern Ireland and Scotland. Find out more at www.nhs.uk and go to 'prescriptions'.

Top tip

A 12-month prescription certificate costs £114.70 in 2024/25 or it can be paid in 10 instalments; if you need two items each month you can save over £100 (and over £300 if you have four items each month). You can do this online via the NHS website or your chemist can help you arrange it.

Going into hospital

Going into hospital can cause people a lot of anxiety. You may be admitted as an outpatient, a day patient (day case), or an inpatient. Many patients are unaware that they can ask their GP to refer them to a consultant at a different NHS trust or even, in certain cases, help make arrangements for them to be treated overseas. Before you can become a patient at another hospital, your GP will need to agree to your being referred. Those likely to need help on leaving hospital should speak to the hospital social worker, who will help make any necessary arrangements. Help is sometimes available to assist patients with their travel costs to and from hospital. Remember to take your phone charger and headphones. If you go into hospital you will continue to receive your pension as normal.

Complaints

If you want to make a complaint about any aspect of NHS treatment you have received or been refused, go to the practice or the hospital concerned and ask for a copy of their complaints procedure. This is the same for GPs, opticians, dentists, hospitals and any care given in the NHS. Full details of how to do this can be found at www.nhs.uk – 'complaints'. You can take the matter to the Health Services Ombudsman should you be dissatisfied after an independent review has been carried out. For further details see:

- Parliamentary and Health Service Ombudsman for England: www.ombudsman.org.uk;
- Public Services Ombudsman for Wales: www.ombudsman-wales.org.uk;
- Scottish Public Services Ombudsman: www.spso.org.uk.

An alternative would be to get in touch with your local Patient Advice and Liaison Service (PALS) office in the event of a problem with the health service. Find out more at www.nhs.uk – 'Patient Advice and Liaison Service'.

Complementary and alternative medicine

Complementary and alternative medicines are treatments that fall outside mainstream healthcare. Although the terms 'complementary' and 'alternative' medicine are often used interchangeably, there are distinct differences between them. Complementary medicine is a treatment that is used alongside conventional medicine, whereas alternative medicine is a treatment used in place of conventional medicine. The best known of these practices are homoeopathy, reflexology, osteopathy, chiropractic, aromatherapy, herbal remedies and hypnosis. Information on the most popular forms can be found on the following websites:

- Association of Reflexologists: www.aor.org.uk;
- British Acupuncture Council: www.acupuncture.org.uk;
- British Chiropractic Association: www.chiropractic-uk.co.uk;
- British Homoeopathic Association: www.britishhomeopathic.org;
- British Hypnotherapy Association: www.hypnotherapy-association.org;
- National Institute of Medical Herbalists: www.nimh.org.uk.

Useful reading on common health issues

The NHS website is the go-to source for more information and explains medical conditions and provides advice. It's best to keep away from other sites as they just make things look scary and that does not help you or deal with the issue.

There are also good sites for specific conditions such as Cancer Research UK that can provide detailed guidance. As a general rule avoid any non-UK sites and chat rooms.

Reminder: Take any action points or follow up points to Chapter 13, Your Plan For A Better Retirement especially those 'start doing' or 'stop doing' lifestyle changes.

Chapter Eleven

Experiences, leisure and holidays

"Twenty years from now you will be more disappointed by the things you didn't do than by the ones you did do. So throw off the bowlines, sail away from the safe harbor. Catch the trade winds in your sails. Explore. Dream. Discover."

MARK TWAIN

If you're on a glidepath retirement and still benefiting from some work-related income you'll have more to spend on experiences, leisure and holidays. Remember that journey may last 30 years or more and you'll be fitter in the early years. As Mark Twain says in my chapter headline quote above "*you will be more disappointed by the things you didn't do*". If you have watched your net wealth grow to the point of <u>now</u> starting your retirement glidepath then <u>now</u> is the time for your life to grow. Don't keep putting off what you want to do. It may may too late as you could be saving money for an experience you may never enjoy. Experiences, leisure and holidays all cost money and sometimes lots of money. By this stage of my book you will understand your net wealth and be planning to save more, earn more and will be working on your well-being. Now it's time for the best bit of the plan- letting your life grow.

You will be more disappointed by the things you didn't do

This could be the first chapter you turn to and maybe a life of 'brilliant new experiences, leisure and holidays' was something that sums up retirement for you? Well, it's certainly all in this chapter but, and it's another big but, maybe it's also about taking a chance to blend a focus on your well-being through mental and physical activity (as per the preceding chapter) which allows us to **'live better'** and enjoy those experiences, leisure and holiday moments even more.

This chapter at a glance

- **Experiences-** you've built up all this net wealth by the time you start your retirement glidepath (Chapter 1 covers your net wealth and plan) and if you have not had the re-set in thinking about this wealth and your plan, then now is the time to start. If there is spare wealth and income use it to have even more brilliant experiences, holidays and time with any children, grandchildren and loved ones. Don't be disappointed by the things you didn't do.
- **Keeping fit** – some reminders of the easy starting points. Then just keep going.
- **Sporting activities**, watching sport and forming your own club. Don't sit around waiting for someone else to do it – it's easy and our three-step model will help get things going.
- **Entertainment and hobbies** – try something different, you just never know what you might ignite. This includes how to access free 'big name' entertainment by getting hold of TV/radio audience tickets – and we all like things that are quality and free (and those two words do not often go hand in hand).
- Keeping **mentally fit** and how to get started on **writing that book** you have had buzzing around your head and how to follow through on any study aspirations.
- Tips and pointers on **holidays, cruises, short UK breaks** and starting to tick off some more European city breaks (especially if you can buy flights for as little as £30- correction £19.99 as I look at the Easyjet big orange sale whilst I'm writing this in December 2024-isn't that an amazing price for a flight to Belfast!).
- In reading this chapter you might surprise yourself at finding a **hidden talent** that has lain dormant until now.
- **Travel insurance** and help if things go wrong on holiday – some essential tips. Don't leave home without them.

Experiences

I remember talking to a friend in 2024 who was approaching their glidepath retirement start point with decent net assets and a small portfolio of properties. Their children were struggling to afford the deposits on their first properties. I said something like *"Who cares if you make a bit of a gain or income on your properties. 40% will go to the taxman when you drop dead so why not sell some properties now and do the things you've always wanted to do with the cash? And, even better, why not help the children with their house deposits or childcare/education by gifting (see Chapter 5, Tax and IHT) at a time when they need it the most."* Harsh, but maybe fair input and it's great that good friends can take each other down a peg or two as I mentioned in **Chapter 10, Well-being and Personal Relationships**. I'm a bit more subtle when talking to tax clients but you get the basic message.

Even better is the fact that some of the best experiences are free (or almost free) so it's not all about money. I think the point I'm trying to get across is Mark Twain's brilliant quote so here it is again to underline the point.

Top tip

"Twenty years from now you will be more disappointed by the things you didn't do than by the ones you did do. So throw off the bowlines, sail away from the safe harbor. Catch the trade winds in your sails. Explore. Dream. Discover."

MARK TWAIN

Let your life grow. Get it right and you will achieve a better retirement.

What are the experiences that you owe yourself? Start a list of the experiences you'd love to achieve and keep coming back to it. Pause, think deep and start below.

Experiences wish list
(don't be disappointed by the things you didn't do)
1.

2.

3.

4.

5.

6.

7.

8.

9.

10.

Leveraging Artificial Intelligence

Subject to the tiny caveat of the piece in italics immediately below not a word of this book (unlike other books!) has been generated by Artificial Intelligence ("AI"). It is, however, a powerful tool and it seems daft to not at least allow it to help you plan your experiences journey. I typed into Chatgpt.com the following random example:

"I am 61, male, living in Northampton and retire this year. I like travel, beaches, entertaining cities and would like a wish list of top experiences to achieve in the next 5 years"

In 5 seconds I received back a 850 word list of activities to pursue. It wasn't perfect but it was really really good and quite clever. It began:

"That's exciting! With retirement approaching, there's a world of possibilities ahead for you to explore. Here's a wish list of experiences that combine your interests in travel, beaches, and vibrant cities, focusing on both adventure and relaxation: ..."

I was enticed by the first recommendation and that's where I'm heading in May 2025!

Keeping yourself fit

Unsurprisingly the healthier you are the better equipped you may be to tackle a wider range of experiences. In addition, if you have managed to **start your retirement glidepath 5 years earlier (as per Chapter 1)** you will be in better condition than if you had waited another 5 years. It's a simple formula.

Am I going to pull on my rugby boots again (they are still stored in the attic- I just can't throw them away) and take run out again at Ravenhill or Twickenham? Absolutely not! So your health and condition will limit your experiences wish list. But the earlier you start the experiences process the more you may be able to cope with. An Eighty Five year old may just decide that they can't cope with a long held ambition to fly long haul to Sydney, Australia from London. That would be an example of being disappointed by the things they didn't do as the health time clock just overtook your capacity to achieve the experience.

Looking then at fitness levels and keeping yourself fit, a good starting point is the fairly basic rule that, generally speaking, the fitter you are the better and longer your quality of life. More at Chapter 9, Health and Relationships and remember to speak to your doctor / GP before embarking on a radical change / increase in exercise.

Walking and running

Walking costs nothing, doesn't require expensive equipment and is the best form of natural exercise. It keeps you healthy, prolongs your life and improves your mental health. There is walking (in the park), hiking (in the hills), rambling (across country), hill walking (in mountainous areas), fell walking (particularly in the Lake District and Yorkshire Dales – fell meaning high, uncultivated land) and scrambling (sometimes applied to mountain walking).

Why not join a small group, which may even have a side benefit of introducing a new circle of friends. Get onto the web and see what might be available locally or take a few soundings from friends and acquaintances. Failing that, try the Ramblers' Charity at www.ramblers.org.uk. If you are more enthusiastic, try running as a hobby. You can do this indoors (at the gym) or outdoors, by yourself as a solo activity, with a group or by joining a club. For those keen to get running try the 'Couch to 5k' app or the following websites for more information:

1. England Athletics: www.englandathletics.org;

2. Run England: www.runengland.org;

3. Association of Running Clubs: www.runningclubs.org.uk.

4. Your local area for park 'fun runs' or up a level to www.parkrun.org.uk for 5k community runs on Saturday mornings.

Get a dog

A dog forces you to walk, improves your fitness and increases social interaction. Select your breed carefully as the span of behaviours is vast and a good trainer is vital at the start. The trainer will train your dog and you. As Graeme Hall, the Dogfather, says in TV's Dogs Behaving Very Badly it's usually not the dog but the owner that needs the training! Common problems include: Dog aggression, pulling on lead, separation anxiety, dog recall, dogs jumping up, excessive barking, toilet training. Get them all resolved early and discover your new best friend!

Costs to budget for are the original fee to any breeder, vet's fees, food and boarding when you are away.

Swimming

Swimming is also one of the best forms of exercise; it builds strength and it is beneficial for your metabolism and the cardiovascular system. Swimming as a hobby, is a great way to relax and get fit. For more information see British Swimming at www.britishswimming.org.

Sporting activities

The list of possibilities is virtually endless and popular leisure sports are golf, tennis, boating, cycling and fishing and there is a further endless list of activities. A bit of research and asking around friends could spark that 'oh, why not, I'll give it a try' moment!

Watching sport and forming your own club

There is excellent coverage of sport on TV but it is really enjoyable to get out and watch live sport. There are many different opportunities – you can watch your local football, netball or rugby team, and of course there are also the big international events which all provide a good day out with a bunch of friends. The main thing is to get off the couch and get out and support your favourite or local team in person or even try something new. Transport and cost issues can be solved by forming your own 'club' – just follow these three easy rules:

1. Find three or four like-minded friends – that is all you need to get started.
2. Agree the briefest of 'rules'– going to events, enjoyment, friendship and sharing the cost.
3. Manage the money. The rules require everyone to chip in £100 (or whatever amount is needed to cover your event, travel and maybe a meal) which the 'treasurer' keeps. You then top it up after each event so that the pot always comes back to number of members times £100. The 'secretary' identifies the event, date and cost and maybe an 'interesting' detour on the way there and people decide if they want to go or not. If you don't go the £100 in the pot is

rolled forward. Every group need a 'chairperson' who just makes the final decision if there is a split vote – then you get on with it. You'll soon find the group of four extends to six and then 10; at some point you'll have to call it a day on new members as part of the fun is the friendship of a smallish group.

> **Top tip**
> **Don't wait for someone else to get your own club going. An informal club can apply to anything – sports followers, entertainment viewing or even a club that follows both! Just get on with it, agree a few simple rules and off you go.**

Entertainment

Approaching – and reaching – retirement means you will probably have increased opportunities to head off for a night's entertainment. Why not try something new? Look beyond your local mainstream cinemas and then also try local drama groups.

A bit of culture – opera, ballet, concerts and museums

Love, hate or don't know? Some of the gems of the UK are its museums and music concerts (from punk to a full orchestra). If you have never tried a ballet or a night at the opera then why not give it a go?

TV and radio audiences

Participating as members of studio audiences and making contributions to programmes is entertaining and free. Tickets for very popular shows can be hard to obtain but you never know – and a new show could be the next big thing. Check out:
Applause Store (www.applausestore.com)
BBC Shows (www.bbc.co.uk/showsandtours/tickets)

Hobbies and other interests

Wikipedia has compiled a great 'list of hobbies' page which lists literally hundreds of possibilities along with their usual click-through facility to reveal more. They range from Acting to Zumba. If something in particular takes your fancy then do a bit more specific exploring on the web and then locally. Don't be worried if you then find it is not for you, just move on to something else – you have time to get it right and find something that really sits with your time, skills, values and beliefs. Below are seven selected as random examples and literally this book could have been filled with lists of hobbies. Who knows where the hobby could lead and remember it's never too soon to start that new hobby if active retirement is years away and you are still in the planning phase.

Gardening

Views differ on where to classify gardening – is it a hobby, a pastime or a necessity? Whatever view you may take, most of us do have gardens and either enjoy looking after them or are forced to do so. If you are already a keen gardener who really enjoys working and relaxing in the garden then keep the good work going and you will enjoy the fact that you now have the time and opportunity to do even more. If you are amongst the less enthusiastic, perhaps due to a busy working schedule, now may be the opportunity to devote a little more time to it. Don't regard it as a chore, and just concentrate on the simple things at first. A nice lawn is the centrepiece to many gardens and the fact that you will now have the time to give it a weekly trim rather than a quick cut when time permits will work wonders for the appearance of your garden.

Mentor

You could help young people in your area. There are many government backed schemes and one is Mosaic a national charity mentoring network backed by the Prince's Trust (www.mosaicnetwork.co.uk).

Model railway clubs

Enthusiasts include Warren Buffett, Eric Clapton, Tom Hanks, Bruce Springsteen, Rod Stewart, Ringo Star and Pete Waterman. Clubs provide a social scene and new members can benefit from the experience and wealth of knowledge and good clubs always adapt to the needs of their members.

Museum volunteer

From the Imperial War Museum to the National History Museum to local museums. The opportunities are abundant for paid and unpaid roles. Check out your favourite museums for opportunities and if it follows one of your passions then even better.

Painting

Get those creative genes flowing onto canvas and try exploring those skills that may have lain dormant since those art classes in your school days. It's never too late to take up this hobby and find your preferred media (watercolour, pastel or ink etc.) and style. Local clubs can be found by an internet search or from your circle of friends where someone will know someone and can introduce you. New member events are usually held throughout the year where the novices can started in a nice friendly environment.

Zookeeper

Zoos and animal welfare charities depend on volunteers and training will be provided. It keeps you fit and will be sociable as there can be lots of interacting with the public.

Write that book?

Why not write that book you've had buzzing around in your head? You might discover a hidden talent and write a bestseller, but for many it ends up as an unfinished project. If you are determined then just start at the beginning, with a fair idea of the ending, and take your readers on the journey. Your motto will be to write, read, rewrite (and repeat). It may end up being self-printed for family and friends or self-published for a wider audience. Or you may find yourself in the realms of working with a publisher, either with or without the help of an agent. As far as top tips go, you will find that lots of people have lots to say on the internet about writing. So we will leave you with just two suggestions. First, make writing a habit; it requires perseverance. Create a routine and write at the same time every day; if it just isn't working one day then give up that day and go and do something else. Then buy a guidebook to help steer you through the maze of options and opportunities – try the *Writers and Artists Yearbook 2025* (more at www.writersandartists.co.uk). Once you are established as a writer, and if you meet their criteria, the Society of Authors is the 'must join' organisation (www.societyofauthors.org). In the meantime a check online should find any local writers' groups in your area which is another good starting point.

Mentally fit- more study?

You may well feel that during your working life you have done enough studying and attended enough courses and are due a break from all of that. However, when the pressure of being almost forced to do something disappears, you can study what takes your fancy, and of course you now have time to do so. Old dogs can learn new tricks!

You may enjoy holidaying abroad in a particular area but miss out on a lot because of language barriers – maybe now is the time to try to pick up the basics (is that a nudge to putting a point down in the 'start now' section of your plan as Chapter 13). Maybe your computer and IT skills are a bit rusty – again, you now have time to put that right. Although there is a cost to their learning courses I do like the vast range of earning opportunities and ability to learn remotely at learn.direct.com. They are a UK based learning organisation with the aim of inspiring people to realise their potential. Learn Direct is packed with skills based courses if you want to retrain (nursing, animal care, book-keeping) and then it has other courses that can give access to Higher Education diploma courses. Or you can dive into health and fitness courses or take some short lifestyle courses.

There are also a wide range of part-time vocational-type courses available at local Further Education Colleges and other institutes of learning throughout the UK. Take a little time to find out what is available in your own area. Your local community/ council may also offer various social and learning activities, so visit the premises (for any helpful community noticeboards) or the websites of your local council, leisure centre, church, community centre or library to find out what's available. Libraries are an endangered species these days so pop in – you never know what or who you might spot, see or meet. Perhaps new contacts via U3A may point you in the right direction- more immediately below.

You're not alone in your hobby or learning with U3A

The University of the Third Age (U3A) isn't a university at all it's just a shorthand for a sort of grouping of like minded people that are in the glidepath through retirement that want to learn, laugh and live. It offers group activities and interest groups throughout the UK and there will be a group near you. Then within that group there could be literally a hundred sub-groups based around hobbies and interests. You might find one like the brilliantly named 'Rubbish friends' as they have in North Down where a group meets for a walk, chat and to do some litter collecting on beaches and scenic spots (that's what I call a win: win: win- as it brings activity, socialising and doing some good locally!). Maybe your interest is badminton, car appreciation, foreign language improvement, pilates, singing, wine tasting and so on- there are hundreds of groups and U3A is growing. If you have an interest and there isn't a group formed already you will be encouraged to form one as chances are that others will be interested or will give it a go. There is no age limit on joining, the only condition is that members should no longer be in full time employment so those on a glidepath part-time employment are welcome. The strap line of U3A is 'learn, laugh and live'. It is committed to lifelong learning, can help combat loneliness with social interaction, and offers a huge range of activities and courses. Membership fees are kept to a minimum (£15 to £20 per year) and members are encouraged to share their skills and interests with each other. There are plenty of U3A branches around the United Kingdom, so you should be able to find one near you. For more information, visit www.u3a.org.uk.

Top tip

If you are no longer in full time employment check out your local University of the Third Age and rekindle some old hobbies or find new ones. This can work well if you have moved to a new area and new social networks will open up.

Holidays

This may well be the part of retirement that you are really looking forward to. With all that time now available you might be thinking about a world cruise, more overseas visits to relatives and close friends, taking an expedition to some remote corner of the world, visiting cities on your must-see list, or maybe just long, leisurely days somewhere in the sun. Retirement really does give you additional options. You are no longer stuck with set holiday dates, which has the additional bonus of allowing you to take advantage of last-minute offers and cheaper rates at off-peak times. Also, of course, you now have time to shop around for the best bargains. So, get out there and start looking for your ideal holiday or adventure at the best price. If you are reasonably competent with computers and the internet you can do a great deal of your business in that way and it frequently represents good value for money. But don't ignore a tried-and-trusted travel agent, many of whom are very knowledgeable about locations and prices.

Here are a few examples just to get your mind working on the endless opportunities.

Bus travel and coach and rail holidays

You may be entitled to concessionary travel in England, Wales, Scotland and Northern Ireland with different rules in different countries and even regions. Just jump onto www.ageuk.org.uk and 'free bus pass and transport concessions" and take whatever you get and enjoy! The Senior Railcard can save a third of the cost on standard or first-class fares (www.senior-railcard.co.uk) and National Express offer a Senior Coachcard that entitles you to a third off ticket prices (www.nationalexpress.com).

Cruising

The cruise market continue to break records after a gap during the Covid-19 pandemic. It is driven on by new and often larger ships constantly being launched. Cruising is firmly on the agenda again in 2025.

Cruising can take you to virtually anywhere in the world or around the British Isles and our wonderful coastline. The big advantage is that your own hotel travels along with you. You can simply relax in the sun of the Mediterranean or the Caribbean; explore a range of classic cities; get to know the Scandinavian countries or Alaska; explore the mysteries of the Far East; or visit Australia and New Zealand. The possibilities are endless, as can be seen from a quick browse of cruise brochures in any travel agents. Or get online and type in the names of a couple of cruise lines.

There are various reasons why so many people enjoy cruising: many operators have ships leaving from the UK, reducing air travel; seeing multiple destinations but unpacking only once; the wide choice, as cruise ships come in all shapes and sizes. Cruise holiday are easy to plan, they are social and there are activities and entertainments galore. If you want to take a closer look at the range on offer from cruise companies and what their individual ships are like, get hold of a copy of the latest year edition of Berlitz Cruising and Cruise Ships, which is regularly updated and provides lots of valuable and dependable information on all aspects of cruising and cruise ships.

Top cruising tips

- *Inside cabins* can be an absolute bargain for those on a budget **but** wanting exceptional itineraries. However, there is no natural light, which can play havoc with your body clock and they can be in poor locations (corridor, lift, engine or other noise) – but don't dismiss them as an option.
- *Buy early or buy late*: Experienced cruisers know the form. Buy early to get the best cabins in the best locations and deep discounts or hang on to the last minute to get a bargain on an under-booked cruise. Shopping around or staying with the same agent (loyalty bonuses and trusted knowledge) can both help with the price you pay. Try negotiations around the amount of on-board spend they will credit to your room as part of any 'deal'.
- *How much!* Many cruises make deep profits on the price of drinks and that final day when you settle up your bill can be sobering. Think about pre-paid drinks packages; some cruises offer these free as an inducement.
- *Repositioning cruises* are made by all the major cruise lines where the ship moves between continents and seasons. They are cheaper than other cruises **but** there are more days at sea and less ports visited which can get a bit boring.
- *How much (part 2)!* Cruise lines also make deep profits from **excursions**. The bonus is that their ship probably won't leave port if your coach breaks down and you miss the scheduled departure time. On the other hand you can more than halve the cruise excursion price by going with a local alternative, and enterprising organisations have set up 'shore excursion' companies offering trips that mirror the cruise company offering. You can also do it yourself via google maps, whatsinport.com and a few taxis.
- *Cruise from the UK or a European port?* We know our lovely UK weather but who has crossed the Atlantic or the Bay of Biscay when it's been rough? The passage to warmer, smoother seas may eat up four or five days of your precious holiday. Why do people do this in late September and October when the seas are rough and the weather is cold? So is it worth it? Or do you **fly out of the UK and pick up a cruise from a Mediterranean port in the more challenging months.**
- **Some useful websites** are www.whatsinport.com for overviews and hints and tips on what is in and around the port area with maps and suggestions that may help if you don't want to go on excursions. Another useful website is www.cruisecritic.co.uk for port and ship overviews and user reviews.

Cargo ship cruises

Seeing the world by cargo ship doesn't offer the trappings of a conventional cruise, but being aboard a freight ship as a paying passenger is like being in another world. Many carry up to 12 non-crew members on routes from a week to months long. Securing a berth can be complicated, and periods in port tend to be brief, but life on board is uneventful – perfect for reading and writing. See Cargo Ship Voyages: www.cargoshipvoyages.com.

River cruising

This type of cruising has some similarities to ocean cruising but there are very big differences.

Riverboats are much smaller and tend to be more intimate, which some people prefer and the client age average seems to be 70 plus. Because of their size there tends to be less concentration on entertainment. They do, however, give an excellent opportunity to explore inland towns and cities. Frequently the mooring is very close to the city or town centre.

Short breaks

The UK is a brilliant place packed with diversity and places of interest - that's why the world flocks here as a must see destination. So as a quick reminder and a starter for ten you could start planning those weekends:

- shop in London (as it's better than New York, Paris or Milan);
- take in the pretty gardens and villages in the Cotswolds;
- Caernarfon Castle;
- hit the Lanes and seafront at Brighton;
- take in the rugby, shops and restaurants in Edinburgh:
- take a hot bath in Bath;
- have a titanic experience in Belfast;
- stride the Giant's Causeway;
- tackle the Lake District;
- drive Bwlch y Groes (Hell Fire Pass) in Wales;
- put a bet on at Newmarket racecourse;

- take a steam train to historic York;
- rediscover the Beatles and more in Liverpool;
- see and experience the world class theatres and museums in London.

The list is literally endless just google 'what's on' in different areas and start your own list. You may already have taken advantage of weekend breaks during your working life. A short trip of three or four days is attractive due to relatively low-cost air fares. If you book early and can travel mid-Tuesday or Wednesday afternoon with only hand baggage, you can nab some of those £30 seats. Next best is to try starting your trip on a Sunday night – it's usually the cheapest time for hotel rates. Again, the list is endless and the budget airline websites carry decent overviews and tips. To get your list going try visiting or revisiting :

- **Amsterdam** – tulips, art, culture and wacky cafes.

- **Barcelona** – excellent flight connections make this a must-see city with its Olympic stadium, beach and Las Ramblas all combining very well. Gaudi's La Sagrada Familia Cathedral will stop you in your tracks (oh, and there is that football team as well).

- **Belfast** – according to the New York Times "an eye watering experience in the best possible way".

- **Any island in the Canaries** - for a long weekend and some proper Winter sun between November and February.

- The walled City of **Dubrovnik** – nearly every roof was replaced following the shelling it endured less than three decades ago but the city is standing tall again.

- **Prague** – exceptional value and perhaps one of the most beautiful places you will visit.

- **Rome** – culturally outstanding.

- **Stockholm**- for everything ABBA and simply stunning at every level.

- **Venice** – enchanting.

- **Reykjavik** – highlights include the Northern Lights and National Parks. Timing can mean lots of daylight or darkness.

Top tip
Some city festivals are truly stunning and world class,

leaving an indelible memory. Try La Mercè in Barcelona in September to see what I mean. Prices may go up so plan and book your flights and hotel early and enjoy!

Activity holidays

Holidays that involve your hobby can be a double bonus. Rambling, sport, war tours, history club tours, motor racing, art, reading, painting, yoga retreats – the list is endless. Check with your local contacts and look online.

Holidays for people with disabilities

Affordable, accessible and enjoyable holidays for the disabled are many and varied. Airlines, hotels and resorts are providing people with disabilities or mobility issues the opportunities to travel, enjoy holidays and see the world. Specially designed self-catering units are more plentiful and of a higher standard. Also, an increasing number of trains and coaches are installing accessible loos. An elderly or disabled person seeking a holiday must explain clearly what their care needs are, not only in terms of getting to and from, but also with regard to accommodation requirements. Some people take companions/carers with them. There is a great deal of information available on the internet, so do take time to research carefully. Organizations that can help you include:

- Age UK: www.ageuk.org.uk;
- Able Community Care: www.uk-care.com;
- Accessible Travel: www.accessibletravel.co.uk;
- Disabled Holidays: www.disabledholidays.com;
- Disabled Access Holidays: www.disabledaccessholidays.com.

Hotels and Airbnb

Airbnb (www.airbnb.co.uk) has come into everyday use and helps you find homes and rooms in holiday hotspots for much less than hotel room rates. The quality can be amazing but there has been an incidence of scam accommodation so check for a history or reviews (both quantity and quality) over a few years.

Big hotel groups have loyalty programmes that can stack up and beat price comparison websites prices and the 'loyalty' also helps ensure you don't end up with the nightmare room (above the kitchen, no sea view, beside the lift etc).

Top tip

Rock bottom prices from comparator websites without a room type guarantee usually means a rock bottom room without a view. Try the hotel direct and get a guarantee on the room class - generally the more you pay the better the room. Every hotel has some rooms that no one wants to end up in.

Holidays on your own

When it comes to travelling there are many single people who want to see the world but are daunted by the prospect. Many people travel solo; some may be single, others not. There are companies specialising in singles holidays, tour holidays, exploring holidays and relaxing escape holidays - try searching for 'holidays for solo travellers' and www.friendshiptravel.com for an idea of the offering. Singles holidays should help improve safety, security and the certainty of help and support when needed. There is advice for single travellers on the Age UK website – visit www.ageuk.org.uk and go to 'Tips for single travellers' (including tips on breaking the ice, making time for yourself and staying safe).

Home-swapping holidays

House-swapping with someone on the other side of the world is easy and saves money on accommodation and the bonus for those who dare to do this is the experience of living life as a local, not a tourist. Check with your insurance company in case they place restrictions or exclusions on either your home contents or buildings cover. Some broker sites are:

- Exchange Holiday Homes: www.exchangeholidayhomes.com.
- Home Exchange: www.homeexchange.com.

Travel insurance

As you age you are far more likely to have a pre-existing medical condition that needs to be declared and covered on travel insurance. Some tips on buying holiday insurance follow:

- Adequate *personal liability cover is essential*; a minimum of around £1 million is advisable.
- For safety, *medical expenses cover* should be around £2 million and review conditions that apply to Covid-19.
- Your policy should have appropriate *cancellation and curtailment cover* in case you fall ill or cut your holiday short – read the small print for limitations and exclusions.
- *Don't leave arranging cover until just before you depart*, in case anything happens between booking and departure.
- If you're planning a few breaks over the next year, it could be more cost-effective to buy *annual worldwide cover*. Have a look at some of the comparison websites.
- *If you have a packaged (paid-for) bank account, check if it includes travel insurance.* Some bank accounts include a family travel policy, or winter sports cover.

A cost-effective idea may be to extend any existing medical insurance you have to cover you while abroad. Then take out a separate policy (without medical insurance) to cover you for the rest of your travel needs.

The basic advice is that it can be a complex field and you do need to shop around to get the cover that suits you at the best price.

Things can go wrong

For complaints and assistance when things go wrong, and for the framing of a complaint, see Chapter 7.

Plane delays and missed connections can ruin a holiday but if you are armed with insurance and information about your rights from Citizens Advice you might just save the day.

Some final holiday tips

- Check your passport expiry and the countries' entry requirements. Some require six months' validity from arrival. Have a photocopy of your passport tucked away and write an emergency contact name and number on it - just in case.

- *Safety.* For more official information check the Foreign Office's latest advice at www.gov.uk and go to 'foreign travel advice' where there is detailed country-specific information and advice. Your travel insurance may not cover you if you travel against Foreign Office advice so ask 'is it really worth it?' before you go ahead.
- Check with your mobile phone provider to see what fees apply and how to avoid them.
- *When organising travel always pay by credit card* (if you have paid more than £100, credit cards give increased protection if things go wrong or a contract is broken). More information on these rights (which I call the 'Section 75 magic wand') can be found in Chapter 7, which also explains that a second-best route is to use a debit card because of the protection known as 'charge back'. Unless vital, don't transfer funds from bank account to bank account as this route offers no protection.
- *Always check the small print of your insurance.* Going for the cheapest option can come back to haunt you under the 'what you pay is what you get' rule of life. Take a copy of your insurance policy with you.
- *Use that 'notes' function in your phone app to keep a short 'essentials to take on holiday' reminder list so it's always there as a reminder.*
- *Make sure that your carrier/travel company is ATOL (Air Travel Organiser's Licence) registered if your purchase involves a flight and a hotel.* There is also the Association of British Travel Agents (ABTA), which deals with rail, cruise and self-drive holidays. Note that ABTA has an arbitration scheme for breaches of contract, which can be cheaper and more efficient than going to court. ABTA also has a mediation service for disputes about personal injury and sickness (see www.abta.com.
- Pack any regular medicines you require and take a copy of a prescription and any relevant medical history. Even familiar branded products can be difficult to obtain in some countries. In addition, take a mini first-aid kit with you. If you are going to any developing country, consult your doctor as to what pills (and any special precautions) you should take.
- *Be careful of the water you drink.* If the local water has a reputation for being dodgy watch out for ice, salads, and any fruit that you do not peel yourself.
- *Have any travel inoculations or vaccinations well in advance of your departure date.*

Useful reading

The list of hobbies on Wikipedia and associated links.

The Foreign Office's latest advice at www.gov.uk and go to 'foreign travel advice' There is detailed country-specific information and advice.
Insight Guides or Lonely Planet travel guides on all countries.

Reminder: Take any action points or follow up points to Chapter 13, Your Plan For A Better Retirement.

Chapter Twelve
The sandwich generation and wills

*"Ageing is an extraordinary process, whereby you become
the person that you always should have been."*

DAVID BOWIE

The sandwich generation is the shorthand I use to describe the people that are looking after <u>both</u> dependent young adults and dependent elderly relatives. It's a growing issue in terms of the number of people affected due to life expectancy increasing and younger adults taking longer to find financial independence (compared to those 'flying the nest' in their early twenties as happened in the 1980s). The scale of the financial issues and emotions involved can be immense. It is even more challenging in 2025 because many in the 'sandwich generation' may have wholly or partly lost out on those gold-plated *'final salary'* pension schemes. In 2025 they may also be paying significantly more in mortgage interest if their mortgages renewed in 2023 to 2025. Add in cost of living pressures and frozen tax allowances and thresholds and it's starting to hurt. If this all rings true then this final chapter is the one for you.

This chapter concludes the **'live better'** essential step of this book as there are many things that you can retune and help achieve a better retirement and build on the action plan points that you have already developed from the preceding 11 chapters. It's all about obtaining better knowledge and taking time out to think straight and make better choices by acting on the opportunities and avoiding the risks.

One significant point that most people caught up in the sandwich generation will immediately recognise is a debt-laden younger generation, with university leavers from the 2012 entrance year and beyond potentially racking up £50,000 in student loans which have onerous interest rates. Buying a first house will be challenging for them and many sandwich generation parents may feel that their children in their late 20's or early 30's may still need a helping hand in the near future. The prospect of helping shield them from some or all of the student loan impact may also create financial (and emotional) stress that increases if you have two, three or more children entering this phase of their lives.

Those same children may go on to get married with the sandwich generation parents looking to follow in their parent's footsteps and foot the £20,000 to £30,000 bill or part of it.

Another pressure point on our younger people is unaffordable housing which has led to home ownership halving and, instead, our young people paying out 'dead money' in rent and not acquiring an asset base early enough. The size of the deposit may be too much and the lending deal may simply be unaffordable or impossible to achieve, irrespective of help to buy schemes, and especially if you live in London or the South East or other property 'hot spots'. Relatively high interest rates will create further affordability issues on our young people.

The up-shot is **'boomerang kids'** who will be living with parents a lot longer than their parents lived at home with all the associated emotional and financial factors that arise from this fact.

Looking up a generation to the parents of the sandwich generation, the pressures are, again, both emotional and financial and both are interlinked as quality care has a significant cost (or put another way 'you pay your money and make your choice'). With local authorities spending less on care and the cost of care rocketing it presents an almost perfect storm scenario. With residential care costs now running at anywhere between £40,000 to £100,000 per year depending on location and the extent of medical assistance needed you can see the predicament. Care in a home environment may be cheaper if that can meet the individual's needs. The sandwich generation may find the financial pressures of their children are compounded by the financial pressures of **elderly relatives** where the state funding or the relative's assets are insufficient. The third phase of retirement that I covered in Chapter 1 and called 'the retirement with care phase' may be approaching for your relative when home maintenance issues and costs start to run away with themselves and perhaps even raise questions of safety and welfare. The garden may get to be too difficult to cope with. There may also be medical factors which are making things not as easy as they used to be. Their being alone in a house, however cherished, may also bring pressures of loneliness and depression. There may be a difficult but necessary discussion and then decision to be made about moving into a care environment.

This chapter at a glance

- Some facts about the retirement prospects of our younger people.
- **Boomerang children** returning back to home after University / College and the need for space.
- **Helping millennials and generation Z** on the way with pensions planning and funding.
- Planning for the **big events that may be just round the corner**: university fees, weddings, house deposits and grandchildren.
- Planning for **care home** fees.
- **Maintaining independence** for as long as possible and the ways quality of life can be preserved, via help from local authority services, healthcare professionals and specialist services.
- Accommodation, **housing options** and costs.
- **Voluntary organisations** that can help.
- Practical help and information on **benefits and allowances** and how to obtain financial assistance, if eligible.
- **Intestacy, powers of attorney and wills**.

100 years of changing generational outcomes

The **Silent Generation** (born 1925 to 1945) were disciplined and grew up expecting a hard life. The **Baby Boomers** (born 1946 to 1964) were part of a huge population increase and forged new conventions and broke down old ones. **Generation X** followed (born between 1965 and 1979) with **Millennials** (born 1980 to 1994) believing they could achieve anything and are very self-sufficient. **Generation Z** (born 1995 to 2012) are more tolerant of others.

Millennials and Generation Z are a very relevant age group to 'sandwich generation' parents. The retirement outcomes of the Millennials and Generation Z put many of our own concerns into sharp focus and are worth thinking through as the sandwich generation may need to rethink priorities and retirement planning.

The Resolution Foundation undertakes research on living standards in the UK. Their research in 'An intergenerational audit of the UK' (published 21 November 2024) showed some very relevant key findings with implications for our younger people in terms of wages, housing and pensions which may help explain what the 'sandwich generation' are encountering in seeking to help their younger adult children.

- *The proportion of younger adults (under-35s) living with their parents has risen from one-in-four (26 per cent) at the turn of the century to nearly two-in-five (39 per cent) in 2021-2022.*

- *15 per cent of under-35s living with their parents are unemployed (against 5 per cent for other under-35s), and 33 per cent of those in work are low paid (against 16 per cent for others). This raises concerns that young people who live at home may become 'trapped' in areas with limited opportunities.*

- *However, our analysis suggests otherwise. While the 'live-at-homers' start out as a relatively disadvantaged group, they tend to catch up over time. After five years, young adults who began by living at home are just as likely to be employed as their peers, and no more likely to be low paid.*

- *Mothers are working more than in the past – especially those with young children. In 1992, only four-in-ten mums with a child under five worked; by 2022 it was seven-in-ten.*

- *But motherhood still routinely disrupts careers. The proportion of mothers of under-fives whose employment status is shaped by having children (whether through economic inactivity or part-time working due to family commitments or simply being on parental leave) is around 30 per cent. For fathers, the comparable proportion is 3 per cent.*

- *While formal childcare has expanded to meet the childcare gap created by more mothers moving into work, grandparents also play a crucial role. In total, grandparents provided an estimated 766 million hours of childcare to their grandchildren in 2022-23. If this support had replaced nursery care, its value would amount to approximately £3.5 billion.*

- *Support flows up the generations as well, particularly in the context of rising demand for adult care in an ageing UK. Yet, resources haven't expanded to meet growing need: age-adjusted local authority spending on adult social care was 7 per cent lower in 2022-23 than in 2009-10, while residential care costs have surged 30 per cent in real terms over the past nine years.*

- *Informal care, often provided by relatives, is filling the gap. While middle-aged adults still provide the most care for adults overall, younger adults are also stepping up: millennials are 30 per cent more likely to provide at least five hours of care a week than previous generations did at similar ages.*

- *Care intensity is rising: the share of carers providing over 20 hours a week nearly doubled from 15 per cent in 1991 to 28 per cent in 2021-22. This can limit labour market participation, with carers facing a 70 per cent higher likelihood of leaving employment if their responsibilities intensify.*

- *Our final intergenerational flow – inheritances – has become increasingly significant. Across the 2010s, the number of adults receiving an inheritance over a two-year period rose from 1.7 million in 2008-10 to 2.1 million in 2018-20.*

- *Recipients of inheritances are often in their 50s and 60s, and this can have significant implications for labour market decisions. Among the non-retired over-50s, those who received an inheritance of £50,000 or more were 4 percentage points more likely to retire early than those who did not receive an inheritance. This suggests that more frequent large inheritances may act as a headwind against high employment.*

Boomerang children and the sandwich generation

The term boomerang children describes those who flew off to University or College and then return 'home' after completing their course or graduating. They may be saddled with debt and the employment opportunities in terms of income, security and pension and other benefits is eroding in real terms. Many can't afford to rent and can't afford to buy a house so the benefits of several years back home may assist although this may be countered by a lack of opportunity if 'home' is in a more remote or economically challenged region of the UK. This can allow them to save a deposit for a house and/or may help them progress in their initial career steps to earn enough to rent. The issue for the sandwich generation of homeowners may be gaining sufficient space for each other under one roof and sandwich generation parents may, therefore, be interested in home adaptions or home expansion as a way to a solution, more in Chapter 2, Your Home and Property.

Pensions for the millennials

Pensions knowledge and retirement planning can be poor amongst millennials at a time when disposable cash is limited as life is fun and opportunities are many. Government initiatives around automatic enrollment is finally starting to see improved amounts being saved into pensions and the millennials are recognizing the benefit of 'free money' as the employer is compelled to contribute as well as the employee. But it remains short of ideal levels and only impacts the employed and, therefore, the self-employed or unemployed millennials are still left struggling and may not be funding their pension at adequate levels or at all. Could this be where grandparents, parents and close relatives help millennials with contributions into a pension or LISA (see **Chapter 4, Savings and Investments**). This is either to top up the employer / employee contributions or to kick start pensions for other millennials. This has half an eye on inheritance tax planning as gifting and surviving seven years can (under current tax rules) reduce inheritance tax and the question is whether those with large estates should be gifting earlier (see **Chapter 5, Tax**)?

Planning for big events – university fees, weddings, house deposits and grandchildren

How else can sandwich generation parents help (and, indeed, cope)? The first thing that will hit parents of younger millennials is the levels of debt involved. In very rough terms university fees soared overnight in England from around £3,500 pre 2012 to around £9,000 a year. Add on top off this about £5,000 a year for accommodation and about £3,500 for maintenance (basically food, drink, entertainment, travel and hopefully some books). So in England (for example) more than £50,000 of debt could be racked up over three years but less if you stay at home. At the same time the interest rate applied to the loans (depending on the type of loan) currently (December 2024) ranges from 4.3% to 7.3%.

The basic theory goes like this. If your children don't earn enough the loan will eventually be written off. But if it's likely your children are going to pay off their loans then should you look around at alternative forms of finance for part or all of the loan especially if you have the money tucked away or can access lower interest rate finance in alternative ways such as the equity in your home via a remortgage?

Then we have the wedding. The website hitched.co.uk shows that the average bill for wedding arrangements in 2023 was £20,700 (2022 £18,400). Hitched explain that 65% of the 1,800 couples they surveyed spent over £15,000 on their weddings but added that you can still get married for £10,000 or less with their handy guide- that guide might be worth having a look at! Alternatively, could there be another way with the sandwich generation parents and/or grandparents looking to help things out with clever use of their own pension tax free lump sum planning or playing the tax rate bands with pensions planning or inheritance tax planned 'gifting' to ultimately provide more money at the right time. Gifting probably needs an underline here as those in the sandwich generation that have built up significant wealth and might be hit by inheritance tax issues might have a better alternative. On the one hand and following traditions they may be minded to leave a slice of wealth in their will as an inheritance- but typically inheritances are not received until the individual is in their 50's or 60s. But why not rethink your strategy and instead gift the money when the young adults really need it and it might just fall outside of inheritance tax issues. More research and maybe help from your financial adviser and solicitor may be needed?

Martin Gorvett, a Chartered Financial Planner, of Lavender Financial Planners Ltd, has helped hundreds of individuals understand the interaction between wealth, your children and gifting. Martin advises:

"Simply put, we can't take our assets with us when we die (there are no pockets in a shroud etc). If you want to ensure that your wealth is preserved for future generations and passed on efficiently, an estate plan is crucial. Failing to take appropriate action to protect wealth from Inheritance Tax will cost families thousands of pounds. With Nil Rate Band levels being frozen for several years (another stealth tax), latest UK government figures show receipts of £ 4.3bn in the six months between April 2024 and September 2024 (up £400m from the previous six months). So, even without considering the changes to in the Autumn Statement 2024 (which brings defined contribution pensions in the mix from April 2027, and has hit UK farmers very hard), this is big ticket money spinner for the HMRC!" Martin Gorvett continues to underline the issues.

"Even with recent changes to Agricultural Property Relief and Business Property Relief there are still various strategies and solutions to legally avoid paying this tax – nothing illegal, and all within the rules. While some of us may want to spend it while we can (and godspeed to you), there will be others who want to pass on some of the wealth they've worked hard for. For these people, managing any Inheritance Tax liability is paramount, as is making sure the money they leave ends up with the right people at the right time (and doesn't leave the current chancellor as the largest beneficiary at the reading of the Will). With careful planning it is possible to significantly reduce the need for your estate to pay Inheritance Tax. We spend a lifetime generating wealth and assets but not many of us ensure that it will be passed to the next generation. It's becoming increasingly important for more people to consider succession planning and intergenerational wealth transfer as part of their estate preservation planning."

Still struggling on limited earnings and having moved out of the family home will millennials and generation Z choose to rent a bit longer in 2025 rather than become first time buyers if house prices are falling? Again, the sandwich generation parents or grandparents could look to help things out with clever use of gifting into LISAs for the lucky couple to help them save for a house deposit whist they rent and wait for when the 'price is right' (more about LISAs is outlined in Chapters 4 and 5).

Related to purchasing a home the sandwich generation parents could consider lending their names to the new home mortgage. These are called 'Joint Borrower, Sole Proprietor' mortgages which take the income of two borrowers into account (parent and child) but only puts the child's name on the deeds. This should avoid the extra 5% or more stamp duty that a property owning parent would incur if their name was on the deeds but the maximum age (maybe 70 to 75?) at the end of the mortgage term may limit the availability of this solution. A solicitor should be consulted to review what happens if the relationship does not work out and how everyone's interests can be protected.

The next big event will be grandchildren. The Child Poverty Action Group (cpag.org.uk) published their annual "The cost of a Child" report in December 2024 which showed the cost of raising a child to 18 is £260,000 for a couple and £290,000 for a lone parent. The report highlighted that in-work families are struggling with a lone parent with two children working full time on the minimum wage only being able to cover 69% of the cost of a child. A similar couple can only cover 84%. Out of work families are struggling even more.

Sandwich generation parents can help again at this stage – maybe financially or just basic advice to new parents to review their wills and life cover (more on these below).

Planning for care home fees

In managing potential care home planning for elderly relatives the potential positive is that there is likely to be some capital (in the form of a house) to fall back on and there may also be state help available. If you are in the position of caring for an elderly person, be that a parent, relative or loved one, you will contribute to make their remaining years happy, comfortable and meaningful. As the 'meat' in the sandwich between younger and older generations you can be that little bit more effective with some improved knowledge.

It will be down to you, your relatives, close family and the family solicitor to determine policy and planning around the use of the home and care fees. As a reminder from Chapter 5, Tax tread carefully if someone offers you a magic wand to 'protect your assets from the taxman' or schemes to shelter assets from 'claims for care home fees' based loosely on schemes involving trusts. The ideal scenario is that you would want to be dealing with the trusted family solicitor regulated by the Law Society in your jurisdiction (for instance in England and Wales at www.lawsociety.org.uk) and you would want a solicitor accredited on their Wills and Inheritance Quality Scheme (WIQS). If you depart from this route there are some questions set out in Chapter 5, Tax that may help you steer a safer course.

Maintaining independence

Being able to remain independent for as long as possible, and living in our own home, can be hugely important as you get older. The challenge is the cost, safety and convenience of the home as the years roll by. The cost is relatively straightforward if you face the facts – are the maintenance costs of the house and garden, insurance and council tax too high? On top of that, have you the time and ability to maintain both the house and garden or the funds to pay someone to do it? Perhaps more importantly, it is a simple fact that decent suitable housing underpins health and well-being, particularly in later life. The English Housing Survey found over a million homes occupied by those over 55 where there is significant risk to health (such as excess cold or injury from falling on poorly designed steps). These findings emphasise the importance of **'future-proofing' your home as you grow older** so you can live safely and independently for as long as possible.

Local authority services

Local authorities have a responsibility to help elderly people and provide services that vulnerable people and those with disabilities may need.

After an initial discussion with your GP who may be able to assist with some local knowledge, hints and tips, you then need to approach your adult social services department, explaining you need to arrange a 'care assessment'. Find your local council at www.gov.uk – go to 'find your local council'. They will be able to advise you about what is needed and how to obtain the required help. Your relatives should be assigned a social worker who will be able to make the necessary arrangements or advise you on how to do this. Some of the services available include:

- practical help in the home, with the support of a home help;
- adaptations to the home, such as a ramp for a wheelchair;
- provision of day centres, clubs and similar;
- blue badge scheme for cars driven or used by people with a disability;
- advice about other transport services or concessions that may be available locally;
- assistance with preparing meals, bathing and washing, getting in and out of bed and cleaning.

There is a range of support personnel that you may encounter and they include:

- *Occupational therapists* have a wide knowledge of disability and can assist individuals via training, exercise or access to aids, equipment or adaptations to the home.
- *Health visitors* are nurses with a broad knowledge of health matters and specialised

facilities that may be required.

- *District nurses* are fully qualified nurses who will visit a patient in the home, change dressings, attend to other routine nursing matters, monitor progress and help with the arrangements if more specialised care is required.

- *Physiotherapists* use exercise and massage to help improve mobility and strengthen muscles. They are normally available at both hospitals and health centres.

- *Medical social workers* (MSWs) should be consulted if patients have any problems on leaving hospital. MSWs can advise on coping with a disability, as well as such practical matters as transport, aftercare and other immediate arrangements. They work in hospitals, and an appointment should be made before the patient is discharged.

Following the assessment a care plan will be agreed and written out for you. Most councils charge you for care costs they provide at home; this remains an item high on the political agenda and costs are subject to both change and limits. Amounts, limits and caps vary depending on where you live. You might be able to claim Attendance Allowance or a Personal Independent Payment. Age UK advise:

> *"Most local councils charge for the services at home they provide. Some place an upper weekly limit on the amount you have to pay. Before charging you for services, your local council must work out how much you can afford to pay and this amount should leave you with a reasonable level of income. Check your local council's website for their charging information."*

Follow this advice and check back for updates at www.ageuk.org – go to 'finding help at home'.

Council Tax

There may be deductions available to you in the amount of Council Tax you have to pay (or in Northern Ireland the equivalent rates scheme). Typically these can include: 25 per cent reduction if living alone; if the property is empty as the resident is in a care home; disability deductions, including for severe mental impairments such as dementia. Contact your local council and enquire about help.

Special accommodation for the elderly

The time to start looking for appropriate accommodation for elderly parents or relatives is before they need it. A lot of research will have to be done, and there will be a better (and happier) outcome for all concerned if this process is not rushed. The earlier you make an assessment of their needs, the more choices and control you all will have.

At first glance, the loss of some level of independence can be overwhelming for many older people and thoughts may turn to feelings of shame, fear and confusion. But with your help and increased knowledge you may be able to tilt these initial feelings towards the opportunities and choices that may come with the change, such as increased safety, companionship, new views, closer proximity to a town's amenities and more. Brainstorm with family and trusted friends, and involve their medical team. Often the older person may listen more readily to their doctor or an impartial third party.

A good place to find information about options and funding is FirstStop Advice (www.firststopcareadvice.org.uk), an independent, impartial and free service provided by the national charity Elderly Accommodation Counsel (www.eac.org.uk). This service is for older people, their families and carers. It aims to get elderly people the help and care they need to live independently and comfortably for as long as possible. You will also find first-rate independent help from the Carers Trust via www.carers.org. You are not alone and are treading a well-worn path so start improving your knowledge and options on one of the most vital pieces of support you will provide in your lifetime.

Housing options

The following is an overview of the different types of housing for elderly people.

Living with family

This might at first seem the simplest option, but will the elderly relative have friends and social amenities after moving in? What would happen if the family relationship broke down? Talk with the rest of the family and others that have done this (local networks at www.carers.org should be able to help place 'issues' on your list of things to think about). Sit down with your solicitor and consider any financial or legal implications that could arise before selling the person's home and building expensive annexes or extensions.

Sheltered or retirement housing

If your elderly relatives are able to buy or rent a retirement property from their own private means, the choice is entirely theirs. Prices and types of property vary enormously, from small flats to luxurious homes on sites with every amenity. The majority of properties are sold on a long lease (typically 125 years). It is advisable to check that the management company is a member of The Association of Retirement Housing Managers and therefore bound by its Code of Practice. There is usually a minimum age for residents of 60 or sometimes 55.

Some points to consider when assessing this option could include:

- Do they allow pets?
- Location and proximity to local amenities.
- Guest suites that can be rented (cost?) for visiting families and friends.
- Camera entry and 24-hour call system for added peace of mind.
- The availability of a homeowners' lounge for relaxing with other home-owners in a 'neutral' environment, which can also be used for events.
- Is there a house manager who takes care of the day-to-day running of the site and any organised activities? How accessible are they?
- Is there a complaints book – can you have a look at it?
- Quality of the communal gardens.
- If the property is rented what is the percentage cap on annual rental increases? 'Stealth' increases above the rate of inflation can seem very unfair once you are settled in. Ascertain the increases over the last 3 years
- And most importantly, what is the annual service charge for amenities and shared costs (and what has it been over the last 3 years which, importantly, will indicate a 'trend' line)?

Home care or care at home

This is where the elderly person remains in their home and receives support during the day and/or at night. The time may come when elderly people are no longer able to cope with running their homes and caring for themselves without a bit of assistance. There are various options, some more expensive than others. If approaching agencies, it is well worth asking friends and neighbours for personal recommendations, as this can give a lot of peace of mind. Some of the agencies listed at 'other assistance' in this chapter specialise in providing temporary help, rather than permanent staff. Others can offer a flexible service and nursing care, if appropriate. Fees are normally paid by private funding but, depending on individual circumstances, public financial assistance may be available. There are some things to bear in mind when hiring a carer:

- Should you organise home care for your elderly relative, you or your relative actually becomes an employer, which brings obligations around administering a payroll and, potentially, a pension for the carer. Search 'payroll help' for local help on this or ask around for recommendations. Another alternative is to try it yourself by downloading HMRC's basic payroll tool (www.gov.uk – go to 'basic payroll tool'). If you employ the carer, undertake a DBS check. Criminal Records Bureau (CRB) checks are now called Disclosure and Barring Service (DBS) in England and Wales with slight amendments in terminology in Northern Ireland and Scotland. Help is available with these at www.gov.uk – go to 'DBS checks'.

- Elderly people organising care themselves also have the responsibility for checking eligibility to work in the UK and conducting a 'DBS' or equivalent check.

- Carers need clear guidelines as to documentation, medication, care plans and dietary guidance.

- There must be a contingency plan should the chosen carer fall ill or be unable to work for other reasons.

Ukcareguide.co.uk estimates the cost of overnight care at home in the UK, or day care in the home (December 2024) to be anywhere between £15 and £30 per hour. With home care you have the advantage of being in familiar surroundings. Find more information at www.thenationalcareline.org and www.carers.org.

Housing with care

This is a newer form of specialist housing, sometimes referred to as extra care housing. Properties can be rented, owned or occasionally part-owned/part-rented. They are fully self-contained homes, usually with one or two bedrooms. To find some options just google 'housing with care' and your region.

Care homes

Deciding whether a care home is right for an elderly relative is a difficult decision that sometimes has to be made in a hurry. All care homes in England are registered and inspected by the Care Quality Commission (CQC) and must display their CQC rating (outstanding, good, requires improvement or inadequate) throughout the home and on their website – see www.cqc.org.uk.

In Wales, the inspectorate is called the Care Standards Inspectorate for Wales – www.cssiw.org.uk.

In Scotland it is called the Care Inspectorate – www.careinspectorate.com.

In Northern Ireland it is the Regulation and Quality Improvement Authority – www.rqia.org.uk.

Top tip

The oversight organisations listed above provide thorough independent information and reports on each care home in the UK. You simply cannot do your relative any justice if you do not access, compare and review the information they have for the areas being considered for your relative.

The next step is to start visiting some care homes – possibly by yourself at first – and just doing a drive past to get a feel for a possible 'shortlist' from a longer list established from a review of the above websites and, of course, the care home's own website if they have one. Then download the Age UK care home checklist and start your visits (www.ageuk.org – 'finding a care home'). There are lots of invaluable hints and tips; use the checklist together with a few of our own tips:

- Overall, recognise that often it comes down to fees, and generally speaking rooms with a view and high-quality services and amenities all come with a cost – the better the standard, the higher the price.

- Recognise that all of your relative's belongings will probably need to fit into one room.

- Look at any entertainment schedule and pop along to see it for yourself.

- Is there free internet access?

- How do they meet religious/pastoral needs?

- Ask about special situations such as dementia – what is their approach for both those that have it and those that do not?

- Ask to see sample menus and, better still, ask to pop in to see the kitchens whilst mealtimes are in progress. Visit two or three times and reconsider this point; the quality of food reveals a lot. Can they cater for special diets?
- Ask about visiting times – are there restricted hours?
- Is contents insurance included in the fee?
- Ask about links to a hospital and any assigned doctor.
- Ask how personal care is addressed and at what cost – typically this is hairstyling and care of fingernails and toenails.
- Ask if you can bring your/their pet in to visit your relative.
- Trust your instincts about your overall feelings about the home and how it may be suitable for your relative.

There are two main types of care homes: residential and nursing homes:

- **Residential homes** can range from small in size with a few beds, to large-scale facilities. They offer care and support throughout the day and night. Staff are on hand to help with personal care. Carehome.co.uk report (December 2024) states that the average cost of residential care in the UK is £60,320 per annum (£1,160 per week) while average fees at a nursing home are £73,320 per annum (£1,410 per week). Care homes that offer specialist care, such as dementia care, tend to charge a higher fee.
- **Nursing homes** offer the same type of care as residential homes but with the addition of 24-hour medical care from a qualified nurse. Carehome.co.uk report (December 2024) states that the average fees at a nursing home are £73,320 per annum (£1,410 per week).

Care homes costs and help

There are currently over half a million older people living in residential and nursing homes in the UK and around half of these fund their care themselves (according to carehome.co.uk). Care homes vary in cost, and fees rise depending on how complex the needs of the elderly person are.

The funding aspect is complex and can be subject to political pressure and change. Funding may be available for part or all of the nursing/medical care element of any fees. There are then fees for the 'accommodation aspect'. Carehome.co.uk provide useful hints and tips and summarise (December 2023) the capital/asset thresholds that cause you to pay the full cost of care in the UK.

- *England and Northern Ireland: assets of more than £23,250 (if you have assets of more than £14,250 you will have to pay some of your care costs).*

- *Scotland: £35,000 (below £21,500 for maximum support).*

- *Wales: anyone with capital under £50,000 will receive fully funded care.*

If your savings or income falls below the threshold or you start to run out of money, the local authority should begin paying for your care costs. The UK Conservative government had announced that from October 2025 (this was originally due to come into effect in 2023 but had been delayed), no one in England will have to pay more than £86,000 in care costs during their lifetime. Carehome.co.uk reports (at December 2024) that *"These reforms were scrapped by the new Labour government on 29 July 2024. Chancellor Rachel Reeves said she needed to tackle a spending 'black hole' inherited from the Conservative government."*

If you give your home away to a child or relative in an attempt to exclude it from the test on income and capital limits it may count as a deliberate 'deprivation of assets'. This is the technical term used by Councils; it means that you still pay the same level of care fees as if you still owned the home.

Top tip
Take care if an organisation seems to be promising to shelter your home and finances from the grasps of the local authority with schemes and arrangements involving trusts and tax planning to remove your home from your ownership to avoid care home fees being paid by you. There are suggested questions and checks in Chapter 5, Tax in the section on Inheritance Tax.

Other assistance

In addition to the services provided by statutory health and social services for elderly people living at home, there are a number of voluntary organisations that can offer help, including:

- lunch clubs and day centres;
- holidays and short-term placements;
- aids such as wheelchairs;
- transport;
- odd jobs decorating and gardening;
- prescription collection;
- family support schemes.

You will be able to find out more via your local Citizens Advice Bureau (www.citizensadvice.org.uk) but some of the key agencies are:

- Age UK: www.ageuk.org.uk;
- Age Scotland: www.ageuk.org.uk/scotland;
- Age Cymru: www.ageuk.org.uk/cymru;
- Age NI: www.ageuk.org.uk/northern-ireland;
- Care Information Scotland: www.careinfoscotland.scot;
- Centre for Individual Living, Northern Ireland: www.cilbelfast.org;
- Contact the Elderly: www.contact-the-elderly.org;
- Disability Wales: www.disabilitywales.org.

Practical help for carers

The UK has 6.5 million carers and whilst your elderly relative is reasonably active and independent – visiting friends, able to do his or her own shopping, enjoying hobbies and socialising – the strains of caring for them may be light. However, when this is not the case, far more intensive care may be required. Make sure you find out what help is available and how to obtain it and entitledto.co.uk can provide help on benefits in addition to the help available through Citizens Advice.

> **Top tip**
> Download, review and follow through on the advice and
> information in the free guide 'Looking after someone:
> information and support for carers', available from
> www.carersuk.org

Help and support in the first few days and weeks following a death

The laws vary slightly in England and Wales, Scotland and Northern Ireland. Your
solicitor will be able to provide you with an information pack which will usually give
you guidance on how to register a death, what happens if the coroner is involved,
arranging the funeral, carrying out any personal wishes made, choosing a funeral
director and help on paying for the funeral. The guidance pack will usually then
provide pointers to the essential help and support in the first few weeks following a
death.

Laws of intestacy

If you die without leaving a will your finances are dealt with under the rules of
intestacy. Again, the rules differ slightly between England and Wales, Scotland and
Northern Ireland but that should not detract from the following key message. An
intestacy is basically a great big mess that will take time, money and effort to sort out
and even then things won't follow a smooth path. Rules set by the government (the
laws of intestacy) will determine who inherits the deceased person's estate
(possessions, property and money). There is no guarantee that the deceased person's
wishes will be carried out or that their estate will go to those they intended. Promises
made will count for nothing and may only cause confusion and perhaps upset. Only
married or civil partners (actually married at the time of death) and close relatives can
inherit under the rules of intestacy. An unmarried partner and stepchildren have no
automatic rights. Possessions, including the home, may have to be sold to split the
proceeds between the heirs and if there are no relatives the Crown gets the lot.

All is not bleak, as usually a close relative will have the legal right to step in, prove their position and relationship and seek to sort out the estate of the person who has died intestate. To administer someone's estate you apply to the deceased's local Probate Office for a 'Grant of Letters of Administration'. You can ask your solicitor to help you with applying for a grant or you can make a personal application. When you get the grant you become the 'administrator' of the estate. The grant provides proof to banks, building societies and other organisations that you have authority to access and distribute funds that were held in the deceased's name. If Inheritance Tax is due on the estate, some or all of this must be paid before a grant will be issued.

Top tip

Intestacy is a mess so don't put your relatives through it. Make a will (an action point for Chapter 13?) and use that as an opportunity to revisit other matters covered in this chapter. Bear in mind the motto "Tough discussions and decisions are often not so difficult once the subject is broached."

Wills

A will is a legal document that sets out a person's final financial wishes. There are six main reasons why you should make a will if you have not done so already:

- The alternative is the mess of intestacy as above.

- It means your wishes are known with clarity (after all you won't be around to clarify things!).

- It helps avoid disputes between relatives. Some relatives may not agree and some may still seek to make a claim on your estate but the fact that you have clarified what you want goes a very long way to prevent disgruntled relatives disputing things.

- It can protect assets for future generations. If you are fortunate to have assets that can stay in the family the will can be directed to put certain assets or funds into a trust to help preserve them for the benefit of future generations. This may help prevent the next generation blowing the lot and can be useful in large and complex estates or family situations that appear chaotic.

- Inheritance tax. If you leave your estate to your husband, wife or civil partner then no inheritance is paid. Anything left to a charity is also exempt from inheritance tax. Armed with some of the information on gifts from Chapter 5 (Tax) you will also see how you could be more tax-efficient with more knowledge and advice.

- Clarify the funeral that you would like and provide for the costs of the funeral and any after event (catering and venue hire) to be paid from your estate. This allows you to specify what you would like and also anything that you do not want, and removes significant stresses from those left to make the arrangements.

Having a will is essential if you live with an unmarried partner, have divorced, remarried, or need to provide for someone with a disability. You can write your will yourself or with the assistance of do-it-yourself will-writing kits available online or from stationery shops. Both routes can be prone to error and misinterpretation and therefore advice and assistance really should be sought.

There are several different types of wills, amongst which are:

- a *single will* relates to an individual;

- *mirror wills* are designed for couples who have the same wishes;

- a *property trust will* places the estate into trust for beneficiaries;

- a *discretionary trust will* allows trustees to decide what is best at the time of your death.

There is no 'one size fits all' answer to deciding which sort of will is best. Specialist advice is essential and researching your circumstances (personal and financial) will reveal what kind of will is right for you. Your will should be stored carefully where the relevant people can find it and needs to be formally witnessed and signed to make it legally valid. If at any time you wish to update your will, this must be done officially, by means of a 'codicil'. If your circumstances change (divorce, death of a loved one, or new family members) you should review the position and decide if a new will is necessary.

Keep with your papers at home a list of your 'assets'. Where is the treasure buried? By keeping this information up to date you can save your executors hours of work pursuing wild goose chases. Ultimately, those you wish to benefit will get more if your paperwork is accurate.

Tom Bottomley of Ewart Price Solicitors of Hertfordshire shares his top five tips for a successful will:

1. Think carefully about what you own (your assets); are there any unusual things about them that you need to consider?

2. Whom do you wish to benefit? People might have expectations, for example close family members. If you are not benefiting them, why not? Seek advice about whether a disappointed individual might have a claim against the estate.

3. Meet with a solicitor and instruct him or her to draft a will for you.

4. Carefully check the draft, and ask for an explanation about anything you do not understand. There is no point signing a document you do not understand.

5. Leave the original will with the solicitor and keep a copy. You can register the will with the National Will Register, officially recognized in the UK, who will be able to say from their database who has the will (www.nationalwillregister.co.uk).

Banks

Some banks offer a will-writing service. Make sure that you can choose your own executor or understand in advance the bank's charges for acting as executor as fees can be relatively expensive if banks undertake the executor service.

Professional will-writing specialists

A will-writing service can be cheaper than using a solicitor, and more reliable than a DIY will. A will-writing service could be a good choice if you understand the basics of how wills work, you wish to pay less than a solicitor would charge, and your estate is not complex. Before you instruct a will-writing service make sure they have professional indemnity insurance, because if they get it wrong there may be nobody to sue.

Solicitors

The best solution is usually through an appropriately qualified solicitor who will ensure your will is interpreted the way you want and may tease out tricky issues that you may not have anticipated. If you do not have a solicitor, ask friends for a recommendation, or ask Citizens Advice. You can budget for around £200 to £500 plus VAT for this help – more if you have very complex financial affairs.

What to include and terminology

Your will should explain the main assets you own (your 'estate') and indicate your debts (what you owe). This is not an exhaustive list but it will be helpful to detail any homes, significant assets, investments, savings and life policies, their location and the main debts owed (usually mortgages, loans and a listing of credit cards). Jointly owned property should be clarified and remember 'joint tenants' will see your share automatically passing to the other joint tenant(s) on death and 'tenants in common' means you can leave your share to someone else. 'Executors' are the vital people who make sure your will happens as you intended – more on them below.

'Beneficiaries' are the people you name to receive something in your will; remember to give their full names and precise relationship to you to make sure they are correctly identified. 'Legacies' is the name for gifts you make to beneficiaries. A 'residual beneficiary' is the person or charity that receives the remainder of your estate once specific gifts have been paid out.

'A letter of wishes' can often accompany a will as an annex and can be helpful in avoiding cluttering up a will with a long list of people who are to be given specific assets. It can be useful for clarifying desired funeral arrangements but it is not a legally binding document. Particularly where you have created a discretionary trust in your will, a letter of wishes can flesh out the bones of a dry legal document. Typically, where young parents are worried about their children becoming orphans, they wish to say how they would like their children to be educated.

> **Top tip**
> Ask for a quotation for completing the will and the costs of any anticipated extras (for instance lasting powers of attorney – see below). If using a solicitor, check that they are a member of the Law Society's Wills and Inheritance Quality Scheme and that anyone else entrusted to write your will is a member of the Society of Trust and Estate Practitioners (STEP).

Deeds of variation

A deed of variation can be used to change a will up to two years after the date of death where all those affected by the alteration agree to the change. But only a beneficiary can re-direct their own inheritance. You cannot vary others' entitlement. Typically, it is used to redirect the stated benefit in a will from, say, a child to a grandchild to keep down the inheritance tax potential on the child's estate; specialist advice should be obtained from a solicitor on this potentially useful tool. The effect of the deed of variation is to rewrite the will as if the deceased person had made the new and altered instructions in their will.

Executors

An executor is the person you appoint in your will to be responsible for handling your estate and making sure your wishes are carried out after you die. Think of a best man or chief bridesmaid at a wedding, only this time it's 10 times more important, so choose wisely. It is usual to appoint more than one executor and they should be over 18, so perhaps it could be your husband, wife or civil partner and a child, brother or sister. This could take some of the pressure off your husband, wife or civil partner in the initial period when emotions and loss are so significant.

Bear in mind that a complex estate can involve the executor in a significant amount of work and possibly stress. If the estate is complex and the will includes trusts, appointing a professional executor to act with lay executors is worth considering.

The main duties of the executor are:

1. Registering the death at the Register Office (find your relevant one at

www.gov.uk) and locating the final will. You will need to take the medical certificate signed by a doctor when you register the death. Once you register the death you will get a Certificate for Burial or Cremation (the 'green form') and a Certificate of Registration of Death. Think about how many copies of the death certificate you will need.

2. Arranging the funeral. The costs will usually be payable from the deceased's estate. Check on funeral wishes in any will or 'letter of wishes' or in any funeral plan (perhaps left with an undertaker) and with close family on the preparations. Notices may need to be placed in newspapers and social media informing people of funeral arrangements and any donation wishes (or the fact that donations should not be made). Emotions will be high and time is short, making this a difficult time, and so funeral specifications provided in the will can prove a blessing.

3. Valuing the estate. Gather in and ensure you have control of everything the deceased owned and also establish everything they owed. Obtain valuations from a professional valuer of expensive items and any residential property.

4. Apply for probate which gives the legal right to deal with someone's estate (for instance to sell their house), complete the relevant Inheritance Tax form and pay any tax due. The process varies between England and Wales, Scotland and Northern Ireland; the specifics can be found on www.gov.uk (go to 'probate').

Tom Bottomley of Ewart Price Solicitors shares some suggestions and pointers on executors:

"Taking on the role is a serious undertaking. It is one thing for a spouse to manage their deceased spouse's estate – they will have an intimate knowledge of their affairs and will likely be the sole/only beneficiary; it is quite another to appoint, say, a family friend to deal with a portfolio of assets and multiple beneficiaries. Even with the help of a solicitor it can be difficult and stressful to deal with assets, sell property, and keep a contingent of (potentially upset and impatient) beneficiaries informed and happy. People commonly leave gifts to their executors for taking on the role and more often than not, the executors are residuary beneficiaries anyway. This is up to the testator's discretion, but it makes sense to appoint someone as executor who has an interest in the estate as they will be motivated to get everything sorted. A professional executor will either charge by the hour or by a percentage of the estate."

Lasting power of attorney

Dementia can develop slowly or suddenly, especially following a stroke or an accident, and the emotional turmoil will be substantial. There are one or two very simple procedures that can and should be done to ease the situation. The first is to set up a Lasting Power of Attorney (LPA); some solicitors consider this to be just as important as making a will. This has to be done before losing mental capacity, otherwise it is invalid. Before doing anything it would be wise to discuss the options with family or someone they trust to see what they think and whether they can help. To find out more about mental capacity and making decisions use www.gov.uk and go to 'make decisions for someone'.

An LPA gives someone you trust the legal authority to make decisions on your behalf and therefore you retain control through that person, known as the attorney. The attorney could be a husband, wife or civil partner, a son or daughter, a brother or sister, nephew or niece or just someone you trust. The person allowing the LPA to be drawn up is known as the donor. There are two types of LPA: one for *property and financial affairs* and another for *personal welfare*. It is safest to have both types. A health and welfare LPA allows others to make decisions about the donor's day-to-day care, where they live, who they should have contact with and, if desired, their choice for end-of-life care. The property and financial affairs LPA covers paying bills, collecting benefits, selling property and investing money. Without an LPA the only way a person can take charge of another person's finances is via the Court of Protection which is a lengthy, costly and stressful process.

Once you have made your LPA it is very advisable to register this immediately with the Office of the Public Guardian. This process takes at least two months, so if things deteriorate quickly an unregistered power is not valid.

The right time to draw up an LPA is while the individual is in full command of his or her faculties, so that potential situations that would require decision making can be properly discussed and the donor's wishes made clear. If you are considering setting up an LPA for yourself or an elderly relative it is important to consult both the relevant GP and the family solicitor as well as members of the family. When making an LPA make sure the attorneys can be relied upon to always and 100 per cent place your best interests at heart. Lasting Powers of Attorney were introduced in October 2007, replacing the old system of Enduring Powers of Attorney (EPA). An EPA created before October 2007 remains valid.

The personal welfare LPA could save endless amounts of angst amongst family and friends when dementia and then the end of life occurs. According to Compassion in Dying:

> *"Seventy per cent of us want little or no medical intervention at the end of life; 53 per cent believe family can make healthcare decisions on behalf of a loved one; and only 4 per cent of us have made our treatment wishes known in an Advance Decision."*

Being prepared will also allow more quality time with loved ones, particularly when those precious final months, weeks or days come. It will also relieve lots of strain and stress so consider incorporating the following in either your LPA or in a 'letter of wishes' appended to your will; your solicitor will be able to guide you on the best route:

- your end-of-life care plan;
- where you wish to be cared for;
- advance decision to refuse treatment (do not resuscitate (DNR) form);
- organ and tissue donation;
- planning your funeral.

The NHS website gives general advice on end-of-life planning at www.nhs.uk (go to 'end-of-life care') and there is also quality information available from Age UK: www.ageuk.org.uk.

Important wealth warning

This chapter is only a guide and it is neither legal nor taxation advice. Any potential tax advantages may be subject to change from the position as at December 2024 and will depend upon your individual circumstances, so individual professional advice should be obtained.

Useful reading

The cost of care is an area subject to considerable pressure and potential change. Quality advice and updates can be found at www.citizensadvice.org.uk, www.ageuk.org.uk (go to 'paying for permanent residential care'), www.independentage.org (go to 'paying care home fees' to download their latest factsheet) and 'How to fund your long-term care - a beginners guide' (at www.moneyadviceservice.org.uk). Support is available for carers at both the national level and their local groups via www.carers.org.

Cruse Bereavement Care: www.cruse.org.uk or phone 0808 8081677;

Care for the Family and their specialist bereavement support:
www.careforthefamily.org.uk (go to 'bereavement support' or phone 02920 810800);

Samaritans: www.samaritans.org. With Samaritans remember their motto:
'Whatever you're going through, call us free any time, from any phone on 116 123.'

Reminder: Take any action points or follow up points to Chapter 13, Your Plan For A Better Retirement.

Chapter Thirteen

YOUR PLAN FOR A BETTER RETIREMENT

It's up to you- it's your '**re-set**' moment as you start a glidepath towards a better retirement. You can make a big lifestyle change but take the issues one or two at a time and become obsessed with them for 10 weeks. Share them with your partner and close friends and the new lifestyle change will help your retirement plan.

LIFESTYLE- I'M GOING TO START DOING

	Page No.	Issue
1		
2		
3		
4		
5		

LIFESTYLE- I'M GOING TO STOP DOING

	Page No.	Issue
1		
2		
3		
4		
5		

Glidepath retirement action plan. Things to action straight away

	Page No.	Issue	Priority: High Medium or Low
1			
2			
3			
4			
5			
6			
7			
8			
9			
10			
11			
12			
13			
14			
15			

Notes:

List of points in this book to follow up and research for a better retirement

	Page No.	Issue	Website or source of more help
1			
2			
3			
4			
5			
6			
7			
8			
9			
10			
11			
12			
13			
14			
15			
16			
17			
18			
19			
20			

www.ingramcontent.com/pod-product-compliance
Ingram Content Group UK Ltd.
Pitfield, Milton Keynes, MK11 3LW, UK
UKHW021411080725
6787UKWH00033B/684